Praise for
*Joyful Learning*

"Kerry McDonald's vision for education entrepreneurship is both inspiring and urgent. This book is the roadmap for anyone tired of the status quo and ready to make a difference in how we teach the next generation."
—John Mackey, cofounder of Whole Foods Market and *New York Times*–bestselling author of *Conscious Capitalism*

"With her rich background in economics and education policy, and her experience as a mother of four, Kerry McDonald is the perfect person to document today's schooling revolution. I recommend *Joyful Learning* to all parents seeking the best educational opportunities for their children, to all enterprising souls who want to help provide those opportunities, and to anyone interested in understanding the future of American education."
—Peter Gray, author of *Free to Learn*

"It's hard not to feel like we're at the dawn of a new era when you read this book, pulsing with ideas, makers, dreamers, and plenty of plain old fed-up parents who decided it was time to change the world by changing the way kids get educated. Want to be amazed and inspired and hopeful? Want to see just how wide the word 'school' can stretch? Want to nurse that glimmer of 'I can do it, too,' flickering in your heart of hearts? Dig in!"
—Lenore Skenazy, author of *Free-Range Kids*

"The way we teach our kids is stuck in the past. Illuminating and deeply reported, *Joyful Learning* thoughtfully considers the innovative educational models being pioneered by parents and teachers frustrated with one-size-fits-all schooling and offers helpful advice to parents seeking outside-the-box learning opportunities for their children."

—Todd Rose, author of *Collective Illusions*

"*Joyful Learning* reveals the possibilities that arise when we break free from traditional educational constraints and champion a future where every child can thrive on their terms, shining a particular spotlight on Black school founders whose resilience and commitment to education reform are both inspiring and instructive."

—Denisha Allen, founder of Black Minds Matter

"A fair-minded exploration of how fed-up parents, despondent teachers, and other concerned citizens are reimagining what schooling looks like in today's America—and how you can get involved in the ongoing education revolution."

—Corey DeAngelis, author of *The Parent Revolution*

# Joyful Learning

# Joyful Learning

## How to Find Freedom, Happiness, and Success Beyond Conventional Schooling

### Kerry McDonald

PUBLICAFFAIRS
New York

Copyright © 2025 by Kerry McDonald
Cover design by Emmily O'Connor
Cover image copyright © Robert Kneschke/Shutterstock.com
Cover copyright © 2025 by Hachette Book Group, Inc.

Hachette Book Group supports the right to free expression and the value of copyright. The purpose of copyright is to encourage writers and artists to produce the creative works that enrich our culture.

The scanning, uploading, and distribution of this book without permission is a theft of the author's intellectual property. If you would like permission to use material from the book (other than for review purposes), please contact permissions@hbgusa.com. Thank you for your support of the author's rights.

PublicAffairs
Hachette Book Group
1290 Avenue of the Americas, New York, NY 10104
www.publicaffairsbooks.com
@Public_Affairs

Printed in the United States of America

First Edition: August 2025

Published by PublicAffairs, an imprint of Hachette Book Group, Inc. The PublicAffairs name and logo is a registered trademark of the Hachette Book Group.

The Hachette Speakers Bureau provides a wide range of authors for speaking events. To find out more, go to hachettespeakersbureau.com or email HachetteSpeakers@hbgusa.com.

PublicAffairs books may be purchased in bulk for business, educational, or promotional use. For more information, please contact your local bookseller or the Hachette Book Group Special Markets Department at special.markets@hbgusa.com.

The publisher is not responsible for websites (or their content) that are not owned by the publisher.

Print book interior design by Sheryl Kober

Library of Congress Cataloging-in-Publication Data

Names: McDonald, Kerry, 1977– author
Title: Joyful learning : how to find freedom, happiness, and success beyond conventional schooling / Kerry McDonald.
Description: First edition. | New York : PublicAffairs, 2025. | Includes bibliographical references and index.
Identifiers: LCCN 2024046771 | ISBN 9781541705524 hardcover | ISBN 9781541705548 ebook
Subjects: LCSH: Non-formal education—United States | Home schooling—United States | Education—Aims and objectives—United States | Educational change—United States | Student-centered learning—United States
Classification: LCC LC45.4 .M32 2025 | DDC 371.04/2—dc23/eng/20250425
LC record available at https://lccn.loc.gov/2024046771

ISBNs: 9781541705524 (hardcover), 9781541705548 (ebook)

LSC-C

Printing 1, 2025

*To the entrepreneurs creating joyful schools and spaces,
and those they inspire.*

# Contents

Author's Note ... ix

Introduction ... 1

## Part I. Imagine

**Chapter 1.** Changes ... 13
**Chapter 2.** Alternatives ... 35
**Chapter 3.** Founders ... 59
**Chapter 4.** Families ... 83

## Part II. Seek or Build

**Chapter 5.** Startups ... 107
**Chapter 6.** Searches ... 135
**Chapter 7.** Solutions ... 155
**Chapter 8.** Metrics ... 173
**Chapter 9.** Challenges ... 201

## Part III. Transform

**Chapter 10.** Expansions ... 229
**Chapter 11.** Intrapreneurs ... 247
**Chapter 12.** Trends ... 267

Afterword ... 285

Acknowledgments ... *287*
Appendices ... *289*
Notes ... *297*
Index ... *309*

## Author's Note

Much of the inspiration for this book came from hours of podcast and article interviews and in-person visits with hundreds of education entrepreneurs since early 2022. If you listen to my *LiberatED* podcast, you may recognize some of the founders featured in these pages while also enjoying fresh perspectives and updates from them. You'll also be introduced to new founders and families not profiled elsewhere. If you are not a regular listener of *LiberatED*, or reader of my related articles at Forbes.com, The 74, and FEE.org, the founder stories and strategies presented here will show you what you can build as an education entrepreneur, or find as a parent looking for the best learning environment for your child.

In passages where I have quoted founders from the podcast, I have taken the liberty in some cases to slightly alter the spoken dialogue to remove its choppiness while fully retaining an interviewee's words and intent. In most instances, I conducted supplemental interviews with podcast guests to gain new information. For complete podcast episodes featuring some of the founders in this book, please visit LiberatedPodcast.com.

Education entrepreneurship, like any professional endeavor, has risks and rewards. This is especially true with innovative, unconventional, and emerging educational models, where founders may be creating schools and spaces that don't fit easily into established regulatory frameworks meant for traditional schools. Regulations in some states are starting to catch up, as I discuss in Chapter 9; but you'll want to do your homework on what is required for compliance with local, state, and federal laws and regulations—both as an entrepreneur and as a parent.

The content provided in this book is for general informational purposes only and should not be construed as legal, financial, or investment advice. You should do your own research regarding complying with homeschooling laws, private schooling regulations, or alternative education requirements in your area. If you are a new or aspiring entrepreneur, I recommend consulting with experienced professional service providers as you start or scale your small business. If you are a parent looking for a school or space for your children, be sure to do your own due diligence when evaluating a program's quality.

# Introduction

*All humans are entrepreneurs not because they should start companies but because the will to create and take control of our destiny is encoded in human DNA—and creation is the essence of entrepreneurship.*
—REID HOFFMAN (COFOUNDER OF LINKEDIN),
*THE STARTUP OF YOU*

Coi Morefield never expected to be an education entrepreneur. She'd worked as a classroom teacher in both Chicago and Memphis public schools but grew increasingly disillusioned by the standardization and regimentation of conventional schooling. It wasn't the people that were the problem. It was the system. "We weren't focused on the learners and their families and how best to support them, to put people first before checking our boxes," said Coi, who created the Black Inquiry Project in 2020 as a way to encourage crucial conversations in schools around race and culture.

She knew that she didn't want to enroll her four young children in any of the local public schools, and she was unimpressed with the traditional private education options in her community. "I was looking for a school with racial and cultural diversity, a progressive curriculum, and a highly customized experience for them," Coi said. "I thought I found it, but instead what I got was a staff that was all white and this one-size-fits-all experience that was essentially a really expensive public school, even though it was private," she said.

Like so many entrepreneurs, Coi realized that she had to build what she couldn't find. In the fall of 2021, she opened The Lab School of Memphis, a secular, mixed-age, low-cost elementary microschool—a contemporary one-room schoolhouse—that prioritizes childhood freedom and autonomy. The state-recognized, accredited private school opened with six students and today has more than sixty. It's continuing to grow and attract families like Coi's who are looking for a creative, curiosity-driven, culturally relevant learning environment for their children. Nearly two-thirds of her students attend the school nearly tuition-free with the help of a targeted Tennessee school choice program. Implemented in 2022, the choice program enables some low- and middle-income students to access a portion of state-allocated education funding to use toward various educational expenses—including schools like Coi's. In early 2025, Tennessee joined more than a dozen other states in extending private school choice eligibility to all students.

At the same time that Coi opened her Memphis microschool, another Tennessee education entrepreneur was preparing to launch a hybrid homeschool program in Chattanooga. Rebecca Ellis was growing weary of independently homeschooling her youngest children, and she was dissatisfied with the rigidity and frequent testing that her oldest child, then a fourth grader, was encountering in a traditional school. Rebecca wanted an affordable, faith-filled, child-centered learning environment for her children that would blend the best of conventional schooling and homeschooling. She couldn't find it, so she built it.

In the fall of 2022, Rebecca launched Canyon Creek Christian Academy, a hybrid homeschool blending both on-campus class days and at-home days. She opened with thirty-two homeschooled students in elementary and middle school grades, growing to more than fifty students the following year and over sixty-five by the fall of 2024. Unlike traditional homeschool co-ops, where parents often stay onsite and take turns doing the teaching, hybrid homeschool programs like Canyon Creek are drop-off programs without parent participation during on-campus days. Canyon Creek students attend the teacher-led program three full days each week, learning through a curriculum centered around the Charlotte Mason educational philosophy. An influential British Christian educator at the turn of the twentieth century, Mason developed an educational approach that focuses on respecting children and nurturing their curiosity in core content areas using works of high-quality, engaging literature, as well as immersive nature study and short lessons with frequent breaks. Children in Rebecca's program spend the remaining two days each week working on their curriculum at home with their parents. At an annual tuition of $3,750, Canyon Creek is significantly more affordable than most other private education options in the area.

Coi and Rebecca are two of the hundreds of K–12 (kindergarten through twelfth grade) education entrepreneurs I have had the privilege of meeting and interviewing since 2020. They represent a tiny sliver of the enormous variety of people and programs fostering individualized, accessible, joy-filled education across the United States. Most of these entrepreneurs are parents who wanted a different educational experience for their school-age kids. When they looked around for new or different learning options, they couldn't find what they wanted, so they created their own schools and spaces. Stories of these everyday entrepreneurs are what inspired me to write this book, and—I hope—will inspire you too. The following pages blend these stories with practical strategies to help you find or build a joyful learning environment for the children around you. Coi's school is estimated to be one of the approximately 125,000 low-cost microschools now operating in the United States, serving upward of 1.5 million full-time students—including many who are low-income and from historically marginalized groups.¹ Rebecca's hybrid homeschool is creatively meeting the needs of homeschoolers, a population that has swelled in size over the past decade.²

Entrepreneurial teachers and parents like Coi and Rebecca are building innovative education programs such as low-cost private schools and microschools, hybrid homeschools and homeschooling collaboratives, small co-learning communities sometimes known as learning pods, and personalized online learning platforms all across the country. In some places, such as the greater Fort Lauderdale area, these programs are serving an estimated ten thousand children annually with affordable, learner-centered options.³ In other areas, such as around the Las Vegas Strip, roughly twenty-five microschools currently educate about 750 students, with growth projected to climb.⁴ "Demand is surging," Laura Meckler wrote of these unconventional learning models in the *Washington Post* in 2023. "For a growing number of students, education now exists somewhere on a continuum between school and home, in person and online, professional and amateur."⁵

This book tells the stories of these education changemakers and their entrepreneurial efforts. From the cosmopolitan corners of South Florida to the rural recesses of southern Idaho, and from Detroit to Omaha to Austin, everyday entrepreneurs are introducing innovative, community-based educational models that prioritize and protect a holistic view of childhood and learning. Most of the imaginative educators who are building these new models are working outside the public school system, but some are trying to change the system from within by pioneering new programs—and even disrupting entire school districts—to be laser-focused on individualized learning and student agency.

These entrepreneurs are breathtakingly diverse, from their geography and demographics to the students they serve, to their distinct educational philosophies and worldviews; but they share a dedication to meeting each child's personalized educational needs with low-cost learning options and enabling young people to flourish as individuals outside of a conventional classroom. A majority of these founders are former public school teachers who love teaching but became fed up with the standardization and regimentation of established schooling. Many are people of color, and a desire to reach low-income or marginalized families is often a top motivator for prospective founders.[6] Some education entrepreneurs are opening learning spaces specifically for neurodiverse students or those with dyslexia. Others are creating nurturing environments for LGBTQ+ youth or launching microschools that celebrate the experience of BIPOC (Black, Indigenous, and people of color) youth. These ordinary parents and teachers are part of an extraordinary, bottom-up movement that is transforming US K–12 education in sweeping and profound ways.

Is your story reflected in these pages? Perhaps you are a dad like James Lomax who didn't like that his daughter's pricey preschool was focused more on formal academics than on childhood play, so he opened his own learner-driven microschool for his children and others in his Nevada neighborhood. Maybe you are a mom like Amber Okolo-Ebube who couldn't find a diverse and inclusive homeschool co-op or microschool in her Texas community, so she built both. You might be a public school teacher like Imani Jackson in Philadelphia, Alycia Wright in Richmond, or Greg Brown in Portland, Oregon, who have built alternatives to standard schooling.

You might be a pharmacist like Dallin "Doc" Richardson, a Head Start advocate like Danna Guzman, an attorney like Gaby Narvaez, a soil scientist like Jen Granberry, a physician associate like Sharon Masinelli, an accountant like Elmarie Hyman, or a retired United States Air Force officer like Todd Hepworth—all of whom spotted local demand for new and different ways of approaching K–12 education and built sought-after solutions. You may even be currently working within the conventional public school system, like Cory Steiner in North Dakota, Sherrilynn Bair in Idaho, or Robby Meldau in Arizona, and want to shake things up from the inside.

Maybe you want to find—not build—a new school or space. Perhaps you are like grandparents Cheryl and Randy Mynatt in Missouri who sought a school that was more aligned with their faith-based values and viewpoints, or like parents Sara and Brandt Elliott in Massachusetts who were thrilled to find a school where their gender nonbinary children would be welcomed and affirmed. Maybe you are a mother like Melissa Shah in Arizona who wanted a setting that would work best for her gifted and autistic teenager, or a dad like Tim Tran in Texas who wanted a school that prioritized learner autonomy and responsibility. Maybe you are like Regina Birdine in Nebraska who wanted to see her daughter's love of learning restored. Whoever you are, if you are curious about outside-the-box education possibilities—or are perhaps itching to create your own—this book is for you.

My previous book, *Unschooled*, was published in the spring of 2019 and told the story of homeschoolers and microschool founders who embraced one particular educational philosophy—self-directed education—that empowers young people to be fully in charge of their education. One year later, as millions of students were suddenly displaced from their classrooms and sent home to wait out a global pandemic, more parents were attracted to homeschooling, microschooling, and other schooling alternatives, and more of these unconventional education options began to emerge. These options weren't new, but they gained new appeal during the COVID crisis and have continued to blossom in the years since. As the Nobel Prize–winning economist Milton Friedman said: "Only a crisis—actual or perceived—produces real change. When that crisis occurs, the actions that are taken depend on the ideas that are lying around."[7] Unconventional education was one of those ideas lying around.

For the purposes of this book, I define unconventional education models broadly as K–12 schools and learning spaces that prioritize the distinct needs, talents, and ambitions of each child in creative and often novel ways. These schools and spaces reject the standardization and stagnation characteristic of traditional schooling—both public and private—and instead embrace individualization and innovation. They may incorporate time-tested educational models, such as Charlotte Mason or Montessori, and often embrace nontraditional schooling methods like homeschooling, self-directed approaches like unschooling, hybrid homeschooling, microschooling, forest schooling, and virtual schooling. We'll see real examples of these models and methods throughout this book. Some are secular, others are faith-based. Some serve a handful of children, others serve hundreds.

What distinguishes the schools and spaces featured here from other alternative and traditional schools—and what makes them particularly disruptive to the schooling status quo—is their low cost and lean operations. Most are a fraction of the cost of typical private schools in a given location—even established alternative ones like Montessori and Waldorf schools—and are usually priced well below what local public school districts spend per student each year. (There are also public Montessori and Waldorf schools operating in some communities throughout the United States.) The average tuition of all US private schools, including both secular and religious ones, was estimated to be $13,133 in 2024, according to data from Private School Review, while the average K–12 per pupil expenditure in US public schools reached $15,633 in 2022, according to the US Census Bureau.[8]

By contrast, nearly three-quarters of today's microschools, or intentionally small, highly personalized learning environments, charge less than $10,000 a year, and only 3 percent charge more than $20,000, according to data collected by the National Microschooling Center.[9] Additionally, these creative schooling options are founded and led by regular parents and teachers who in many cases never thought they would become entrepreneurs. In the pages ahead, I share the experiences of these entrepreneurial parents and teachers who are reimagining learning in their communities—showing you what is possible for your children and perhaps stirring some of you to take your own enterprising leap.

School founders are one type of education entrepreneur, but there are countless others across the United States and the globe who are creating amazing products and services that promote individualized, joyful education. Some are running educational technology companies. Others are offering tutoring or coaching services, educational therapies, afterschool enrichment activities, or summer camps. Still others are providing high-value curriculum or classes to homeschoolers and microschoolers ranging from salsa lessons to STEM (science, technology, engineering, and mathematics) programming. Some are running traditional private schools. These founders are every bit as entrepreneurial as the founders featured in this book, and their offerings are instrumental in fostering a thriving education landscape. Those aspiring to develop similar programming will discover a great deal of inspiration and information in the chapters ahead. Some may even expand their current camp or class offerings into a microschool or similar model. This book welcomes all education entrepreneurs, but it is primarily meant for parents and teachers in the United States who are looking to launch or explore creative, individualized alternatives that can serve as a complete substitute for traditional K–12 schooling.

In Part 1, "Imagine," I explore the unconventional education ideas that were "lying around" before 2020 and explain some of the reasons for their escalating appeal in the wake of the COVID crisis. School closures and prolonged remote learning led many parents and teachers to wonder about—and create—new educational options in their communities, accelerating a shift away from standard schooling that began years earlier. These initial chapters invite you to wonder what less rigid, more joyful learning can look like while offering snapshots of the everyday entrepreneurs who have launched innovative schools and spaces. I also describe the boom in American entrepreneurship since 2020 and how a growing number of education entrepreneurs are starting their own small businesses. I share why more parents are interested in alternatives to standard schooling for their kids and what happens when they switch to a different educational setting. Throughout the book, you will find that I use the terms *founder* and *entrepreneur* interchangeably, as well as the terms *unconventional, innovative,* and *alternative education* to refer to today's creative schooling options.

Part 2, "Seek or Build," digs deeper into the startup journey with step-by-step strategies for launching your own bottom-up learning solution or finding one that works well for your child. It highlights schools and spaces created for neurodiverse learners and those with special needs, as well as those catering specifically to BIPOC and LGBTQ+ youth. It addresses common startup challenges and offers tips for overcoming them, including how to deal with failure and setbacks. In addition to reimagining conventional classrooms and curriculum, education entrepreneurs are also defining success beyond standardization. I examine how founders measure outcomes in an innovative education setting. Traditional testing may be one way, but what about gauging success based on kids' desire to go to school—even on snow days?

Part 3, "Transform," offers a vision for the future of learning, as parents and teachers just like you imagine, build, and scale new educational offerings—including as "intrapreneurs" within the conventional school system. This final section offers predictions for the future of learning, describing the dominant trends that are converging to remake American education from the bottom up. Throughout the chapters, you will find reflective questions, checklists, and recommendations to help you navigate your education options as a parent and consider your path forward as a founder. These tips and tools will help you uncover your own values and viewpoints to find or shape your preferred learning environment.

I have been working in education for more than twenty years, and I have never felt more exhilarated or optimistic than I do right now. Young people today have the opportunity to enjoy personalized learning experiences where they are truly able to discover their own human genius.

Families are able to access these innovative education environments in unprecedented numbers. Entrepreneurial parents and teachers are creating more solutions every day. As Becky Elder, a Kansas education entrepreneur who homeschooled her children decades ago and later launched a microschool, told me: "The fringe is becoming the cloth."

## Part I

# IMAGINE

## Chapter 1
# Changes

*To me, entrepreneurship is about creating change, not just companies.*
—Mark Zuckerberg (cofounder of Facebook)

Jill Perez had seen how disruption could change education. She was just a few days into working her first job as a middle school mathematics teacher in the Jersey City Public Schools system when she and her eighth graders looked out their classroom window across the Hudson River as two buildings went up in flames on September 11, 2001.

Two of her students fainted. Everyone was scared and uncertain. All planned lessons were scrapped. In that moment, Jill relied on her experience as a yoga instructor. She led breathing and meditation exercises with her students, helping to restore calm and regulate emotions. She wanted her students to feel safe.

The district canceled school for the remainder of that week. The following Monday, Jill continued to incorporate breathing and mindfulness exercises into her classes, helping the children process the trauma that had occurred—pre-algebra wasn't the only priority. The tragedy of 9/11 forever changed Jill as a teacher. "It made me reflect on a lot of things about what it means to be an educator. I realized that there were fundamental pieces of teaching children that I really didn't get in my teacher preparation," she said. She began to see education as much more than schooling, and to view her experience as an educator as much more than teaching and testing.

Jill carried those newfound insights with her over the subsequent decade that she spent as a classroom teacher before moving into a role in higher education, first at Rutgers University teaching introductory education courses and later at Seton Hall University supervising student-teachers. She was working in this latter role when COVID hit. Like other schools across the United States and around the world, the K–12 schools that Jill's four children attended shut down in the spring of 2020, and she had to help her student-teachers navigate a new remote-learning world. When it became clear that schools would not open normally, or at all, in the fall of 2020, Jill knew she had to take action, responding once again with ingenuity to unforeseen educational disruption.

Like thousands of parents that year, Jill unenrolled her children from traditional schools and opted for independent homeschooling while forming a "pandemic pod" with several local families to enable ongoing learning and social interactions in a small, safe environment. She cobbled together a curriculum and created lesson plans, and parents took turns hosting the mixed-age learning pod at their homes during the week. Each day began with movement and abundant outside time before focusing on academic content and enrichment activities. Word got around. Neighbors started seeing these pod children learning and playing freely outside of a conventional classroom. They wanted in. That was how Jill became an education entrepreneur. She spotted the mounting demand from parents in her community for an alternative education environment, and transformed her informal pod into an established microschool.

The word *microschool* is frequently used as a catch-all term to reflect many of today's creative schooling options. What one founder calls a learning pod or hybrid homeschool, another might call a microschool. This can reflect the preferences of the founder and the families they serve, or it can relate to various state or local regulations regarding what can and cannot be classified as a school—even a micro one. Microschools may be state-recognized private schools or full-time or part-time programs geared toward homeschoolers. They are designed to be small, typically serving fewer than fifty students, but can grow to more than a hundred learners. They take place in a variety of settings, from private homes, offices, and places of worship to commercial spaces and educational facilities. They are usually drop-off programs (meaning parents don't stick around) with a flexible, individualized curricular approach and paid educators. Microschools are generally lower in cost than traditional private schools, deliberately avoiding many of the accoutrements of conventional schooling, such as layers of administrative staff, large buildings, and afterschool sports teams—although they regularly partner with local sports and extracurricular organizations.

Tranquil Teachings Learning Center opened as a microschool in the fall of 2021 with about three dozen prekindergarten to eighth grade (PK–8) students in a leased commercial space in Monmouth County, New Jersey. Jill recruited experienced teachers from New York City public schools who were burnt out from a year of online and hybrid schooling and eager for a change. "They're loving what they are doing in a way that they hadn't in years," Jill said of her teachers, most of whom work part-time at the microschool, given its nimble scheduling.

As in many microschools, students at Tranquil Teachings are legally recognized as homeschoolers but can attend the program up to five days a week as a full-time schooling alternative. Homeschooling provides the legal designation for parents to assume full control and flexibility over their children's education but, in most states, that doesn't mean parents have to be the ones directly teaching their children. They can often outsource all or part of that instruction to various educational providers, including microschools, tutors, online learning platforms, and so on. State laws vary on how directly involved homeschooling parents must be in their children's teaching and learning, but microschools like Tranquil Teachings exist all across the United States. They are typically much less expensive than most traditional, secular private schools and far lower than what public schools spend on students each year. Many of Jill's students attend full-time, but some choose a part-time enrollment option, attending the two enrichment days that feature classes in art, music, languages, gardening, and movement while completing their academic content at home or elsewhere on the remaining days. "Every family has a unique situation, and I get to know the families and what they value. Having that flexible component is really important," Jill said.

Her program was so popular that Jill decided to purchase a property for the microschool in 2022, choosing an agricultural lot with an old farmhouse and gardens that would allow for extensive learning outside. She now has more than fifty learners, although, like many microschool founders, Jill plans to keep Tranquil Teachings small to foster the kind of individualized, child-centered education that she believes is most valuable and effective. "We are at such a pivotal moment in education," Jill said, as she's seen more families seeking the personalization in education that they experience elsewhere in their lives, such as the fitness tracking apps on their smartphones or the movie recommendations on their Netflix profiles.

Jill was my very first podcast guest. For the previous two years, I had been writing about the creative approaches some parents and teachers were taking in the wake of COVID-induced school closures. I was captivated by their stories and their latent entrepreneurial spirit that began to emerge, first out of necessity and later out of a passion to do school differently. I shared these stories in my column on Forbes.com and elsewhere, but as an avid podcast listener, I thought that it would be even more powerful to hear the actual voices of these innovators.

In February 2022, the *LiberatED* podcast launched with Jill's story. Six months later, I had such a backlog of recordings of entrepreneurial parents and teachers across the country who had launched innovative education models—most over the previous two years—that I bumped the podcast from weekly to semiweekly. Now, hundreds of episodes later, I still have a backlog.

There is no doubt that the pandemic brought us to this pivotal moment in education. While interest in alternatives to conventional K–12 schooling was growing prior to 2020, as I documented in *Unschooled*, the education disruption caused by nationwide school closures and prolonged remote learning supercharged that interest. In 2020, parents were jolted by an educational upheaval that led many of them to question the schooling default. They became more open to other ways of teaching and learning beyond the conventional classroom. They chose private schools at far higher rates than they did previously, often because those schools were more likely to reopen for in-person learning faster than local public schools.[1] They saw that virtual learning could remove constraints around how, where, and when one learns. Their opinion of homeschooling rose.[2]

At the same time, entrepreneurial parents and teachers like Jill were constructing clever learning solutions in their own backyards and bringing others along with them. They were rejecting an outdated, top-down mass schooling model and instead embracing do-it-yourself schooling alternatives. Together, these small-scale solutions are having a big, enduring impact on education all across the United States.

## BIG DISRUPTION, BIG CHANGE

As devastating as the pandemic was, upending the lives of millions of students and their families, it prompted systemic change in education and unleashed innovative ideas. Many of those ideas have stuck and are steadily reshaping K–12 education. A similar educational renewal occurred on a smaller scale in the wake of the massive disruption caused by Hurricane Katrina in 2005, when that storm pummeled the city of New Orleans.

In January 2020, I was at an education conference in Florida that featured a keynote presentation by Stanford University professor Terry Moe. He was talking about his latest book, *The Politics of Institutional Reform*, that explained how Hurricane Katrina not only destroyed homes and schools and the overall infrastructure of New Orleans, but also how it destroyed the unseen bureaucratic barriers that prevented systemic, citywide educational change. With the school system shut down for many weeks, new ideas emerged that challenged the way schooling had always been done in the city. Specifically, the havoc brought by Katrina led the Louisiana Department of Education to take over the entire school district and begin to convert every district school into a charter school—a tuition-free public school that is taxpayer funded but privately run, usually by an independent nonprofit organization.

Charter schools were gradually making their way into New Orleans before Katrina, but the hurricane accelerated the charter shift. The point, as Moe explained, is not whether this change was positive or negative, but the "fact that major change of any kind happened at all—and that an entrenched institutional status quo, long resistant to change, was transformed."[3] Data do suggest that the charter shift in New Orleans led to improved student outcomes over the subsequent decade; but regardless of those outcomes, the disruption caused by Katrina transformed education in New Orleans in deep, long-lasting ways.[4]

I left that presentation intrigued by what had happened in New Orleans but resigned to the idea that large-scale, sustained change in education was improbable. Hurricane Katrina was a once-in-a-lifetime event. We weren't likely to see that level of education disruption again any time soon. Or so I thought.

Three months after I heard Moe speak, it was clear to me that the level of educational disruption initiated by COVID would dwarf anything we had seen before. One hurricane overhauled one city's entire education system. What would a global pandemic do? On March 11, 2020, the day the World Health Organization declared COVID a pandemic, I wrote in my Forbes.com column about "the world's homeschooling moment." It was roughly one week before most US schools shut down, but globally the pandemic had already sent home more than 300 million students, and domestic closures were coming. Like many of us at the time, I suspected, and hoped, that school closures would be temporary—a few weeks at most. But I also suspected that even those few weeks of displacement would fundamentally change education, just as Katrina's closures had fifteen years earlier. Most schoolchildren would return to their conventional classrooms post-COVID, I wrote in my column, but some families "may start to wonder if homeschooling or other schooling alternatives could be a longer-term option."[5] Sure enough, many families did wonder that. Some of them even built those alternatives.

Aside from the sheer scale, the key difference between the systemic educational change occurring today after COVID and the change that occurred after Katrina is that the latter was centralized while the former is entirely decentralized. After Katrina, the State of Louisiana took over the New Orleans school system to orchestrate educational change from the top, albeit with the goal of eventually returning it to more localized control—something that would take more than a decade to do. Today, it's entrepreneurial parents and teachers who are spontaneously and independently creating education solutions in their own communities. There is no central plan, only grassroots possibility.

Felicia Rattray saw this possibility. She and her husband, Amnon, had recently gained custody of their young nephew when COVID hit. Felicia's sister had died tragically in a car accident when the boy was just nine days old. Since then, he had been living with his grandmother, who was growing increasingly frail, so Felicia and Amnon took over their nephew's care. He was in the third grade in a Florida public elementary school when schools shut down in 2020, but Felicia, a public school teacher and counselor for more than a decade, soon discovered through the boy's remote learning that he was academically much further behind, barely above a kindergartener in reading and math ability. This was unacceptable to Felicia. She set out to create her own microschool for her nephew, who has autism, and other local children that would focus on core academics as well as incorporate a relevant curriculum on Black history and culture, reflecting and respecting her students' experiences.

Felicia wasn't sure where to start, so she reached out to Laurel Suarez, a microschooling pioneer in the Fort Lauderdale area who launched her program, Compass Outreach and Education Center, in 2019. Born and raised in the US Virgin Islands among a family of educators, Laurel was a classroom teacher and worked in charter school administration in Florida before launching her own tutoring business on the side in 2014. "While I was working in the high school setting, I started to see students coming into school and there was no more love of learning," Laurel told me. When she worked with homeschooling families in her tutoring program, she noticed those children had a very different, much more positive relationship with learning. Laurel began imagining a learning center for homeschoolers that would serve as a one-stop shop, providing regular classes and social connection. It was something she would have loved to have for her own children, who were then grown. When she mentioned the idea to some of her tutoring families, they jumped at the possibility, urging her to make it a reality. She wasn't sure exactly what her program would look like, but she knew the type of environment she wanted to create. "I wanted to hear kids say, 'I don't want to go home yet,' versus 'What time is it? Is my mom here to pick me up yet?'" Laurel said.

On a sunny fall morning, Laurel greeted me as I arrived at Compass's one-story white building on a quiet, residential side street. It was instantly clear that her students adored being there and were indeed sad when the day was over or weekends came. Two eight-year-old girls told me how much they loved Compass before they both ran off to join a group of peers playing outside in the expansive lot and manicured gardens that surround the school, which is adjacent to a local public school property. It seemed like an ideal location for the type of learner-centered, outdoor-focused educational environment that Laurel tries hard to foster.

Finding this location wasn't easy for Laurel. She had looked at more than thirty potential properties before settling on this one due to its generous outside space and appropriate zoning for educational purposes. The building, though, was a wreck. It was an abandoned church in total disrepair. The ceilings and walls were crumbling. The plumbing didn't work. There were squatters living in the rooms at the time. Nevertheless, Laurel saw the property's potential and labored with her family members to renovate and rejuvenate the building and grounds.

She opened Compass as a microschool for homeschoolers, eventually converting it to a recognized, accredited PK–12 (prekindergarten through twelfth grade) private school so that low-income students would be able to attend tuition-free using Florida's tax-credit scholarship program, a school choice policy that enables low-income students to access funding to use on private education options.

Laurel continues to offer part-time enrollment options for homeschoolers, but she's found most learners want to be there full-time. "I've had students enroll with us who have experienced bullying and similar issues, and they are looking for a different kind of environment," Laurel says. "Parents often want to homeschool and attempt to commit to it fully, but because they have to work, it doesn't always go as planned. Schools like ours are perfect for these families because we can partner with them and provide the support they need."

This close parent partnership, along with small class sizes and a focus on individualized learning and content mastery, is leading to powerful educational outcomes. Like many other innovative educators, Laurel downplays the role of testing at Compass. She saw in conventional schools how teachers would often teach to the test and students would tense up ahead of testing. At Compass, it's different. "Our students don't even know they're being tested," Laurel told me. "We don't put any pressure on them because we really just want to see how they organically perform." She explained that this created confusion when members of a school accrediting agency toured her school and asked the students how they felt about the tests they take. The students responded with blank stares, saying they didn't take tests. Laurel then had the students log in to a particular computer program that they use regularly that also serves as their assessment platform.

The visitors were impressed and granted Compass its educational accreditation, a voluntary, third-party designation that some founders and families value but that the majority of today's microschools (as well as many traditional public and private schools) choose not to pursue. I'll talk more about accreditation in Chapter 7.

Laurel has watched her students quickly accelerate academically and often score above grade level in core subject areas. While her curriculum is aligned with traditional state standards and she uses standardized tests strategically throughout the year, Laurel values whole-child development at Compass and embraces both conventional and unconventional metrics of success. Are the children spending lots of time playing outside and in nature? Are they happy? Are they learning to collaborate with and support each other? Are they developing an entrepreneurial spirit? In Chapter 8, we'll explore more of the academic and nonacademic outcomes measured in today's innovative schools and spaces.

Laurel has seen how happy and successful her students are at Compass and tries to support the growth of more schools like hers—something that has become more urgent since 2020, as her program hit capacity with nearly fifty students and eight hired educators. Like many microschool founders, Laurel says the "micro" piece is crucial for personalizing learning and fostering strong connections with families. She doesn't want to grow bigger, but she enjoys collaborating with other educators, helping them take the leap to become entrepreneurial educators and launch their own programs.

Laurel's school has already served as a community incubator for several successful microschools—including Felicia's school, Permission To Succeed Education Center. When Felicia was beginning her efforts to build a learning program for her nephew, she connected with Laurel, who offered to sublease a small classroom space at Compass so that Felicia could begin to bring her vision to life. She says she benefited greatly from Laurel's encouragement and mentorship.

That was in 2020. One year later, Felicia moved to her own leased space in a Salvation Army building less than two miles from Compass. She opened her microschool that fall with 20 mixed-age students and four teachers spread across two classroom spaces. Tuition was set at $700 a month, significantly less than other local private education options; yet all but two of her students attended tuition-free through the state's low-income scholarship program. Today, Permission To Succeed Education Center serves more than seventy students, with all of them receiving tuition assistance through Florida's expanded school choice programs that are now universal, meaning all K–12 students are eligible, regardless of income or special needs. Felicia hopes to have one of her small schools in every county in Florida. With the 2024 opening of her second microschool location in St. Lucie County, she is well on her way to achieving her goal.

## EDUCATION AS AN INNOVATION LAGGARD

A bit over a year after I first visited Laurel's Compass Outreach microschool, I was driving with her on the way back to Fort Lauderdale from Coral Springs where we had visited another new microschool. A British male voice was hollering driving directions from the car stereo. I asked Laurel how she got the voice on her iPhone to sound so different from the factory-default version I knew. "Oh, there are now so many new voice options to choose from," she explained, describing how to easily change the settings on my device and select from a variety of British accents and a host of other voices. It got me thinking about the extraordinary innovations we've witnessed over the past few decades in many areas—such as communication and navigation—while innovation in education lags.

We see innovation everywhere, from the applications on our phones that give us access to the precise meals, music, and media we prefer, to personalized medicine that is tailored to our distinct genetic makeup. Today, we benefit from so much individualization and innovation in nearly every part of our lives; yet, our dominant education system remains largely standardized and stagnant.

My grandmother was a teacher. Born in Vermont in 1915, she attended public schools throughout New England, trained to be a teacher at Perry Normal School in Boston, and then taught in both private nursery schools and in public elementary schools in Massachusetts. I remember as a child playing in her attic with the mimeographed math and language arts worksheets that she held on to through the years. I still recall the feel of the waxy paper with the purple print. Aside from their musty smell, the worksheets were nearly identical to the photocopied ones in my public elementary school classrooms in the 1980s.

Over the course of her long life, my grandmother witnessed countless extraordinary innovations, from the television and commercial flight to a man walking on the moon, to the internet and the iPhone. (She told me the dishwasher was her favorite invention.) When she died in 2010, just shy of her ninety-fifth birthday, my grandmother's world looked very different from the one she was born into, with a staggering amount of invention and personalization; yet, schooling remained largely one-size-fits-all. Age-segregated classrooms, children sitting passively at their desks waiting to be called upon, bells and buzzers, hall passes and detentions, curriculum and testing meant for the masses—these have been the defining traits of American schooling for more than a century. For all the astounding progress and innovation seen over my grandmother's lifetime, K–12 schooling stayed stubbornly the same.

Now, that is finally changing. Education entrepreneurs like Coi, Rebecca, Jill, Laurel, and Felicia are building the creative schooling options that treat each child as a unique human with specific needs, interests, and preferences. Passionate parents and talented teachers across the country are jolting education away from standardization and stagnation and toward individualization and innovation.

As we increasingly coexist with artificial intelligence, it's more crucial than ever to embrace education models that prioritize originality over obedience, creativity over conformity, and curiosity over compliance. Originality, creativity, and curiosity form the essence of human intelligence and are often sadly weakened through years of conventional schooling. These are the defining qualities of the new schools and spaces that are replacing a stale schooling model with a vibrant learning one reflecting the progress and possibility of the twenty-first century. While there were previous pockets of experimentation in education that valued individualization and innovation, the COVID pandemic is what thrust these ideas from the margins to the mainstream—from the fringe to the fabric—and created the conditions for new models to emerge.

## OPENNESS TO NEW PERSPECTIVES

Both Jill in New Jersey and Felicia in Florida say that they never would have thought to become education entrepreneurs if it wasn't for the COVID disruption and the window it opened to alternative education models. Now, they can't imagine doing anything else. The pandemic experience prompted many parents and caregivers to pause and reflect on their children's education in ways they hadn't before.

Beginning in 2020, more parents became aware of learning options beyond their local traditional schools and became more receptive to different types of teaching and learning methods. According to a 2023 analysis by Stanford University economist Thomas Dee, more than 1.2 million students left local district schools between the 2019/2020 and 2021/2022 school years.[6] Many of them chose homeschooling, private schooling, and charter schooling—and remained there even as schools reopened after the pandemic.[7]

In October 2023, an article in the *Washington Post* declared that homeschooling is "America's fastest growing form of education," with some areas of the country seeing astonishingly high post-COVID homeschooling growth rates.[8] The new Johns Hopkins University Homeschool Hub estimates that homeschoolers comprise approximately 5 to 6 percent of the overall US K–12 student population—or more than three million children in 2024. That puts homeschoolers nearly on par with charter school and private school students, who are about 7 and 9 percent, respectively, of the overall school-age population.[9]

The expansion of school choice policies across the United States is also contributing to rising demand for innovative education options. Between 2021 and 2024, twelve states enacted universal or near-universal education choice programs, making all K–12 students eligible to access a portion of state-allocated education funding to use toward a variety of approved education expenses. In several states, these expenses include microschools, pods, homeschooling centers, tutoring services, educational therapies, and curriculum resources. As of 2024, an additional twenty-one states, plus Washington, DC, and Puerto Rico, had a private-school choice program that applies to certain categories of students, such as low-income students or those with special learning needs.

According to data from the nonprofit advocacy group EdChoice, by the end of 2024 nearly twenty-two million students—or 40 percent of the US K–12 student population—were eligible to access funding to use toward schooling alternatives—including Coi Morefield's Tennessee microschool and Felicia and Laurel's microschools in Florida.[10] Regardless of how you might feel about school choice policies, the reality is that these programs are rapidly expanding, and many parents now have far greater financial access to innovative educational models, encouraging even more entrepreneurship.

Parents are looking for new and different education possibilities. They desire alternatives to traditional schooling, as author and former Harvard Graduate School of Education professor Todd Rose revealed in polling conducted by the think tank he founded. "Americans don't want 'better'; they want different," Rose said. "They want a way out of the one-size-fits-all approach driven by standardized testing models and elite institutions making us compete in a zero-sum game and instead an educational framework geared towards individualized learning, practical skills, and preparation for a meaningful life."[11]

We have witnessed a remarkable shift in American educational perspectives and patterns since the spring of 2020. In some cases, school closures and remote learning gave families the nudge they needed to move away from a learning environment that wasn't working well and find something better. In other cases, parents might have been quite satisfied with their children's learning environment, but the pandemic disruption opened their eyes to other possibilities. The latter was what happened to our family.

## OUR FAMILY'S EDUCATION DISRUPTION

It was two years into the pandemic when I suddenly realized that everything I was saying about other families also applied to my own. My four children were thirteen, eleven, nine, and six when COVID hit. They had always been homeschooled, or more accurately, unschooled. With unschooling, and related self-directed educational approaches, young people are granted the freedom and responsibility to steer their own learning without being tied to a predetermined curriculum. Adults act as facilitators and guides, connecting a child's interests to available learning resources and offering support as needed. My children attended a nearby microschool two days a week that embraced self-directed learning, and they all took additional classes that appealed to them in and around Cambridge, Massachusetts, where we live.

The spring 2020 stay-at-home orders stung, although they weren't nearly as tumultuous for us as they were for many families. We had been accustomed to living and learning alongside our children and not being tied to a school calendar or standard curriculum and assessment expectations. My husband, Brian, and I both had flexible work schedules that allowed us to at least partially work from home. We weren't frontline workers or deemed "essential." All of that made the at-home transition smoother, but it was still a huge change. We may have been a homeschooling family, but our children were frequently away from home, learning from others in their microschool and in dynamic programming around town. Their microschool would stay closed for months, as would the martial arts studio that my two daughters attended several times a week. All classes ended and all museums and libraries shut down for in-person visits, in some cases for more than a year. Our family's entire educational ecosystem evaporated.

Like so many other families, we went digital. In the fall of 2020, my oldest, Molly, took an online, year-long literature and composition class through a respected provider that had been offering virtual learning programs to homeschoolers for years. It was the first formal class she had ever taken. She loved it and wanted to explore other online classes on different topics. In spring of 2021, Molly enrolled in history and Spanish classes through Arizona State University (ASU) Prep Digital, an online virtual school that also has brick-and-mortar charter schools and microschools in their Arizona network. ASU Prep is tuition-free for Arizona residents through its charter network and in conjunction with the state's school choice policies, and is a low-cost private option for out-of-staters.

ASU Prep had been building its international virtual program for several years, bringing Julie Young on board in 2017 as its pioneering leader. Julie was the founding president and CEO of the Florida Virtual School, the world's first public, virtual statewide school district that began in the mid-1990s as a small pilot program and grew to serve more than two million students around the world. She oversaw similar growth at ASU Prep, where enrollment swelled to more than 7,500 full-time K–12 students by 2022, as well as thousands of additional part-time students. When school shutdowns occurred, Young and her team were able to quickly adapt and scale their successful virtual program to meet the needs of many more learners, including Molly, who adored her online classes.

With area microschools still contending with various COVID policies in the fall of 2021, Molly decided to take a suite of high school classes through ASU Prep, as well as enroll in their dual enrollment college classes through Arizona State University. She took on an ambitious course schedule, gravitating toward math and science, while continuing to enjoy the freedom and flexibility of being a homeschooler. She knew that this was an educational path she was willingly choosing among various other options and, crucially, she knew that at any time she had the freedom to quit and do something else instead. She also knew that she was in charge of her education and could craft it however she wanted, in pursuit of her own personal goals. Our family's educational embrace of unschooling and the philosophy of noncoercive, self-directed education remained solidly intact throughout the pandemic—but it was starting to look very different than it had before 2020.

With Molly busy learning through her online classes during the 2021/2022 academic year, my three younger children, Jack, Abby, and Sam, continued to feel the ongoing disruption of their unschooling rhythms. They tried online classes but didn't like them nearly as much as their big sister did. They spent a lot of time in the car as we drove out of the city to find homeschooling classes that were open. Some of their local homeschooling friends had moved away or were about to, while others were considering going to a traditional school. There was a lot of uncertainty and inconsistency. Something had to change.

In the spring of 2022, we made that change. Jack, Abby, and Sam enrolled full-time at the Sudbury Valley School, the flagship, self-directed, K–12 Sudbury-model school founded more than fifty years ago in Framingham, Massachusetts. It has since inspired the creation of dozens of Sudbury-model schools around the world. Sudbury schools prioritize noncoercive, self-directed education within a democratically run learning community where students and staff share in establishing and abiding by community policies and practices. It's an educational blend of individual freedom and personal responsibility.

I knew all about Sudbury Valley and wrote about it extensively in *Unschooled*, but never really considered it as an option for my children until the pandemic. For one thing, it's a recognized private school, albeit at one-third the cost of other traditional, secular private schools in our state—including other alternative ones. Until COVID, we had been content to be homeschoolers, exempt from state compulsory attendance laws that applied to both public and private schools. I had also not previously considered Sudbury Valley because it's forty-five minutes away. That's a long drive to do twice a day, five days week; but by that spring, I was already making that drive several times a week to various homeschooling classes. It felt doable. After the kids did a trial week at Sudbury Valley that spring, they fell in love with the school and immediately enrolled full-time.

It was shortly after they joined Sudbury Valley that it occurred to me: COVID had disrupted my children's education as much as it had others'—and in our case it was for the better. For months I had been saying in media interviews how COVID caused many families to make a change to their children's learning environment and inspired teachers to launch their own schools and similar learning models. I had shared how grateful many of these parents and educators were for the schooling disruption that led them to new opportunities, despite the distress of the pandemic. Now, I was one of those grateful parents. We were happy with our family's pre-COVID learning path, but we were even happier with our pandemic-prompted shift. It's possible that Molly might have eventually found her way to ASU Prep and that Jack, Abby, and Sam might have enrolled at the Sudbury Valley School without the COVID catalyst, but I don't know. Sometimes it takes a big jolt to bring about big, lasting change.

*Chapter Reflections for Parents and Founders*

The educational turbulence triggered by the pandemic has led many parents and educators to rethink traditional K–12 schooling and imagine alternatives. It prompted me as a parent to make some educational changes. Maybe you are a parent who is also wondering about an educational change for your kids. Or maybe you can't find what you're looking for or think you can do it better. In that case, you might be well on your way to becoming an education entrepreneur, creating new learning solutions for your community. Below are checklists for parents and founders to consider when seeking or building new schools or spaces.

**Parents:** What are some of your main motivations for seeking a creative schooling option? When I talk to parents seeking or choosing an alternative to a traditional school, the following are some of the common reasons they give for desiring a change. Do any of these resonate with you?

* *I want a happier, more joyful learning environment for my child.*
* *I want my child to retain or reignite their love of learning.*
* *I want my child's mental health and emotional well-being to improve.*
* *I want a more customized, personalized academic experience.*
* *I want my child to be respected as an individual.*

* *I want my child to be part of a welcoming, inclusive community.*
* *I want a more flexible learning option.*
* *I want my child to have more time for play and movement.*
* *I want my child's special learning needs to be adequately addressed.*
* *I want a safe, bully-free learning environment for my child.*
* *I want less focus on standardized testing.*
* *I want my child to have more time outside.*
* *I want a learning environment for my child that is aligned with my parenting preferences, values, and worldview.*
* *I want to have more involvement and input in my child's education.*
* *I want a smaller learning environment for my child.*
* *I want a more culturally relevant educational setting that reflects the background and experiences of my child.*
* *I want my child to be able to learn at his own pace.*
* *I want my child to have more agency over her life's path.*
* *I want my child to be better prepared for the future.*

**Founders:** What are some of your main motivations for building a creative schooling option? Here are ten of the top motivators I've heard from the school founders I've interviewed. Which of these resonate with you?

* *I want a different type of school or space for my child, grandchild, niece, nephew, or neighbor.*
* *I know that school can be done another way.*
* *I know the type of school I want but there's not one nearby, so I need to create it.*
* *I want to help young people develop a deep, lasting love of learning.*
* *I want a school or space that reflects my values and educational philosophy.*

*I want more personal and professional autonomy.*
*I want to help young people have more independence and agency.*
*I want to create a happy, welcoming, inclusive community of learners.*
*I know that my community needs this.*
*I want to help shape the future of learning.*

# Chapter 2
# Alternatives

*Swim upstream. Go the other way. Ignore the conventional wisdom.*
—Sam Walton (founder of Walmart and Sam's Club),
*Sam Walton: Made in America*

When the Sudbury Valley School opened in the summer of 1968, it was part of a vibrant American alternative education movement that would plant the seeds for what is now sprouting more than a half-century later. The 1960s and early 1970s were marked by a countercultural shift away from established institutions and toward homegrown alternatives. Triggered in part by widespread dissatisfaction with the Vietnam War, broad cultural turbulence, and a rejection of traditional schooling policies and practices, the modern homeschooling movement emerged, along with the "free school" movement. Both largely began among political progressives who were seeking alternatives to conventional schooling—public and private.

Homeschoolers, especially those living in intentional, "back-to-the-land" communities, gravitated toward noncoercive forms of learning that promoted childhood autonomy and independence, while others sought to find or create schools that embraced these qualities. Also known as "new schools" or "alternative schools," these so-called free schools were small programs that were "free" in philosophy but not in cost—although, like today's creative schooling options, they were highly affordable, with most offering a sliding-scale tuition based on a family's ability to pay.

Inspired in part by the pioneering Summerhill School in England, founded by A. S. Neill in 1921, the free schools were child-centered learning environments that touted individual freedom and rejected the top-down teaching practices prevalent in standard schooling. The Summerhill School emphasized noncoercive, democratic education in which children weren't compelled to take classes or follow a set curriculum, but they were expected to agree to the school's ethos of "freedom, not license," or balancing freedom and responsibility. Neill's influential book about his school, *Summerhill: A Radical Approach to Child Rearing*, was published in 1960 and became a bestseller, with more than two million copies sold in its first decade. Other notable authors at the time published popular books that amplified Neill's message of freedom-focused education and resonated with homeschoolers and free-schoolers alike.

The author and social critic Paul Goodman wrote *Compulsory Miseducation* in 1964, finding fault with the traditional public school system's coercive practices, such as mandatory attendance, and suggesting alternative educational pathways, including farm schools and apprenticeships. The teacher and author John Holt, who coined the term *unschooling* to refer to a version of homeschooling that is learner-directed, wrote his popular books *How Children Fail* and *How Children Learn* in 1964 and 1967, respectively, pointing out the ways in which traditional schooling can dull students' curiosity and zest for learning. The philosopher and theologian Ivan Illich was influenced by these writers and wrote his book *Deschooling*

*Society* in 1971 to suggest a shift away from institutionalized education toward decentralized, informal learning networks. All these writers, and many more, fueled the burgeoning alternative education movement. The number of free schools in the United States grew from about twenty-five in 1967 to approximately six hundred schools in 1972, with an average enrollment of thirty-three students.[1]

As the Vietnam War ended and the countercultural revolution faded, the free school movement's momentum waned throughout the 1970s.[2] Most schools closed, but some, such as Sudbury Valley School, endured and inspired a new generation of founders over the coming decades. Homeschooling's ascent, however, was just beginning. John Holt's bestselling books in the 1960s focused on reforming traditional schools, but he began to see homeschooling—especially self-directed approaches such as unschooling, in which young people take control of their own education—as the preferred pathway toward individual autonomy and self-determination. Rather than try to change the schooling system from within, Holt looked outside the system and encouraged many parents to do the same. "What is most important and valuable about the home as a base for children's growth in the world is not that it is a better school than the schools but *that it isn't a school at all*," Holt wrote in *Teach Your Own*.[3] Writers such as Neill, Goodman, Holt, and Illich questioned long-standing educational perspectives and practices and helped create a new vision for education beyond traditional schooling.

Holt became a recognized leader in the nascent homeschooling community and, in 1977, began publishing the first newsletter for homeschooling families, *Growing Without Schooling*, which served as a source of support and connection for nearly twenty-five years. During that time, homeschooling grew increasingly attractive to families on both the political left and right, but its popularity among Christian conservatives soared throughout the 1980s, surpassing interest by political progressives. Dissatisfied with traditional public and private schools, including faith-based ones, thousands of conservative Christian families gravitated toward homeschooling in the 1980s.[4] Laura George's family was one of them.

## THE EARLY RISE OF SCHOOLING ALTERNATIVES

"When we started, it was still risky because so few people really understood homeschooling, or very few people had even heard of someone who was homeschooling, so it was a lonely path," Laura said of those early days in the 1980s when she began homeschooling the first of her eleven children in Georgia. Homeschooling was just becoming legally recognized throughout the United States, something that wouldn't be accomplished in all states until the 1990s. Laura recalled being fearful when her children played outside in the yard during school hours, worried that neighbors would judge her or that truant officers would be called. "That was really stressful for me because of our particular lifestyle, but we've come a long way since then. Now, I don't think there's anybody in the world that doesn't know what homeschooling is. They hardly raise an eyebrow anymore," she said.

Laura and her husband, who worked in manufacturing, were drawn to homeschooling out of a spiritual desire to help shape their young children's character. They also wanted the freedom to choose their own curriculum and to allow their children to spend abundant time playing and learning at their own pace. Laura found great joy in teaching her children, but there were challenges. "I often felt like a failure," she said as she described being filled with uncertainty about whether or not she was doing a good job as a homeschooling mother.

Laura joined small homeschool co-ops to help lighten the homeschooling load. Homeschool co-ops, short for cooperatives, are usually arranged between two or more homeschooling families in an effort to share regular teaching and enrichment opportunities and provide time for socializing and connection. Parents may take turns hosting the co-op in their homes or in local community spaces, such as parks, churches, or libraries. They are often no-cost or may include a very small membership or materials fee. As such, co-ops may not be structured as small businesses at all—just groups of families gathering together for a common purpose. There are exceptions, as we'll see in the pages that follow. Some programs today identify as homeschool co-ops but are run as small businesses with set tuition and paid instructors.

Laura found the co-ops in which she participated to be too informal, so she began exploring other schooling models. At one point, she helped get a traditional, private Christian school off the ground but found it too stifling for her children. "I love Jesus, but the way many Christians do school is not good," Laura said. "A lot of Christians want to protect their children from the stains of the world. There's nothing wrong with that, but I didn't want to protect my children's every move," she said, explaining that her kids listened to pop music, dressed casually, and read Harry Potter books—acts that some Christians, and especially certain Christian homeschoolers, rejected at the time. "I've never seen things the way other people do," Laura added, explaining that freedom was her guiding principle.

Homeschool co-ops were too casual for Laura, while Christian schools were too prescribed. She wondered if there was something in the middle—something that could blend the freedom, flexibility, and family-focused learning of homeschooling with the consistency and community of traditional schooling. It wasn't until she was twenty years into her homeschooling journey, and her fourth child went off to college, that she had the confidence to become an education entrepreneur and create her ideal educational model: a hybrid homeschool. Hybrid homeschool programs blend elements of schooling and homeschooling and can operate either as homeschooling programs or registered private schools. Students have full days of structured classes with hired educators—usually two, three, or four days a week—and then work through the established curriculum at home on the remaining days. They are low-cost, drop-off programs.

In 2005, Laura opened Compass Prep Academy, a K–12 hybrid homeschool program in Holly Springs, Georgia, about forty miles north of Atlanta. Fully accredited by the Georgia Accrediting Commission since 2009, Compass Prep's students are recognized homeschoolers who attend the mixed-age program three days a week for core academics and enrichment. They can also attend an optional fourth day, called Mindset Mondays, for tutoring and additional support. With an annual tuition of about $5,000, it is one-third the cost of the nearby private Christian school. Tuition is offered on a sliding scale, with financial aid available and opportunities for families to volunteer at the school to further lower fees. From its origins as a small, two-day-a-week program with Laura's kids and a few others, Compass Prep now serves approximately eighty students—including seven of Laura's grandchildren—with twelve teachers and several additional support staff. Enrollment has soared since 2020, and in 2024, Laura and her talented team opened a second Compass Prep location thirty-five miles north where there is strong demand.

I arrived at Compass Prep's main location on an unseasonably cool January day and was immediately greeted by Laura's radiant smile and lingering hug. She was still reeling from the December death of her husband of nearly fifty years but was eager for the chance to show me one of her life's other great loves. Located in a white wooden church on a busy suburban street, Compass Prep has full and exclusive use of the building and playground on weekdays, including the education center that sits in a separate but adjacent house to the right of the main church. Laura opened the front door into a large, light-filled room with about two dozen young people, mostly in their tweens and teens, talking and laughing as they ate their lunch at one of several rectangular tables in the center of the room. Toward the back corner, a group of younger children were headed outside with their teachers to the playground for some post-lunch playtime.

I took off my coat, and Laura guided me to the right side of the room by the small kitchen where a cheerful, middle-aged woman was placing steaming bowls of homemade minestrone soup and fresh bread onto student trays. Adriana Blanco had been working as Compass Prep's chef for seven years, desiring to stay connected to the place that had been so life-changing for her daughter, Arianne. She moved to the United States from Venezuela in 2001, when Arianne was just three years old. The girl attended public schools in Richmond, Virginia, but by middle school she was suffering. "It was a nightmare," Adriana said of the bullying her daughter endured at school. Data from the Pew Research Center reveal that about one in five students report being bullied at school, with middle school girls among those most commonly harassed.[5] Arianne developed severe anxiety and dread about going to school. "She was a very smart girl, very compassionate, taking advanced classes," said Adriana, who saw her daughter gradually shut down due to the toxic social culture at school.

When Arianne was in high school, the family moved to Georgia and Adriana made the decision not to send her daughter back to public school. "We were looking for something different," she said, explaining that she explored a variety of schools, including private Christian schools. "It was the same thing: big schools with lots of people," said Adriana, who knew that a smaller, more child-centered setting would be better for Arianne. A friend told her about Compass Prep. When she and Arianne visited and met Laura, they knew it was a perfect match. "She was so happy here and had so many friends. When she came here, she was like another child," Adriana said of her daughter, who graduated from Compass Prep in 2016.

"I often say that we're a healing center disguised as a school," Laura remarked as we sat down at one of the lunch tables to enjoy Adriana's delicious soup. She estimates that about half of her students have always been on a homeschooling or alternative education path, while the other half enroll after experiencing some school-related trauma. One of those latter students was Hailey Shirley, a slight, articulate young woman with wispy blond hair who had graduated from Compass Prep a year earlier and was now working there as a teaching assistant. "Public school had been a little rough for me," Hailey said as she joined Laura and me at the table. "It was large and there wasn't much focus on the individual student. I wasn't doing so great," she added.

Behind on high school credits and languishing at school—something that worsened for her during COVID-induced remote learning—Hailey eventually dropped out. She was considering getting her General Educational Development (GED) diploma in lieu of a traditional high school diploma when she heard about Compass Prep. "It's a whole different world that I didn't know existed," Hailey said. "The teachers here are so wonderful, and the small classes made it easier to learn. They made it easier to *like* to learn," she said, explaining that Compass Prep renewed her love of learning and rekindled her longtime desire to be a teacher.

"In the public schools I attended, there were so many worksheets, so many unnecessary things to keep you busy for the hours that you were there," Hailey said, explaining that "busy work" is absent at Compass Prep and the curriculum is relevant and engaging. "The content made a lot more sense to me here. It wasn't pointless. It made the gears in my brain turn," she said. Now in her new role at Compass Prep, she understands more deeply why this model works. "Teachers can cater to each kid's level, so if someone is not so great in math but good at English, they don't have to stay back. Not everyone works at the same pace," Hailey said.

We finished lunch and walked around the two floors of classroom space at Compass Prep as Laura further described her program's use of differentiated instruction, targeting curriculum toward each child's ability. Concepts such as grade levels, which are a standard part of traditional schooling, are devalued in alternative education environments like Compass Prep, where content mastery often takes precedence over arbitrary age groupings. I watched teachers present main lessons to groups of learners, but the way learners worked through those lessons was tailored to each child. Classes were small, with no more than twelve students and ample opportunities for one-on-one attention. Above all, the kids seemed happy.

They were at ease, enjoying the freedom to move around, play, and interact naturally with others. "I really wanted kids to feel like they were home, to feel relaxed here within this community and feel the encouragement of adults," Laura said of her founding vision.

As they move toward graduation, Compass Prep teenagers often take advantage of dual enrollment options, attending select community college classes that give them a head start on a college pathway. Compass Prep offers a state-recognized transcript that enables eligible students to qualify for Georgia's HOPE Scholarship program, providing financial assistance for higher education. But Laura emphasized that college isn't the only route to adulthood. "We also really encourage entrepreneurship here," Laura said, noting graduates who are self-employed.

As part of its accreditation, Compass Prep is required to offer national, norm-referenced standardized testing options every year for families that want to participate, but Laura says these tests don't reveal anything new about a child's academic strengths and weaknesses. Compass Prep teachers and parents have a solid understanding of a child's academic performance going into a test, something Laura says can be lacking in less personalized educational settings. "It's a tragedy when someone is surprised by a test result, because it shows they're not paying attention to that child," she said.

Laura opened Compass Prep just over a decade after the first hybrid homeschools appeared. As more Christian conservatives turned to homeschooling in the 1980s and early 1990s, some homeschooling parents felt, as Laura did, that it would be more enjoyable and enriching if they could create a learning model that incorporated the best of homeschooling and the best of traditional schooling. Hybrid homeschooling was born.

Eric Wearne is a professor at Kennesaw State University's Coles College of Business in Georgia and director of the National Hybrid Schools Project. He has been studying hybrid homeschooling for more than a decade and said that defining these programs can be tricky due to their diversity.

"The operational definition we tend to go with are schools that meet something less than five days a week, but also schools that either dictate or lead most of the curriculum and academics at the school. So, you might think of them as less structured than a five-day school, but a little bit more structured than something like a homeschool co-op or a set of a la carte classes," said Wearne, whose book *Defining Hybrid Homeschools in America: Little Platoons* explains the history and evolution of hybrid homeschooling.

One of the earliest examples of a hybrid homeschool dates back to 1993, when a group of parents in Arlington, Texas, launched Grace Preparatory Academy. That school would eventually form the foundation of a national network of dozens of hybrid homeschools, known as University-Model® schools. Other popular hybrid homeschool networks would follow a similar trajectory, beginning with one small program and expanding into a larger network of affiliated hybrid homeschools across the United States.[6] Some hybrid homeschool founders decide to partner with a network, while others, like Laura, choose to remain independent and retain maximum autonomy over curriculum and customization.

"These are great examples of small groups of civil society coming together and solving a problem," Wearne told me. He went on to say that some hybrid homeschools are legally considered private schools, while others are recognized as homeschool programs. Often this has to do with state and local education regulations in a given area, but it can also be related to a hybrid homeschool's own identity. He shared an example of two nearly identical hybrid homeschools within fifteen minutes of each other that both meet three days a week. He asked each school to describe itself and explain its community. One school identified more as a private school, while the other felt more like a group of homeschoolers. The flexibility to create a learning community with a shared vision and culture, without being tied to traditional expectations and definitions around schooling, is one reason why hybrid homeschooling is becoming increasingly attractive across the United States.

Hybrid homeschools have historically been faith-based, emerging as they did from the modern Christian homeschooling movement, but secular options are also becoming more popular. Even some public charter schools use a hybrid homeschooling framework. For example, the CORE Butte Charter School in California was founded in 1998 and runs as a personalized, tuition-free hybrid homeschool program serving more than a thousand students. Laura's is one of the many hybrid homeschools and microschools that has a statement of faith describing the school's religious principles. She says that can be a draw for some families and is intended for transparency, but it's also not meant to be exclusionary. Many, but not all, of today's emerging schools and spaces use their statement of faith to clearly communicate their values and curriculum approaches to parents and students, while not requiring parents and students to personally subscribe to a certain set of religious beliefs. "We had a student come once who said, 'I'm an atheist. Is that okay?'" Laura explained. "I said, 'Well, I'm a Christian and what we do at school is kind of Christian. We pray with people. We bring out the Scriptures when it's appropriate to do that, but if you can stand us, we can stand you.'" The student acknowledged Compass Prep's religious worldview and enrolled. "He came and was a delight, and it was a wonderful match," Laura said.

## ALTERNATIVE EDUCATION MODELS GAIN WIDER APPEAL

Around the time that hybrid homeschools began to appear in Texas and other mostly southern states, there was a similar but secular movement afoot elsewhere in the United States. In the early 1990s, Kenneth Danford was working as a middle school social studies teacher in an Amherst, Massachusetts, public school and feeling increasingly unsettled. "I felt I was harming many kids: that the rigidity of the school was hurtful and that I wasn't really in a position to change that," Ken told me. He disliked the power dynamic between learners and teachers that resulted from the coercive qualities of traditional schooling, including the compulsion to attend and the over-emphasis on grades and other narrow evaluation measures.

Ken wondered, for instance, why it was that his students would cheer on their last day of school but cry on their last day of camp or when their theatre program ended and the set was taken down. Why didn't they have that same feeling when his history class was over? He tried to make changes within the system but found it futile, saying that administrators were often as constrained in the traditional schooling model as the teachers. "School isn't going to reform in the direction of empowering children and teens to live well," Ken said.

A friend recommended he read Grace Llewellyn's book *The Teenage Liberation Handbook: How to Quit School and Get a Real Life*, which explained how young people could leave school and learn in a more self-directed way as homeschoolers, in charge of their own education. "I knew nothing about homeschooling—zero—and I didn't want to know anything about homeschooling in 1995," Ken recalled. But once he started reading the book, he couldn't put it down. "I was dumbfounded," he said. When he finished the book, Ken knew he needed to act. He imagined launching a learning space that would enable young people to leave a conventional school, become homeschoolers, and be supported several days a week with optional classes, a cohesive community, and ongoing mentoring—all within an educational framework based on consent over coercion. A year later, he and that friend who had recommended Llewellyn's book both quit their teaching jobs to open North Star, a self-directed learning center for homeschooled tweens and teens in western Massachusetts. Homeschool learning centers, sometimes known as homeschool resource centers, are spaces where homeschoolers can gather for regular classes, enrichment activities, and social opportunities throughout the week. They are usually drop-off programs and often have various membership tiers that enable part-time or full-time enrollment, up to five days a week, with paid educators and facilitators. These learning centers are increasingly referred to as microschools.

Adhering to its motto of "Learning is natural, school is optional," which later became the title of Ken's book, North Star flourished. Ken began getting calls from people around the world who wanted to start their own North Star–model programs, so in 2013 he and a colleague, Joel Hammon, cofounded Liberated Learners, a nonprofit network to support and encourage other entrepreneurial educators. Liberated Learners was one of several mostly secular alternative education and microschooling networks that started in the 2010s and have seen soaring interest since 2020.

Around the same time that Liberated Learners began supporting new founders, Acton Academy was expanding from one small school in Austin, Texas, to what a decade later would become a global network of more than three hundred learner-driven microschools serving thousands of learners. In 2014, the Wildflower Montessori network opened its first storefront microschool in Cambridge, Massachusetts, empowering teacher-entrepreneurs to create smaller, more accessible Montessori schools in their communities. Maria Montessori was an early twentieth-century Italian physician whose educational method emphasizes child-centered, hands-on learning connected to individual interests with ample time for play and the development of real-world, practical skills. Montessori schools have existed for decades as both public and private schools, but Montessori microschooling is relatively new and gaining broader appeal.

In 2018, a dad created a microschool in his living room with seven learners, including his son. That quickly grew into Prenda, a national microschooling network that has reached roughly ten thousand learners through hundreds of tiny schools led largely by entrepreneurial parents. I'll share more about these early microschooling networks in the following chapters, but they often began with one parent or teacher who created a single school or learning space and then attracted more parents and teachers who wanted to start their own.

That was the case for Troy Salazar, who found his way to the Liberated Learners network post-pandemic. Like Ken Danford decades earlier, Troy was growing disillusioned with the conventional schooling system. He had been working in the public school system in Des Moines, Iowa, for more than twenty years in a variety of roles, including elementary school teacher, school counselor, special education teacher, gifted learning consultant, and coach. "From my very first year as a teacher I could sense that something was unnatural about our system. It never made sense to me that so many kids didn't like school," Troy said.

He initially thought that tweaking the system from within might work. Troy watched as various curriculum ideas and classroom tools came and went, hoping that one would be the innovation that stuck and made schooling less stifling for both students and teachers. It was thinking about his grandchildren's education that ultimately drove Troy to leave traditional schooling behind. He was in an eleventh grade math class covering for a teacher when he made the decision. "I will never forget the feeling of despair and defeat in that room," Troy said. "I called my wife right then and there from the classroom and told her we absolutely had to find another path for our grandkids." But what were the alternatives?

A short time later, Troy heard about the Sudbury Valley School on a podcast. "I got goosebumps," Troy recalled. He started doing more research on alternative education options and learned that a high school physics teacher in Des Moines was trying to open a Sudbury-model school there but was running into regulatory roadblocks. Iowa is one of the more difficult states in which to open a secular private school, given its approval and accreditation requirements that can prevent nontraditional schools from operating. In 2021, the prospective Iowa Sudbury school founder and his wife gave up on opening their school and eventually decided to move out of state so that their children could attend a Sudbury-model school elsewhere. "They were pretty defeated and deflated," Troy said after reaching out to the couple.

Given their ordeal, Troy chose to avoid opening a private school. Instead, he connected with Ken at Liberated Learners about launching a self-directed learning center for homeschoolers. While it can be challenging to open an unconventional private school in Iowa, the state has very flexible homeschooling laws. In the spring of 2022, Troy resigned from the school district. That fall, he opened Liberty Self-Directed Learning Center in West Des Moines as a low-cost K–12 program with both full-time and part-time enrollment options.

As in all other centers in the Liberated Learners network, the young people who attend are legally homeschoolers. Troy found that most traditional homeschoolers already had their own weekly rhythms and activities and that it was families newer to homeschooling, especially since 2020, who were drawn to his center. He believes it was COVID and extended remote learning that led to a greater awareness of, and openness to, schooling alternatives. "I think it gave parents and families a peek behind the curtain, so to speak, of the conventional system—and some families just decided to do it another way," he said.

## "FELLOW TRAVELERS"

Kennesaw State's Eric Wearne was one of the people to connect the dots. Even though his research centered mostly on hybrid homeschools like Laura's Compass Prep Academy, he recognized that other models—including self-directed, or unschooling, models like Ken's North Star and Troy's Liberty, as well as Sudbury, Montessori, and Waldorf schools, and emerging microschools and microschool networks—were shaping the innovative education landscape. They were, as he put it in his 2020 book, "fellow travelers with hybrid homeschools."[7]

In the spring of 2022, as in-person conferences gradually resumed after the pandemic's peak, Professor Wearne took a chance. He organized a trailblazing conference that he hoped would not only bring together hybrid homeschool founders and education policy advocates from across the United States but would also attract individuals representing a wide variety of unconventional education philosophies and approaches. While various alternative education, hybrid school, and homeschooling conferences had existed for years, Wearne's would bring these "fellow travelers" together. The pandemic had boosted interest in homeschooling and a host of innovative education models. How about getting all these diverse education entrepreneurs in a room? His only concern was whether anyone would show up.

"I was afraid that I would be buying lunch for my friends to get them to come the week of the conference," Wearne laughed. But within a few weeks of opening registration, the conference filled to venue capacity with nearly two hundred attendees. One of them was Tamara Becker. An educator for nearly thirty years, Tamara had held a variety of teaching and administrator roles in both conventional public schools and virtual schools. In early 2021, she was working as the superintendent of Arizona's largest online school but had a yearning to create something new. "I just saw this opportunity for education to innovate itself—for us to do something different and put kids back at the focus of education," Tamara told me.

Tamara took a bold step and quit her job in the spring of 2021 to create Adamo Education, Inc. Less than six months later, she opened her first Adamo microschool with twelve students in kindergarten through seventh grade in a small storefront location in Fountain Hills, Arizona, growing that location to twenty-five students over the next three years. Meaning "to fall in love with" in Latin, Adamo integrates hands-on, project-based learning, as well as mastery-based digital learning tools that enable curriculum to be targeted to each child's individual strengths and weaknesses. This tailored learning approach allows every child to be working at their own level while enjoying the cohesiveness of their small, mixed-age classroom. "There is so much power in students across grade levels learning side by side, and we see that every single day here," Tamara said, adding that the ability to customize and personalize the learning experience for students was why the microschool model was so appealing to her.

It was Tamara's familiarity with Arizona's robust virtual learning options that enabled her to get her microschool up and running quickly. She partnered with an established virtual charter school to become a state-recognized service provider, enabling all her students to attend Adamo tuition-free while also covering her microschool's operating costs. Tamara's partnership with the public charter school also required that she follow the same guidelines and requirements as traditional charter schools, including periodic reviews by the state's charter school oversight board. Adamo students are also required by the state to do frequent benchmark tests—something that Tamara supports. Those tests revealed dramatic academic gains, including nearly 70 percent student growth in both English and math in Adamo's first year of operation.

"It's not just the academic growth, it's the social growth too," Tamara said. "We've seen students who have had severe anxiety really flourish in this environment. They become more comfortable with their peers, and then they're able to feel more connected to the space as well," she said, explaining that Adamo welcomes neurodiverse students as well as those with special learning needs. "We have students who struggle with dyslexia learning side by side with students who are accelerated readers, and we all learn to support one another. That type of support helps students grow academically and socially," she said.

I interviewed Tamara for an article on Forbes.com in November 2021, just three months after Adamo's launch. My story was about teacher burnout, something that was making headlines as pandemic policies and precautions continued into a second school year.[8] The RAND Corporation had released survey results showing that 23 percent of teachers said they were likely to leave their jobs by June 2021, which was "more than in a typical prepandemic year and more than employed adults nationally," according to RAND.[9] I was curious what some of these teachers were doing instead. Tamara had told me that she felt "re-energized" upon leaving her job and becoming an education entrepreneur. It was a sentiment echoed by other teachers I spoke with who also left their jobs to become school founders. But it wasn't just the pandemic that was leading to higher levels of teacher burnout. In 2023, RAND's survey results revealed that the same number of teachers—23 percent—were likely to leave their jobs by June 2023.[10] Teacher burnout may have been hastened by COVID, but it didn't appear to be abating as schools returned to normal. Neither was teacher enthusiasm for entrepreneurship.

I met Tamara in person the following April at Professor Wearne's conference. She was on a founder panel moderated by Beth Seling, chief of operations at VELA, a philanthropic education fund and founder network created to support education entrepreneurs. In 2019, the fund began issuing grants to founders like Tamara who were starting or scaling unconventional, individualized K–12 learning models. Since then, VELA has supported thousands of such founders through its grant programs and vast entrepreneur resource platform. Like Wearne, the VELA team recognized the many new and longtime "fellow travelers" working within the alternative education space and wanted to support them as they grew. Most of these founders were running fee-based programs, but Tamara uncovered novel ways to use existing educational policies and platforms, such as tuition-free virtual charter schools, to make unconventional education models more accessible.

Interest in Tamara's Adamo microschool model grew. In August 2022, one year after her initial launch, she opened her second school in Queen Creek, Arizona, with twenty students. This time, it was in her own home. Students recited the Pledge of Allegiance in her living room, did math around the kitchen table, and gathered in the sun-filled dining room for English language arts. Tamara didn't plan on having her home be the site of a second microschool, but it was the fastest way to get her program launched in response to rising local demand from parents. She soon discovered that the cozy, relaxed setting put children at ease, enabled them to form closer relationships with each other, and led to positive academic outcomes. So, a year later, when the tenants moved out of a rental house she owned just a half mile away, Tamara converted that house into a fully dedicated space for her microschool, which now serves forty-four students.

I pulled into the driveway of the tan, one-story home in a quiet residential neighborhood of the fast-growing Phoenix suburb. Other than a small sign on the window to the left of the door that read "Adamo," there were no indications that this was a school of any sort. Yet, once Tamara opened the door, it was clear that this was a space intended for deep, lasting learning. I walked into an immaculate open-concept living and kitchen space with high ceilings and curtain-clad windows. Colorful classroom decorations, inspirational posters, and student projects lined the walls as a mixed-age group of fourth through eighth graders worked quietly on their core subjects.

Off to the left, some students sat on cozy couches with laptops, working on language arts through an online curriculum platform that assesses student progress based on mastery, moving them ahead as they achieve proficiency. Another student was sitting on a stool at the kitchen island, a paperback copy of *What Is the Constitution?* beside him. At a small kitchen table in a nook overlooking the peaceful, plant-filled backyard, a boy worked on his reading skills through an online application. One group of students sat in another nook to the right of the kitchen island to read and discuss the nonfiction book *The Boy Who Harnessed the Wind*, while another group sat by the back windows reading the popular fiction book *City of Ember*.

In a carpeted room off the main living room, Rachel Gardea guided a mixed-age class of kindergarteners through third graders. Attentive, cheerful, and mild-mannered, Rachel has the personality and temperament of someone who was born to be an elementary school teacher. After a spelling test, her students spent several minutes practicing writing in response to an essay prompt while I talked to Rachel. She began looking into microschools and various alternative education options during COVID, when remote schooling at her children's local public school wasn't working well for them. She tried out a couple of microschools and then eventually sent her three children back to the public schools; but for her son with attention-deficit/hyperactivity disorder (ADHD) and anxiety, the traditional school environment wasn't a good fit. She found Adamo and enrolled him there as a fourth grader, quickly seeing how the smaller, less rigid learning environment perfectly suited him.

A former teacher, Rachel began volunteering at Adamo during her son's first year there, becoming increasingly passionate about Tamara's individualized approach to learning. She came on as a full-time teacher in 2023, pulling her two daughters from their public school to join Adamo as well. "Everyone is thriving here," Rachel said, noting that while her girls were doing fine at their traditional public school, they tell her how much happier they feel at Adamo. Rachel is happier too. "When I taught previously at a public school, I had so many students and so much to teach them that I didn't really get to know them as much as I wanted to," Rachel said. "At Adamo, I only have ten students in my morning class and five in my afternoon class. I get to have those precious few moments with each one every day to ask them questions and listen attentively. I feel more of a connection and bond to these children and can give them a safe space to be with a trusted adult who understands and cares for them," she said.

In 2022, Arizona became the first in a growing list of US states to enact a fully universal education savings account (ESA) program that enables all K–12 students to access a portion of state-allocated education funding to use toward approved education expenses. These include traditional private schools, but in Arizona, funds can also be used for a variety of alternative education options, including microschools like Adamo. The average ESA amount for an Arizona student is about $7,000 each year, with additional funding available for students with identified disabilities or special learning needs.

For years, Arizona was a leader in school choice policies, with a robust charter school sector, virtual schooling options, and "open enrollment" policies that enabled public school students to attend a school other than the one to which they were residentially assigned—including public schools in other cities and towns. The state also had previous ESA programs that were limited to certain student categories, such as those with special needs. The new universal ESA option is a game changer for many families, including some that Tamara serves. In fact, she is hearing from more parents who want to use their ESA funds toward Adamo's tuition, so Tamara is adapting her model to be ESA-friendly.

Adamo continues to grow throughout Arizona, with a new microschool location set to open in San Tan Valley and more locations on the horizon. Expansion is rooted in local parent demand. "Every parent wants to have a learning environment where their student is successful, where they feel safe, they feel encouraged, and loved and supported. I think microschools provide that opportunity, and I think we're here to stay," said Tamara, who finds that more parents want smaller, more personalized learning options for their children.

*Chapter Reflections for Parents and Founders*
The drive to find or create alternatives to conventional K–12 schooling is not new, but there has been new and growing interest in these alternatives in recent years. Small, low-cost private schools that focus on individualized learning, hybrid homeschools that blend campus-based and at-home learning, and self-directed learning centers for homeschoolers have existed for decades. Today, they are more sought after,

plentiful, and financially accessible than ever. Below are some considerations for both parents and founders pursuing these traditional schooling alternatives.

**Parents:** When you are exploring creative schooling options for your children, look at how each program is structured. Some programs may be legally recognized by your state as private schools, while others might be legally structured as tutoring centers, membership associations, or other types of organizations catering to homeschoolers. For the latter, you may need to register as a homeschooling family with state or local agencies and comply with various homeschooling reporting requirements. Homeschooling is legal in all US states, but requirements related to notifying authorities of your intent to homeschool and reporting student academic progress vary by state, as do requirements related to curriculum coverage, instruction, and testing. If you are considering enrolling your child in a program that requires you to register as a homeschooling family, the founder and staff members should be willing to guide you through that process. If they are not, it could be a sign to keep looking for other alternatives.

In some states, such as Georgia, Texas, Utah, and West Virginia, microschools or learning pods have their own statutory definitions. You'll want to know the legal structure of your new school or space, but as Professor Wearne explains, that's only part of the picture. A program could be a state-recognized private school but see itself more as a homeschooling program, and vice versa. Talk to the founder and other parents in the program to get a better sense of the community spirit—and whether or not it feels like a good fit for you and your child.

**Founders:** How do you plan to open and market your new school or space? Will you run a state-recognized private school; a homeschool resource center; a microschool, co-op, or learning pod; a hybrid homeschool that could either be a private school or homeschool program; or some other type of educational program? There is much overlap between these different models, and these terms are often used interchangeably. How you position your new program may depend on state and local regulations or on the services you want to offer. Chapter 5 provides more detail about the startup process, but it will be helpful to consider early on what type of model will work best for you and the families you want to serve.

## Chapter 3

# Founders

*What entrepreneurs do is they imagine what feels impossible to most people, and take it all the way from impossible, to improbable, to possible but unlikely, to plausible, to probable, to real!*
—Vinod Khosla (cofounder of Sun Microsystems; founder of Khosla Ventures)

When Tamara Becker founded Adamo in 2021, she was one of the 5.4 million Americans who started a business that year—the highest level of entrepreneurial activity since the US Census Bureau began tracking such data in 2004.[1] In fact, 2021 broke the record set a year earlier, when more than four million entrepreneurs requested Employer Identification Numbers (EINs) from the Internal Revenue Service (IRS) for their new ventures. With 5.5 million new business applications, 2023 again smashed the startup record, signaling an ongoing entrepreneurial surge.[2] Despite the social and economic turbulence of the COVID era, many individuals found it to be an ideal time to pursue their entrepreneurial dreams. Even as our pandemic memories begin to blur, the entrepreneurial cascade that COVID helped unlock becomes clearer to see.

Education entrepreneurs are part of this swell in American entrepreneurship that began in 2020. Indeed, the majority of the education entrepreneurs I have interviewed and visited have opened their new schools and spaces since 2020. In 2023, Babson College's Global Entrepreneurship Monitor (GEM) report revealed that nearly 20 percent of Americans were either in the process of launching a new business or had launched one since 2020—representing the highest level of entrepreneurial activity since the annual survey started in 1999.[3]

The uptick in US entrepreneurship reverses a yearslong dip prior to COVID and places the United States in the lead for startup activity among developed countries. "The COVID-19 pandemic triggered an unexpected boom in entrepreneurship, as Americans opted to start businesses at record rates. Just as unexpected has been the boom's durability," wrote Kenan Fikri and Daniel Newman in the *Harvard Business Review* in 2024. They noted that the pandemic prompted many Americans to re-evaluate their lives and livelihoods and create new personal and professional goals. "It's a testament to something deeply ingrained in American culture that, confronted with all that 2020 threw at us, so many people chose entrepreneurship," they wrote.[4]

American entrepreneurship has been particularly strong among certain demographic groups since 2020. For instance, data from the Kauffman Foundation shows that Latinos launched more new businesses in 2021 than any other racial or ethnic group, and immigrants were particularly entrepreneurial.[5] "Americans are starting and running their own businesses at record rates, part of a post-pandemic shift toward entrepreneurship led by women and people of color," the *Washington Post* reported in 2023.[6] It's not surprising, then, that women and people of color are also the ones leading the way in launching new schools and spaces as education entrepreneurs.

## FOUNDER DIVERSITY

Denisha Allen has been documenting this entrepreneurial momentum, specifically among Black school founders. After George Floyd's death in the summer of 2020, as "Black Lives Matter" signs proliferated and the United States grappled with a racial reckoning, Denisha penned a viral op-ed calling on Americans to cherish Black minds as well as lives. "Those committed to protecting black lives cannot simultaneously refuse to nurture black minds. Our essence and our being deserve life. Our black minds matter," wrote Denisha, who was born to a teenage mother and grew up poor in Jacksonville, Florida.[7] She failed the third grade twice and her future looked bleak. Denisha recalled that teachers would sigh when she walked through the classroom door. They expected her to become a statistic. She began to expect it too. "I come from a family of high school dropouts," Denisha told me. "Many women in my family have given birth to kids as a teenager, and I thought that would be my same trajectory."

But then her godmother heard about a small private school at her church that participated in Florida's school choice scholarship program, enabling low-income students like Denisha to attend. It was life-changing. "The teachers at the new school created this community for me. They helped me realize that I wasn't a failure, that the system of education had failed me. It really helped me understand that when a kid receives a great education, when a kid receives a good community, when they receive love and comfort and they're nurtured, then they are really able to do anything," Denisha said.

At her new school, Denisha excelled academically and went on to college and graduate school—accomplishments that she doubts would have happened had she stayed in her local public school. She became a vocal advocate for school choice policies like the one that helped her, while championing Black school founders who create new education options for families.

After her July 2020 article gained widespread attention, Denisha created BlackMindsMatter.net to promote education entrepreneurship and choice. Over the next year, she expanded the website to include the first national directory of Black school founders. Today, that searchable directory has grown to include hundreds of entrepreneurs who have created private schools, microschools, charter schools, learning pods, and homeschooling co-ops and collaboratives. In 2022, Denisha hosted the first annual Black Minds Matter Summit, bringing together Black school founders from across the country to share their experiences, gain insights about the business side of running a school or learning program, and build community with other entrepreneurs. "Many of the school founders that I've spoken to felt isolated and alone and like they had to figure it out by themselves," said Denisha, who also manages a Facebook group for Black founders and connects them to training and grant opportunities.

She thinks that we're just at the beginning of this post-2020 entrepreneurial surge. "I believe that there are going to be way more education entrepreneurs—not just African Americans—people just trying their hand at doing something different," she told me. In 2024, Denisha gathered the first cohort of McLeod Society Fellows, named after Mary Jane McLeod Bethune. An American educator, entrepreneur, and civil rights activist who founded the National Council of Negro Women in 1935, Bethune served as an advisor to President Franklin D. Roosevelt and started a private school for Black students in Florida that later became Bethune-Cookman University.

LeDonna Griffin was one of the inaugural McLeod Fellows, joining fifteen other Black education entrepreneurs across the United States who are working to create and expand learning options for families—especially low-income, Black families. LeDonna grew up as a fourth-generation resident of North Omaha, Nebraska, the youngest of five children raised by a single father after her mother passed away when she was three years old. Having grown up in what she described as a marginalized African American community, LeDonna knew that she wanted to work with others from similar backgrounds. She saw education as a means to both individual and community empowerment. "I saw firsthand some of the things that marginalized communities consider as constraints, but I see them as opportunities. Moving into education gave me the opportunity to work directly with families in marginalized communities from day one, back in 1993," LeDonna told me during our first interview in 2023. A first-generation college graduate who later earned a doctorate, LeDonna became a teacher and principal in the Omaha Public Schools system. Her career in urban public education ultimately spanned more than two decades.

LeDonna loved teaching and was proud of some of the initiatives she was able to implement as an elementary school principal, especially a no-suspension policy that addressed social and behavioral issues within the school rather than contributing to what she saw as a school-to-prison pipeline. "It was so evident to me," LeDonna said regarding this pipeline. She explained how children in her elementary school, especially Black and brown boys, would get into trouble at school, get suspended, and then internalize the idea that they were "bad," which would perpetuate the behavior-suspension cycle. "This leads directly to dropping out," LeDonna said. "Hope is pulled away from our youth as they go through school. Eventually they wonder why they should even bother coming to a place where they have no success."

Regularly suspended children have a much higher likelihood of being incarcerated as adults. In 2021, researchers from Harvard University, Boston University, and the University of Colorado Boulder reported a causal link between adolescent school suspension rates and adult jail time. "Our findings show that early censure of school misbehavior causes increases in adult crime—that there is, in fact, a school-to-prison pipeline."[8] Moreover, the scholars found that negative outcomes related to strict school disciplinary policies were worse for boys and students of color, and that these policies can exacerbate existing racial and socioeconomic achievement gaps. A law passed by the Nebraska state legislature in 2023, and championed by LeDonna, prohibits school suspensions in most instances for children in prekindergarten through second grade.[9]

Despite some in-system successes as a principal, LeDonna grew frustrated. "I thought that there was a better way to do this," she said, adding: "The bottom line is, when you work for a public school district, there are mandates." These mandates can include curriculum to be covered at certain times and in certain ways, "seat time" requirements that dictate the number of classroom attendance hours and days and can limit scheduling flexibility, and standardized testing protocols that often create a teach-to-the-test atmosphere. The desire to be an entrepreneur also kept tugging at her. She watched as her father, who dropped out of school in the eighth grade, built up his own successful cleaning business over the years, creating jobs for family members and instilling in LeDonna and her siblings an entrepreneurial spirit and commitment to hard work and self-reliance.

So, in 2018, while still working as a public school principal, LeDonna created Leaders to Legends LLC. It began as a small side project, providing educational consulting services to local families. In 2019, she left the district and began running Leaders to Legends full-time. When COVID arrived a year later and schools closed, LeDonna was inundated with requests from parents looking for homeschooling guidance.

To support those families, most of whom were Black and low-income, LeDonna began leading homeschooling online information sessions and established a faith-based homeschooling co-op in the fall of 2020 that met several days a week at the local public library. "We quickly outgrew the library," LeDonna recalled. The expanding co-op, which LeDonna named Leaders to Legends Academy, moved to a dedicated space in a historic church building in northeast Omaha, where the group continues to meet three days a week from 9:00 a.m. to 3:00 p.m. Today, Leaders to Legends Academy serves about twenty students ranging from prekindergarteners through high schoolers, with a waitlist. Nearly all the students were previously enrolled in an Omaha public school.

When I arrived at Leaders to Legends on a Thursday morning in April 2024, all the co-op members were engaged in a martial arts lesson taught by an expert instructor. Next, the "littles," as the prekindergarteners through fifth graders are known, broke off into a separate large classroom space flooded with sunlight beaming through huge floor-to-ceiling windows. They worked on individualized math lessons with several mom-instructors. The "bigs," as the older learners are called, went into a different, though equally bright, classroom where they worked on an aquaponics project. The students enthusiastically explained to me in-depth how they had created an ecosystem in which the fish they hatched from eggs fertilize the hydroponic plants in their aquarium habitat in an elegant, regenerative cycle.

"My kids were told they were failing, but really it was the system failing them," said Regina Birdine, one of the co-op parents with whom I spoke when I visited. A mom of nine children, her three oldest were given an individualized education plan (IEP) early on in public school, but Regina said it wasn't followed. Her sixth grader learned to read while in a preschool that was part of the federal Head Start program for low-income families, but she began hating to read in elementary school. Regina knew it was time to make a change. According to national data released by the US Department of Education in 2024, a top reason why parents choose homeschooling is that they are "concerned about the school environment, such as safety, drugs, or negative peer pressure."[10] A 2023 survey by the *Washington Post* found similar results, revealing that concerns about school shootings, bullying, and politics in schools were among the main reasons why parents chose to homeschool their children.[11]

For Regina, Leaders to Legends Academy was just what she needed to support her homeschooling choice. "Nothing else like this exists in Omaha," said Regina, who removed all her children from public school to homeschool them through Leaders to Legends. Her oldest, who was a high schooler when she joined the co-op, initially had some reservations. What would it be like? Would there be enough kids her age? Would she miss her friends? Soon, she couldn't imagine doing anything else. She graduated in 2024 with plans to pursue her gift of doing natural hair and further embracing her entrepreneurial work. Since joining the co-op, Regina's younger daughter rekindled her love of reading, gaining confidence by reading to the younger children and enjoying a more personalized reading approach tied to her needs and interests.

There is rigorous academic content being explored and mastered at Leaders to Legends Academy, but the students are doing it in a relaxed, joyful environment that respects their gifts and talents. Regina told me that when her children were recently ill and had to miss school, they were so upset. "Can't I just wear a mask?" one of her children begged, so eager was she to attend. Her kids had the exact opposite reaction to sick days when they were in conventional schools. LeDonna added that at least some of the explanation for rising rates of chronic absenteeism in traditional schools is because they are not places where many children want to be. In 2022/2023, nearly 40 percent of students enrolled in the Omaha Public Schools system were chronically absent, defined as missing at least 10 percent of school days.[12] Creating more joyful schooling environments like LeDonna's can be a key strategy to combat rising levels of chronic absenteeism.

Through intake assessments, LeDonna finds that many of her students join the co-op several grade levels behind. This isn't surprising, given that only about one-third of students in the Omaha Public Schools system were proficient in reading or math in the 2022/2023 academic year.[13] At Leaders to Legends, students are able to quickly close academic gaps due to the individualized learning approach and the stress-free, child-centered environment.

Although she facilitates the co-op and helps with curriculum and assessment, LeDonna believes that parent-directed education is the key to student success and individual empowerment. Most parents of students at the co-op work other jobs, but they take turns leading classes at the co-op or offer support in other ways. "It's not a re-creation of the public school system. It is where parents are directing the education of their children," LeDonna said. "Parent-directed is so important. I've seen it year after year, over and over again, what happens when parents are leading the way," she told me, explaining that she views supporting North Omaha homeschooling families as one way to address, and hopefully halt, intergenerational poverty.

## TODAY'S ENTREPRENEURS: MORE MICROSCHOOL THAN MICROSOFT

When we hear the word *entrepreneur*, many of us think of Silicon Valley stars like Steve Jobs, Mark Zuckerberg, Peter Thiel, Bill Gates, Jeff Bezos, and others who have created sprawling, successful companies whose products and services seep into our everyday lives. These entrepreneurs may be household names, but they are more the exception than the rule. Everyday entrepreneurs—the ordinary people launching and leading small businesses—form the backbone of the US economy. According to the US Small Business Administration (SBA), small businesses account for more than 99.9 percent of all American companies, employing more than sixty million people. A typical entrepreneur, defined by Merriam-Webster as "one who organizes, manages, and assumes the risks of a business or enterprise," is more like a microschool founder than a Microsoft founder. She is more LeDonna Griffin than Bill Gates.

Everyday entrepreneurs like LeDonna may not be motivated by venture capital investments, rapid scalability, and high-profile IPOs, but they are no less entrepreneurial than the tech titans we admire. They spot unmet needs and create solutions while assuming significant personal and financial risks amidst a high likelihood of failure. Indeed, 20 percent of businesses fail within their first two years and nearly half close within five years.[14] The scope of their risks and potential rewards may vary, but if there is one characteristic that all entrepreneurs share, it's a willingness to jump into the unknown to pursue an idea that just might work. A 2016 paper on "everyday entrepreneurs" published in *Entrepreneurship Theory and Practice* reminds us that entrepreneurship "is not just a pursuit of heroic 'Silicon Valley' entrepreneurs, but it can produce heroes of many kinds: of their own lives, families, communities, and myriad other contexts."[15] Education entrepreneurs are examples of these everyday heroes.

How do you know whether you have what it takes to be a school founder? It's tempting to think of today's education entrepreneurs as possessing certain characteristics that elude most of us. Maybe they are consummate risk-takers or they relish impossible challenges. Perhaps they are astonishingly creative or more ambitious than most of us. The truth is that today's education entrepreneurs share many of the same qualities as entrepreneurs more generally—and most of those qualities aren't as superhuman as we may think. In his surveys of entrepreneurs across sectors, Harvard Business School Senior Fellow Timothy Butler found that the stereotypes of entrepreneurs often don't match the reality. "For instance, entrepreneurs aren't always exceptionally creative," Butler said. "But they are more curious and restless. They aren't risk-seekers—but they find uncertainty and novelty motivating," he said.[16]

The education entrepreneurs I interview are incredibly diverse, but there are several common qualities shared by most of them. They are eager for a challenge and are confident that they can overcome inevitable setbacks. They like to take initiative and are comfortable with unpredictability. They are critical thinkers, questioning the way things are typically done in education and wondering about new approaches. Today's school founders like to learn and do new things, and often have a low threshold for boredom. They work well under pressure and are good at building relationships and collaborating with others. Finally, the founders I spotlight are optimists. They believe that education can be changed for the better and that they can be a successful part of that change.

The word entrepreneur comes from the French *entreprendre*, meaning "to undertake." It is largely believed to have originated with the French-Irish economist Richard Cantillon, who used the word in his eighteenth-century writings; but it was the nineteenth-century French economist Jean-Baptiste Say who elaborated on its meaning, connecting it more closely to our modern understanding of entrepreneurs and their important role in a productive economy.[17]

I reached out to Richard Salsman, assistant professor of political science at Duke University, who coined the term *Saysian economics* in 2003 to fully capture Say's economic philosophy, including his recognition of the central role of entrepreneurs. "Say developed the idea that the labor force and the resources of production have to be brought together by an entrepreneur," Salsman told me. "Say saw this as a very active and intellectual process. He went out of his way to say this work is cerebral, that the entrepreneur's contribution comes from the mind: from intelligence, creativity, and perseverance."

In 1803, Say published his famous *A Treatise on Political Economy*, which laid out his theory for a flourishing market economy, including the importance of entrepreneurs. Inspired by Say more than a century later, the Harvard economist Joseph Schumpeter refreshed the image of an entrepreneur as one who induces innovation and change through what he called "the perennial gale of creative destruction." This is the continual process by which outdated industries, enterprises, and practices are replaced by new models and methods brought forth by entrepreneurship and innovation.[18] According to Schumpeter, "The entrepreneur and his function are not difficult to conceptualize: the defining characteristic is simply the doing of new things or the doing of things that are already being done in a new way (innovation)."[19] Education entrepreneurs are both doers and innovators, creating change by building new learning models and refreshing old ones.

More recently, innovation and entrepreneurship have been associated with the term *disruptive innovation* that was popularized by Harvard Business School professor Clayton Christensen beginning in the 1990s as a way to characterize how some products or services begin on the margins and then increasingly occupy a larger share of a market before ultimately upending incumbents.[20] "Airbnb is a classic case of disruptive innovation," Christensen said, explaining how the startup moved from offering a low-end product to a small, niche group of consumers, to eventually moving into the mainstream and disrupting an entire industry.[21]

The story of Airbnb is not only instructive as an example of disruptive innovation. It also illustrates what prompts many entrepreneurs to get started: the need to solve a problem in their own lives. Brian Chesky and Joe Gebbia needed rent money. Two twentysomethings living in San Francisco, the men had met a few years prior as students at the Rhode Island School of Design and became friends. In 2007, Chesky had just moved to the city from Los Angeles and the pair was struggling to cover the rising rent of the apartment they shared. Then Gebbia proposed an idea: what if they rented out some air mattresses in their apartment to attendees of an upcoming design conference who didn't want to pay hefty hotel costs? Airbnb's founders succeeded in creating a legendary company that transformed the hospitality industry and activated millions of entrepreneurial homeowners. But it all started with creative problem-solving.

Most of the education entrepreneurs I have interviewed launched their new schools and spaces to address a challenge within their own immediate family or community—or both. For Maria Gabriela Narvaez, who goes by Gaby, that challenge was about preserving personal agency and cultural roots for both her children and the wider Latino community in South Florida. Born and raised in Venezuela, Gaby was a good student who went to good schools, got good grades, and eventually became a lawyer because she was told it would be a good job. Yet, she felt unfulfilled. In 2012, as the economic and political situation in Venezuela worsened, she and her husband decided to flee the country, eventually settling in the Fort Lauderdale area of Florida in 2016. "It could sound like a sad story, but it was the perfect moment for me to just discover who I was," Gaby said. She also began to wonder about what else was possible for her future children's education, telling her husband: "I'm not going to just let them go to school to spend twelve or thirteen years learning stuff just because the system says that you need to learn this in order to be that."

Pregnant with her first child in the spring of 2017, Gaby was out for a walk in the park one Monday morning when she noticed a bunch of barefoot school-age children playing and laughing as adults lingered nearby. She wondered why they weren't in school, so she approached one of the moms, Iman Alleyne, founder of Kind Academy, who explained that they were a group of homeschoolers. "I was like, what is this homeschooling? Because, of course, in Venezuela it's illegal to do that. It was shocking for me because I looked at these kids and these moms and they were truly the definition of joyful learning. They were just being themselves, and it was a magical thing," Gaby recalled.

Gaby decided right then that she wanted to homeschool her own children, so as her oldest, Luis Carlos, and later her second son, Joaquin, grew, Gaby began offering bilingual classes for local homeschooled preschoolers in a learning pod she named Popcorn Academy. Learning pods typically consist of small cohorts of about a dozen or so multi-age students, with a paid educator or guide, who gather together for regular, personalized learning, often in a private home or community space. Gaby hoped to continue homeschooling, but as the children in her pod reached kindergarten age, their parents decided to enroll them in Broward County public schools. Luis Carlos wanted to join his friends, so Gaby reluctantly agreed and enrolled him too. When an opportunity arose mid-year to volunteer at her son's school, Gaby jumped at the chance. "¡Buenos días, Valentina! ¡Buenos días, Luis Carlos!" Gaby exclaimed when she entered the classroom and spotted her son and some of his friends from her homeschool pod.

But the children quickly stopped her. "No," they told her. "We cannot speak Spanish here because the teacher doesn't like it when we speak Spanish."

"Are you kidding me?" Gaby asked in astonishment. "What are you saying? ¿Qué estás diciendo?" When the children reiterated that they couldn't speak Spanish at school, Gaby grew indignant. "It's part of who you are, Valentina! It's part of who you are, Luis Carlos! You don't have to be ashamed because you speak Spanish," Gaby told them. "It's a gift. It's something that you should feel proud of. It's an asset. It's not something that you eliminate. Your language, it's deep in your bones," she said. Gaby approached the teacher who confirmed that Spanish was not to be spoken at school. "You don't understand," Gaby responded. "It's who we are." Gaby soon removed her son from school and resumed homeschooling while continuing to run periodic bilingual classes. This passion for language preservation and connection to culture has fed Gaby's entrepreneurial drive and desire to help other families in her community hold on to their heritage.

In the summer of 2023, Gaby teamed up with another local mom, Andrea Hantman, to open PLAY K–12, a storefront microschool in Coral Springs, Florida, that offers full- and part-time learning options focused around a P.L.A.Y. philosophy that stands for Passion Learning Approach Year-Round. Gaby and Andrea had met several years prior when Gaby was running one of her bilingual programs and Andrea was running learning pods to accommodate the needs of her children and others in her community who were diagnosed with autism spectrum disorder. They soon discovered that they were both from the same Venezuelan city of Maracay, and they began collaborating. The pair's new business venture is one of the nearly five million Latino-owned businesses across the United States representing a surging entrepreneurial demographic—especially since 2020. According to Stanford University's 2023 "State of Latino Entrepreneurship" annual report, Latino-owned businesses (LOBs) "continue to grow at a faster pace than White-owned businesses (WOBs)—and American businesses in general—in terms of revenue, number of businesses, employees, and payroll."[22]

For Andrea, becoming an education entrepreneur was also motivated by a personal need that grew into a community purpose. Her eleven-year-old son Danny has unique abilities along the autism spectrum. Despite advocating for changes in the local public school system—and even switching to a different public school—Andrea didn't feel that he was thriving in the traditional system. "The system is failing our kids because every child has a different way of learning," Andrea told me. When 2020 came and schools shut down, Andrea decided to homeschool Danny and his younger sister Sofia. She found that she enjoyed learning at home with her children and that homeschooling worked well for them, so she continued homeschooling even after schools reopened.

When I arrived at PLAY K–12 on a drizzly winter day in 2024, Andrea welcomed me with a big hug and a beaming smile, her long ebony hair contrasting against the vibrant yellow-painted walls. Off to the left of the pristine main classroom space, Gaby led a hands-on equilateral triangle activity with three students that coincided with a project on the Chinese New Year. To the right, a girl sat at a small sensory table in front of a plush sofa while two boys played chess together nearby. A large window on one wall offered a glimpse into one of the three adjacent classroom spaces, where a boy worked one-on-one with his instructor, a retired public school teacher from Pennsylvania. Another teacher worked individually with a different student.

"Each child gets one-on-one instruction time throughout the week," said Andrea, who incorporates a variety of individualized curriculum offerings in consultation with her teachers. "If the families want us to use their own chosen curriculum, we'll do that," Andrea added, explaining that most of her students are legally considered homeschoolers, while some are transitioning from a virtual school to an in-person option. "This is a safe space for the family and the children," she continued. "This is their homeschool experience. For parents who work, we get them involved in other ways, like after work hours, creating connections and bonds between child, family, and school. We are more than a microschool. We're really a family wellness center," Andrea said, adding that most of her students attend her microschool tuition-free, or nearly so, through Florida's universal school choice program.

Andrea and Gaby decided to establish PLAY K–12 in order to combine the best features of homeschooling and traditional schooling, enabling a customized curriculum approach within an intentionally small learning community. There are currently fourteen students enrolled, including the founders' own children. Several students are neurodiverse, gifted, or have special learning needs that qualify them for certain educational supports, such as occupational or speech therapy, that are covered by the families' personal health insurance plans. These specialists join the children at the microschool, seamlessly integrating therapy into the school day. The whole experience has been transformative for her son, Andrea said.

There is a large Latino community in Broward County, and Gaby and Andrea say that they are finding more Latino parents who are intrigued by homeschooling, microschooling, and alternative education options. This reflects national data showing higher rates of Latino homeschooling since 2020.[23] The Latino parents that Gaby and Andrea talk to say they are especially drawn to the concept of personalized, family-focused learning and language preservation. "Parents here want to do homeschooling, but they're immigrants and don't speak English," Gaby said. "It can be scary for them, so we cater to this population." She explained that all their school's promotional and classroom materials are in English and Spanish and that language preservation is part of their school's core mission. "Bilingualism is to be embraced and celebrated. Culture washes away when language is lost."

Growing interest in their school is leading Gaby and Andrea to dream about expanding into the vacant storefront space next door and offering additional services for teenagers, as well as for students with significant special needs who cannot currently be accommodated in the existing space. They see a lot of possibility as education entrepreneurs creating value in their community by offering a more customized, culturally relevant, financially accessible learning option. Andrea says that her entrepreneurial vision is immense but she's optimistic. So is Gaby. "As immigrants, we chase the American Dream," Gaby said, adding, "The American Dream is about building your own dream. It's about what you can do to make your dream life come true."

## PERMISSIONLESS INNOVATORS

Many of today's school founders didn't intend to chase the American Dream through entrepreneurship. It happened largely by accident. In the summer of 2020, jostled by weeks of social isolation and creeping uncertainty about what back-to-school time would look like, some parents spontaneously created learning pods, known then as "pandemic pods." In July of that year, the *Wall Street Journal* shared the story of a mother in Washington who created a Facebook group for families in her area interested in homeschooling pods. Within two weeks, the group had 850 members.[24] Similar stories appeared across the country, including a *New York Times* report on a pandemic pod Facebook group in San Francisco that grew to nearly ten thousand members by August.[25] Whether concerned about back-to-school uncertainty or worried about virus exposure, many of these pod families withdrew their children from school that summer to become independent homeschoolers. A Gallup poll in August 2020 showed a doubling of the homeschooling rate from the previous year, something that would later be confirmed by the US Census Bureau.[26]

The pandemic pod phenomenon helped unleash a spirit of "permissionlessness" in education. Out of necessity, and in the context of a massive national emergency, parents didn't wait around to see if they were allowed to create these home-based learning pods. They just did it. In many places, the rules around such pods were murky—they weren't daycare operations because many of the pods were aimed at school-age children, and they certainly didn't look anything like schools. Also, the nation was in the midst of an unprecedented pandemic event with entire school systems shut down for months. Clearly the old rules didn't apply, pod parents thought. Some states issued hazy guidelines for such pods in 2020, but for the most part, pod parents went ahead and created these small solutions all on their own—without waiting for permission.

In many ways, these pod parents became what author Adam Thierer calls "evasive entrepreneurs," or those who move forward with a new business solution without waiting around for permission from local regulators or public officials.[27] We typically think of "evasive entrepreneurs" as those like the founders of Uber, Lyft, or Airbnb—innovators who leveraged technology to enter static markets by offering lower-cost, more personalized services. They did this initially without asking for permission and have now become mainstays of American life. But during the pandemic, parents who created new pods and microschools were often similarly evasive—perhaps not as intentionally defiant, but also not delayed by questions regarding what they may and may not be allowed to do. They had children at home who needed to learn and connect, and they were committed to making that happen no matter what.

Like nearly every school-age child at the time, Danna Guzman's six-year-old daughter switched to remote learning in the spring of 2020. She didn't like it, so Danna began seeking other options and found a couple of friends whose children were similarly struggling with remote schooling. They decided to create a pandemic pod. Initially, the three families were planning to share educational responsibilities, taking turns hosting the pod at their homes throughout the week. But Danna, who has a background in child development and early childhood education, offered to host the pod at her home with seven children, including her own three kids, during the 2020/2021 school year. The other two families eagerly agreed, and Danna's home in southwest Detroit became one of countless pandemic pods to open that year.

Early in her career, Danna worked with children as a Family Advocate for the Migrant and Seasonal Head Start program, a federal early childhood education service for low-income families. Danna grew up as the daughter of migrant farmworkers, moving from one part of the United States to another depending on the growing season. One of her earliest memories is of being with her parents in the orange groves of Florida around age five. After that, she spent most of her childhood and adolescence migrating to Michigan each spring and then to Texas each fall. As a teenager, she worked in the fields picking cucumbers while becoming more interested in the lives and experiences of migrant families. After college, Danna worked full-time with Head Start and eventually moved to Detroit to help establish a Head Start program there.

As her oldest child approached school age, Danna chose Waldorf and Montessori programs, as she was attracted to the holistic, child-centered methods touted by these twentieth-century trailblazing alternative education philosophies. When she observed in her own pandemic pod that children were naturally curious and learning deeply in a more informal, unstructured way, she began to do more research on different educational philosophies and discovered self-directed education—or unschooling. The idea of granting young people more autonomy and control of their learning, without coercive curriculum tactics, resonated with Danna, and she began shifting her pod to be more learner-directed. Parents and kids liked it. In fact, word got around, and more families asked to join the pod. By June of 2021, Danna had fifteen children enrolled.

She continued the pod into a second year, with all families legally recognized as homeschoolers who were able to choose between full-time or part-time enrollment options. One family that was with her in the first year decided to go back to a conventional school in the fall of 2021 but returned to Danna's pod mid-year. When year three came along, Danna thought for sure that the pod wouldn't continue. After all, schools were getting back to normal, and the pandemic seemed increasingly distant. Yet, families stayed at Big Bad Wolf House, the playful name the children gave their maturing pod.

With enrollment continuing to climb during the 2022/2023 academic year, Danna and her husband, who works for the federal government, decided to purchase a two-family home down the block. I visited Big Bad Wolf House in the spring of 2023 as home renovations were underway to convert the downstairs unit into the pod school space while the family lived upstairs. When I arrived, Danna and the children were planting seeds in the raised-bed gardens of their unusually large urban yard before taking a snack break inside.

In addition to group projects like seed planting, Danna partners with community organizations and instructors throughout Detroit to augment daily learning. Big Bad Wolf House now enrolls twenty mixed-age learners in prekindergarten through sixth grade. Ninety percent of them are from low-income households in Detroit, and nearly all the parents pulled their children out of conventional public schools or entered Big Bad Wolf House in lieu of public schools when their children reached school age. "Letting go of the idea that conventional schooling is the only way to get an education was very tricky for some of them, and we're still working through that," Danna said. She finds parents' comfort levels steadily growing, especially as they see how happy and content their children are and how much they are learning.

Danna also sees a rising community-wide comfort level with new learning models. Homeschooling and alternative education models have become more popular and accepted throughout Detroit since COVID. For example, Engaged Detroit is a homeschool co-op and resource center that serves more than two hundred homeschoolers across Detroit. It was founded by Detroit mother and parent-advocate Bernita Bradley, who in 2020 began supporting about a dozen families who started homeschooling their children during the pandemic. Today, Engaged Detroit is a regular meeting place for homeschooling families to take classes, access curriculum and assessment tools, build community, and receive mentoring from experienced homeschooling parents.

"I don't think it's going to stop. I think it's only going to keep growing," Danna said of the momentum surrounding pods, microschools, and similar learning models in Detroit and elsewhere. She's right. In 2024, an EdChoice/Morning Consult poll featuring a nationally representative sample of more than two thousand respondents found that about one in ten parents said their children are enrolled in a microschool, and one-third or more of parents are interested in enrolling their child in a microschool.[28] It's no wonder more parents are attracted to these creative schooling options. As the following chapter shows, they are having a truly transformative effect on the lives of parents, teachers, and kids.

## Chapter Reflections for Parents and Founders

The American entrepreneurial spirit is on the upswing, and education entrepreneurs are very much a part of the trend toward new business creation. Women, immigrants, and people of color are among those driving the larger US entrepreneurial boom, and it's not surprising to see that they are also the ones creating many of today's new schools and learning models. Like entrepreneurs in other sectors, today's school founders identify educational needs in their communities and invent solutions to satisfy those needs. As a parent searching for these solutions, or a potential founder eager to build them, the following are some suggestions to consider.

**Parents:** Sometimes parents need to take matters into their own hands. Recall how Regina recognized the limitations of a one-size-fits-all schooling system in Omaha and noticed her children's dwindling love of learning. She assumed control of her children's education through homeschooling, with the support of LeDonna's Leaders to Legends Academy. Maybe you are thinking about doing something similar. If so, you may find it helpful to seek out and join homeschool co-ops like Leaders to Legends, or explore similar hybrid homeschools or microschools in your area. They can make the transition from traditional schooling to something more unconventional a bit less intimidating while connecting you to a supportive community of teachers, parents, and learners.

There is currently no reliable, centralized directory of all innovative education options, but there may be resources in your local area. Indeed, hyperlocal networks, such as MicroschoolFlorida.com in the Sunshine State, HUMAcollab.org in Tennessee, WiseTogether.org in Kansas, and OptionsForEducation.com in Oregon, are often the best source to find what you're looking for, as new programs continually sprout. Appendix 1 offers additional local and national resources and websites to explore.

I suggest googling the terms *homeschool*, *microschool*, and *alternative education*, along with your city, county, or state, to find out about creative schooling options near you. You may need to run three different searches with each of those terms to discover what is available, and you can also extend your search to include your closest major city or your region. You should also consider joining local homeschooling, parenting, and education groups on Facebook or other social media sites. Posting in these groups about what you are seeking, even anonymously, can help you discover nearby options.

**Founders:** Just like parents, you may also find it valuable to seek out and connect with local networks. Resources such as Black Minds Matter can be incredibly helpful in gaining support and encouragement along your entrepreneurial journey. Other national networks, such as VELA and the National Microschooling Center, can offer community and advice. Just as for parents, hyperlocal networks can be especially useful for would-be education entrepreneurs. Appendix 1 provides a list of some of these networks, along with startup incubator and accelerator programs for microschool founders, such as KaiPod Catalyst, Launch Your Kind, Prenda, Wildflower Montessori, Liberated Learners, and Microschool Solutions.

## Chapter 4

# Families

*Whatever you do, be different—that was the advice my mother gave me, and I can't think of better advice for an entrepreneur. If you're different, you will stand out.*
—Anita Roddick (founder of The Body Shop)

Most of us likely attended traditional K–12 schools, following a familiar educational path from kindergarten to college or career. Some of us undoubtedly loved our schooling experience, while others sadly didn't. "I hated going to school when I was a kid," Elon Musk said in a 2015 interview. "It was torture." His dissatisfaction with his own schooling experience motivated Musk in 2014 to create a small, project-based school called Ad Astra on his SpaceX campus for his children and those of his employees. "The kids really love going to school," Musk said about Ad Astra, adding that "they actually think vacations are too long, as they want to go back to school."[1]

Regardless of our own schooling experiences, we may just want something different for our children's education. We may dislike the current one-size-fits-all education system and want a more individualized approach for our kids. It turns out, most Americans want this, but we falsely believe we're the only ones who do. In his book *Collective Illusions*, Todd Rose shares numerous examples of the disconnect between what we personally value and what we think others value. These "collective illusions" lead us to incorrectly assume that our opinions are on the fringe when they are actually very mainstream but hidden due to our false perceptions of the majority view.

After working as a professor at Harvard University, Rose founded the nonprofit research organization Populace to dig deeper into data on some of these collective illusions, including as they relate to education. One striking finding from Populace's 2022 nationally representative survey, conducted in collaboration with the polling organization YouGov, is that most Americans personally prioritize individualized education, but they believe that everyone else wants the one-size-fits-all version. For parents specifically, the illusion is even more pronounced. They state privately that "the option to choose courses based on interests and aspirations" is their top priority, but they perceive it as being a low priority (#15) for other parents—an illusion that has persisted since 2019 when Populace began its polling. Relatedly, parents say they dislike standardization in education but think everyone else likes it.

Overall, most Americans want the education system to fundamentally change, with more than 70 percent of Populace's survey respondents stating that "more things about the educational system should change than stay the same," and more than 20 percent of them saying that "nearly everything should change."[2] Polling from Gallup uncovered related findings. Those results showed that Americans' satisfaction with K–12 schooling in 2025 were at a twenty-four-year low, with 73 percent of Americans indicating they were dissatisfied with the quality of US public education.[3]

To shatter the collective illusions surrounding education, parents should be honest and upfront about their desire for difference in education. As more parents realize that they are not alone, more will seek and build different educational options that elevate individualized learning. Tim Tran is one of those parents who is speaking out about wanting a different type of education for his kids. When he came on my podcast in 2024, Tim talked about his childhood and adolescence spent in the Fairfax County Public Schools system in Virginia, just outside of Washington, DC. "I did everything that I was supposed to do," Tim said. "I took Advanced Placement classes and did well enough in high school to get into college. I went to Virginia Tech and got an engineering degree, and did well enough in that to get hired by a big consulting firm in Washington, DC. When I came out, having done everything I was supposed to do, I realized I was ill-prepared for the real world. When my wife and I had our first child, I started to think: Is there anything else?"

While listening to a podcast one day, Tim heard about Acton Academy, a fast-growing network of learner-driven microschools. Jeff and Laura Sandefer cofounded Acton Academy in 2009 in Austin, Texas, when they couldn't find what they were seeking for their own children. Their boys were attending a Montessori school, and they were wondering when the right time might be to enroll them in a traditional school as they grew older. "I went to see the very best teacher in what was reportedly the very best traditional school in Austin," Jeff told me in a podcast interview in 2023. Jeff asked the teacher when he thought the boys should leave the Montessori school and he replied, "As soon as possible." Jeff was startled and asked why. "Well, once they've experienced that kind of freedom, they won't want to be chained to a desk and lectured to all day," the teacher told Jeff, who then responded earnestly: "Well, I don't blame them." The teacher became emotional, saying after a brief pause, "I don't either." Jeff left that meeting and said to Laura later that day: "We're either going to homeschool, or we're going to start a school, because the very best teacher in the very best traditional school in Austin, Texas, just told me not to send our boys there."

That was the beginning of Acton Academy, which now includes hundreds of independently owned and operated schools across the United States and abroad—including the one Tim ultimately found for his children. Laura's book, *Courage to Grow*, details Acton Academy's origin story and has been a source of inspiration for many founders and parents such as Tim. "It wasn't until Acton that I started realizing that children are naturally curious about things," Tim said.

When he first discovered Acton Academy in 2019, Tim was immediately attracted to its individualized approach in which young people take charge of their own education, or "hero's journey," as it's known in the Acton network. Learners set personal academic goals and use a variety of digital and analog learning tools to achieve content mastery. They work on peer projects, engage in thoughtful Socratic discussions, set expectations for behaviors and responsibilities in their classrooms (known as studios), and hold each other accountable. Acton Academy was inspired by Lord Acton's famous 1887 quote, "Power tends to corrupt and absolute power corrupts absolutely."[4] Acton Academy learning communities aim to decentralize power as much as possible to each learner, granting them individual freedom combined with responsibility.

Tim knew Acton Academy was the type of school he wanted for his children, but at the time he was looking, there weren't any in northern Virginia (though there are now). He and his wife decided that the next best alternative would be a Montessori school, so they enrolled their son there. That worked well for preschool, but they eventually needed a change. "Since my wife and I are both entrepreneurs, we crave freedom," Tim said. "That's kind of the reason why we wanted to have our own business. When the business started taking off, we were traveling a little bit more and said let's try to homeschool because the schedule of Montessori didn't really fit into our lifestyle." They soon decided that homeschooling wasn't for them.

"Very quickly we realized we were not homeschooling parents. We didn't have the patience for it," Tim said.

Living in Los Angeles at the time, Tim and his wife revisited the idea of Acton Academy for their son and daughter and decided to move to Austin, Texas—an area rich in Acton Academies due to its origins there. Tim googled Acton Academies near Leander, a suburb where the family was planning to settle, and discovered that Sarah Max was just about to open Invictus: An Acton Academy. "I think it hadn't been more than a week since she posted her business on the internet," Tim said, "So I sought her out and was like, 'Hey, can we have coffee?'"

Like many of today's education entrepreneurs, Sarah decided to launch her microschool because she wanted a different educational experience for her sons and others in her community. As a former fifth grade teacher who worked in the public school system for more than ten years, Sarah became increasingly frustrated by the intractable nature of conventional schooling. "I started experimenting a little bit toward the end with learning for mastery and giving children more ownership of their learning journey, but there are so many constraints within the public school model," Sarah said when she appeared with Tim on my podcast.

Sarah had worked in both low-income, Title I public schools as well as public schools in more affluent communities. She despaired over how quickly children would be labeled as below grade level if they weren't checking certain boxes, and watched as that label followed them throughout their schooling. "It doesn't make sense to group people by age and expect them to all learn the exact same thing at the exact same time," Sarah said. She also noticed a steady decline in children's natural exuberance for learning. "What I saw as a fifth grade teacher was, by the time children came to me, the light had already gone out. It was an uphill battle to try to get them to enjoy learning again, and it was heartbreaking because children come into the world eager. They come into the world curious and wanting to know more. And the educational model just dims that light," Sarah said.

When she was expecting her first child, Sarah decided to quit teaching to be a stay-at-home mom. She knew that someday she would return to education but not to conventional schooling. She also knew that she wanted a different learning experience for her children. A few years later, while still at home with her kids, Sarah was helping her sister find a school for her child when she stumbled upon Acton Academy. Enchanted, Sarah applied to become a founder within the Acton Academy network. She was accepted and launched her school in a rented church space in the fall of 2021 with five learners, including her son, Tim's son, and three others. Today, Invictus has twenty-five learners from ages three to eleven on a large hilltop property on the edge of town, with ample room to add a middle school and high school program as the students grow.

"I think that one of the most beautiful aspects of the Acton model is the confidence and the sense of agency that these young people have," Sarah said. "They know that their opinions are valued. They know that they are becoming adept at problem-solving. They know they're on their own unique learning journey, and it's not a competition against anyone else. They're still excited to learn—and that was ultimately my goal," she said.

Tim agreed, noting the growth in confidence, critical thinking, and communication skills he's seen in his son, and now his daughter, since they started at Invictus. His children have a degree of self-awareness and agency that Tim wishes he had a chance to develop as a kid. "I found that I didn't really understand what my strengths were until I was like twenty-eight or twenty-nine," Tim said. "Being an entrepreneur now, I wish that I had more problem-solving and critical thinking skills very early on and knew my talents a lot earlier. That's why I wanted to provide that for my child."

## WHY PARENTS SWITCH SCHOOLS

I was twenty-one when I met my first homeschooler. An economics major in college in the late 1990s, I began taking more courses in education, intrigued as to why there were such limited choices in that sector of the economy compared to others. For an independent research project during the fall semester of my senior year, I had an opportunity to shadow a local homeschooling family and see an example of alternative education up close. I was completely captivated. The eight-year-old homeschooled girl was so self-assured, so competent, so eager to learn, so well-socialized. My stereotypes were smashed.

That same semester, I did a student-teaching practicum in a local public elementary school with second graders who were the same age as the homeschooler. The contrast couldn't have been starker. The conventionally schooled children lacked autonomy, self-direction, and a passion for learning. They were forced to follow a set curriculum, without regard to their own skill level or interests. They were made to sit quietly at their desks, to color in the lines, to wait to be called on, and to ask permission to use the bathroom or get a drink of water. Obedience and compliance were rewarded above originality and curiosity. It wasn't the teachers' fault. Their originality and curiosity were just as stymied as their students', required as they were to obey top-down mandates and comply with administrative directives.

I shouldn't have been surprised. After all, I had attended suburban K–12 public schools that were almost demographically identical to the one I spent time in that semester. I felt that I had a positive schooling experience, but what did I have to compare it to? Once I saw what learning could look like outside of a conventional classroom, I couldn't unsee it. I couldn't ignore the subtle and not-so-subtle ways that traditional schooling steadily erodes a child's eagerness for and engagement in learning. Indeed, a 2024 Gallup survey found that between a quarter and more than half of Gen Z K–12 students are lacking engagement in school.[5] These findings reinforce previous Gallup polling results showing that students become increasingly disengaged as their school years progress.[6] I couldn't forget the idea that education could be different. A decade later when I became a mom, I held on to this idea. Like Tim and Sarah, I chose an alternative education path for my children before they even reached school age. For many families, though, forgoing conventional schooling wasn't on their radar. It was something they sought only when they soured on traditional schooling. That was the case for the Elliotts.

"We moved to Milton for the schools," Sara Elliott told me. She and her husband, Brandt, a sales executive, had been living in Boston, Massachusetts, but bought a house in an affluent suburb adjacent to the city in 2013, just before their oldest child was about to enter kindergarten. "Initially, it was a really good experience for both of our kids," said Sara, who attended and excelled in traditional public schools in Connecticut and now works as a senior marketing director for a technology company. She expected a similarly conventional schooling path for her two children. But as their elementary years wore on, Sara and Brandt became increasingly dissatisfied. "They were in a big public school," Sara said. "They weren't the superstars, but they weren't the troublemakers. They were doing okay enough to skate by, but I questioned if they were truly realizing their full potential."

While Sara and Brandt may not have been wowed by their children's schooling, they weren't yet seeking other education options. That changed a few years later when their older child identified as nonbinary, switching their name from Caroline to Farrin and adopting they/them pronouns. Sara and Brandt began wondering about alternatives that might be more identity-affirming for Farrin, but they couldn't find anything they liked. Then COVID came, schools shut down, and things for Farrin, then twelve, grew bleak. "Farrin had suicidal ideation during the early months of the pandemic really bad," Sara said. Farrin wasn't alone.

A study released in the fall of 2020 by the US Centers for Disease Control and Prevention (CDC) found a 31 percent increase in emergency room mental health visits for adolescents between the ages of twelve and seventeen that year, compared to 2019. For children ages five to eleven, the increase was 24 percent.[7] A follow-up paper released a few months later provided an even clearer, and more dire, picture of the impact of COVID policies on youth mental health. According to the CDC, beginning in May 2020, emergency room visits for suicidality began to rise for children ages twelve to seventeen. Girls were especially vulnerable. Hospital reports of adolescent suicidal ideation and attempts continued to climb over the subsequent months of pandemic lockdowns and school closures. The CDC found that between February and March 2021, alleged suicidal attempts for girls ages twelve to seventeen were nearly 51 percent higher than they were the previous year.[8] In 2021, nearly one-third of girls between the ages of fourteen and eighteen seriously considered suicide—significantly above pre-pandemic rates of suicidal ideation among this demographic.[9]

Childhood and adolescent mental health had been deteriorating in the decade leading up to 2020, with increasing rates of youth anxiety, depression, and suicide.[10] The isolation and hopelessness brought on by the pandemic response exacerbated that trend. "It was bound to happen," Sara said of Farrin's deepening depression during 2020, for which they received therapy and medication. "We have a family history of anxiety and depression, but it was exacerbated by the pandemic. I think it had a huge impact," she said. It affected Sara and Brandt's other nonbinary child, Nox, as well; Nox was eight years old when schools shut down in 2020. While the first year of COVID school shutdowns was rough, it was mediated slightly by the "pandemic pod" that Sara and Brandt created for Nox and some of their friends. When schools reopened for in-person learning during the 2021/2022 academic year, Nox's mental health tumbled.

"The mask was really hard for such an empathetic person like Nox to not be able to read facial expressions," Sara said, adding that the school had also implemented silent lunchtimes to minimize viral spread, which was also very hard on her fourth grader. "They had severe depression, anxiety, and school refusal," Sara said of Nox. "We were at a crisis moment. That's when we heard about Elements Academy."

Elements is a mixed-age microschool for children ages three to eighteen that stresses self-directed learning tailored to meet each child's needs and interests. It was founded by Heather DiNino, a former special education teacher and department chair who taught in Massachusetts public schools for more than a decade. "When I was teaching, I loved it," Heather told me. "I loved the kids. I loved the community aspect. Starting out, I didn't realize that I was thinking about alternatives per se, even though many would say I was doing things very differently than the norm." As a special education teacher, Heather was always experimenting with different learning approaches and individualizing each student's educational path. She spent endless hours trying to get the system to work for the student. "It got exhausting," Heather said. "It wasn't until I became a mom that I realized I didn't have the energy to go back to that, to always be fighting upstream and trying to do things differently."

Heather stayed at home with her daughter, and soon her son, while doing part-time professional development coaching for several public school districts. Like the Elliotts, Heather and her husband Hank had moved to their neighborhood specifically so that their children could attend the local public elementary school—widely considered the "best" one in town. Within a month of her daughter entering kindergarten, Heather knew they needed a different plan. "Her curiosity disappeared," Heather said. "Her compassion was starting to disappear, which was so innate from day one. She would come home saying, 'I'm not supposed to help other people because I have to stay at my seat,' or, 'I'm not supposed to talk to my friends because I'm supposed to be quiet.' She was starting to learn that these things were normal. They didn't align with our parenting style. They didn't align with what I wanted for her education. Pretty quickly I landed on opening my own school because I wasn't finding that perfect combination. I was like, 'I'm just going to do it.'"

That was in the fall of 2019. Heather pulled her daughter from kindergarten that October and put her back in the Montessori preschool she had previously attended while filing the paperwork to create an LLC and become a state-recognized private school, with part-time enrollment options for homeschoolers. Elements was scheduled to open in 2020. "I never questioned whether or not we would still do it, but of course, we had to reroute. We tried to stay pretty versatile and adaptable," Heather said, explaining that opening amidst the tumult of 2020 helped her be laser-focused on her vision of creating an inclusive, individualized space prioritizing family wellness. Within a few months, it was clear she had succeeded in creating the school she wanted—for her own children and others. "The transformation we see, simply put, is they become themselves," Heather said of the students at Elements.

The Elliotts have observed this transformation firsthand. In the fall of 2022, still straddled with severe depression and anxiety, Nox decided to try fifth grade in their local public school. They only lasted two days. The third day, Nox did a trial day at Elements, where a friend was also enrolled, and said they were never going to return to the public school. "Nox is healthier. They're outgoing. They're realizing what they're interested in, and just becoming a really good person," Brandt said. I asked him if he really thinks it has been the school that has led to this change and not other factors, like therapy and growing up. "I think it's the school, I really do," Brandt said, adding that the peace Nox felt at Elements made them better able to respond well to therapy. "If you think about it, Nox could still be in bed. They could still not have come out of the depression. They might be fighting us at this school. They could still have all those challenges. The school is the differentiator," he said.

Not long after Nox began at Elements, Farrin wanted to join too. It's been just as transformational for them. "Farrin is like a normal teenager now," Brandt said, explaining that Farrin is taking on new challenges and healthy risks—traveling on the subway into the city, talking openly to people, and even performing songs in public at various musical events around town—all actions that would have been unimaginable prior to Elements. Academically, Farrin is also advancing, Brandt said, especially in math and engineering, thanks to the customized curriculum that enables deep, enduring learning in core content areas without top-down pressure. As a sophomore, Farrin is starting to think about college, and Brandt is confident that attending an innovative school like Elements won't hold them back from any college or career path they want to pursue. "I have no concerns about them, or Nox for that matter. Once they know what they want to do, they'll do it. For example, they just started playing the drums the other day because they wanted to. Now they're already good, just three weeks later. They can do anything they want," Brandt said.

"When you really think about it," he continued reflectively, "what Elements is providing is what school used to be. The kids go to a small, one-room schoolhouse. They go to a *Little House on the Prairie*–type of environment where they form bonds and learn life. That's how people were educated for hundreds of years, not this big, factory school thing. That's a modern convention," he said.

## WHAT IS THE JOB TO BE DONE?

Thomas Arnett wanted to know why parents today are switching from conventional schools to microschools. Why are they rejecting the "big factory school" in favor of the "small, one-room schoolhouse"? A senior fellow at the Clayton Christensen Institute, which is named after the renowned Harvard Business School professor, Arnett analyzed parents' microschooling choices using the Jobs-to-be-Done (JTBD) theory developed by Christensen and a colleague, Bob Moesta. This theory holds that consumers "hire" various products or services to do a job for them. Whether that's "hiring" a cup of coffee, or a pair of shoes, or an attorney, or a school, there is a specific "job" that a customer wants performed. Surprisingly, it may not be so obvious what that job is.

In their bestselling 2016 book, *Competing Against Luck: The Story of Innovation and Customer Choice*, Clayton Christensen and his coauthors described a classic example of the JTBD theory. They presented the real-life story of a fast-food restaurant chain that wanted to increase sales of its milkshakes. The chain did all sorts of market analysis, asking customers what would make their milkshake better; but all these product improvements didn't increase sales. Then, Christensen and his collaborators looked at the issue differently, asking what "job" customers were hiring their milkshake to do. After hours of customer observations, a pattern emerged. Many people purchased milkshakes early in the morning. When interviewed, these morning milkshake drinkers revealed that they were in fact "hiring" the milkshake to do a job that was more than meets the eye. Christensen and his coauthors explained that "it soon became clear that the early-morning customers all had the same job to do: they had a long and boring ride to work. They needed something to keep the commute interesting. They weren't really hungry yet, but they knew that in a couple of hours, they'd face a midmorning stomach rumbling. It turned out that there were a lot of competitors for this job, but none of them did the job perfectly."[11] Satisfying customers is not just about perfecting a product or service; it's also about understanding the true "job" that a product or service is performing for certain customers, at certain times and in certain ways.

Armed with this deep understanding of Christensen's JTBD theory, Arnett and his colleagues interviewed parents who switched their children to microschools to figure out what "job" they were hiring the microschool to do. The researchers uncovered three primary "jobs" that Arnett wrote about in a 2024 paper published by the Christensen Institute. These jobs are:

1. When I disagree with decisions at my child's school and I'm feeling unheard, help me find an alternative that will honor my perspective and values.
2. When my child is unhappy, unsafe, or struggling at school, help me find an environment where they can regain their love for learning.

3. When my child's school is too focused on academic milestones and neglects other forms of learning, help me find a balanced educational experience for my child.[12]

I talked with Arnett about his research and findings and asked him where someone like me—or Tim and Sarah from Invictus, described earlier—might fall in his analysis. After all, we knew before our kids were even kindergarteners that we would choose alternative education options for them. Do we show up in any of his school-switching data? Arnett said that we would probably fit most closely with Job #3, preferring a less rigid, more holistic approach to education, thus "switching" from a conventional model very early on. But he also said that there is a different, and potentially much larger, set of parents who are more like the Elliotts or Heather. They are in a moment of struggle in their current conventional school and need their microschool to perform one of those three jobs well.

For Heather, it was likely Job #1 that prompted her to pull her daughter out of the local kindergarten and ultimately create Elements Academy. The conventional school wasn't aligned with her parenting perspectives and values. Not finding a school that would provide her ideal holistic, self-directed, affirming learning environment, she chose to build it. For the Elliotts, it was likely Job #2—improving the happiness of their children who were struggling at school—that led them to seek alternatives and settle on Elements Academy.

Arnett's analysis is also very useful for microschool founders who may be hyperfocused on their overall learning philosophy and curriculum approach and forget that for many families the "job" for which they are hiring the microschool may not have as much to do with choosing a certain educational philosophy as it does with its ability to alleviate a pressing problem. Those families need a solution and they need it now. "One of the things that I think this research helps elevate is that while there are families out there in the world that just have a different mindset of what they want out of schooling, there's a lot of other families where that's not what's driving them," Arnett told me. "It's usually those moments of struggle where conventional schooling is fine until it's not, and then that motivates them to go look for something different," he said.

## LOOKING FOR SOMETHING DIFFERENT

Cheryl and Randy Mynatt desperately needed something different for Gabe. He struggled in his local public schools almost from the beginning, being labeled with ADHD, becoming easily distracted in large classes, and frequently getting into trouble. Throughout elementary school, some grades and teachers were better than others but neither Cheryl nor Randy felt that Gabe was truly able to realize his full potential. Gabe is their grandson, of whom the Mynatts assumed full guardianship when he was three years old while his mother, their daughter, battled bipolar disorder. They later adopted Gabe with the full blessing of their daughter, providing him a safe, stable home in Liberty, Missouri—just outside of Kansas City.

In the spring of Gabe's fifth grade year, COVID hit and his school shut down, soon switching to remote learning. "I think that that's the point where we became aware of the lack of learning that he had," Cheryl said. "They teach primarily to the 80 percent that learn inside the box, and he was in the 20 percent that learned outside the box," she said. Online, and later hybrid, schooling during COVID gave the Mynatts a clearer window into Gabe's learning. "He wasn't reading at the level that he should have been. He was like two years behind, and he didn't know his math facts," Randy said. Gabe hadn't brought home much homework in the years prior to COVID, and even though the Mynatts suspected he might be falling behind academically, when they went to parent-teacher conferences they were told not to worry. "They just kept passing him along because they didn't want to deal with the fact that he wasn't learning the way that he should be, and they didn't want to be responsible for it," Cheryl said. The couple considered private schools, but cost was always a barrier.

The family's mounting dissatisfaction with the local schools came to a head when Gabe entered the seventh grade, returning to full-time, in-person schooling in the fall of 2021. "Middle school was just awful," Cheryl recalled, explaining that Gabe's social skills, which were already underdeveloped, grew worse in the wake of school shutdowns and remote learning. Gabe would sometimes be disruptive in class, and because he was a large kid, he would frequently be taunted by his peers. The inflection point for the Mynatts came midway through that school year after two troubling incidents. The first occurred when Gabe acted poorly in class one day, cackling loudly when a girl spilled some water. Cheryl explained what happened next: "The teacher yelled from across the room, 'Gabe, do you always have to be such a prick?' I just don't think that is acceptable behavior from a teacher. Then the kids began to see that if the teachers can talk that way to Gabe, they can too," she said.

The second incident that pushed the family to pull Gabe from school in the middle of seventh grade happened during a physical education class when Gabe noticed that some of his classmates were on their phones looking at pornography. "Now, why in the world are kids having phones in school? And why aren't they doing what they are supposed to be doing in P.E.?" Randy asked. Gabe reportedly told the teacher, who dismissed his concerns and told him to mind his own business. At that point, the couple pulled Gabe from school, and Cheryl began homeschooling him. While she and Randy had been noticing that Gabe was struggling in school and increasingly unhappy, it was ultimately the disconnect between the practices and behaviors in Gabe's school and their own perspectives and values that led them to make a switch. Applying Arnett's Jobs-to-be-Done analysis, the Mynatts were looking for a schooling alternative that likely fit Job #1.

For the rest of seventh grade and all of eighth, Cheryl homeschooled Gabe as he participated in a remote schooling option offered through the local public school district, in partnership with an established statewide virtual school. The one-on-one approach to learning suited Gabe, and he quickly made progress academically. "Cheryl did a great job, and the teachers were really good with assisting and tutoring on the side as needed. It was really a win," Randy said.

While Gabe was closing learning gaps, the personal dynamic between Cheryl and Gabe grew strained. "The problem became that I was too many things. I wasn't only grandma and mom. I was math teacher, English teacher, science teacher, P.E. teacher, principal. Then because of Gabe's ADHD and the impulsivity, I was constantly bringing him back on task. It was too much. It became a friction in our relationship. I didn't want to have this combative relationship with him for four more years of school. So, I decided we had to do something else," Cheryl said.

The family found a traditional, private Christian school in the area and applied there for the 2023/2024 school year, Gabe's freshman year of high school. Gabe went through all of the school's interviews and testing during the spring of eighth grade, and Cheryl and Randy thought he would attend. Ultimately, the school denied Gabe admission due to his ADHD and related behavior issues. "They were more about performance than people," Randy said. The Mynatts were crushed. "Now I can tell you it was the hand of God at work," Cheryl told me. At the time, however, she didn't know what to do. Gabe was adamant that he didn't want to go to the public high school, and Cheryl knew they needed an alternative to the public virtual school. That's when someone told her about Refine KC.

In August 2022, Refine KC opened in Kansas City, Missouri, as a Christian, faith-based microschool offering a uniquely tailored, personalized learning experience for each student. It was founded by Matt Barnard, a high school mathematics teacher in Missouri public schools for twenty-eight years, and his wife, Amy, who has a degree in elementary education and also taught for several years. They were joined by their friend

Amanda Zaring, who holds a master's degree in secondary education and spent fifteen years in business consulting, along with her husband, Ryan. A year earlier, Matt was preparing for the upcoming school year and was increasingly drawn toward the idea of starting his own school. "I'd realized that there were so many kids that were just lost in the world," Matt said. "I saw kids that would completely change from their eighth grade to ninth grade year—and these were good, solid kids from good, solid families, but they were just getting lost. I also saw that there wasn't a lot of accountability in public education." Matt and Amy decided to pull their son from public school prior to the start of his freshman year. He would have attended the school where Matt was teaching.

At the same time, their friends, the Zarings, also pulled their two children out of public school in a different district, and the two families began homeschooling their children together while contemplating the possibility of opening a school. "It was kind of a dream at the time, and we prayed about it," Matt said. In late January 2022, the four founders established their school, naming it after a biblical story about a place where God performed miracles and "refinement" happened. The founders registered their school as a state-recognized private school, wrote their organizational bylaws, and submitted their application to the IRS for 501(c)(3) nonprofit status while spending hours together in their kitchens writing handbooks, determining curriculum, and preparing for their launch just over seven months later.

"We had an unnatural amount of energy to put toward this," Amy remembered. "It meant so much to all four of us. Our kids had to tell us to stop working on school. We just knew that it was necessary, and we felt like we were on a clock in a way, too, because we had three school-age kids at that time, and homeschool was just a patch for us. It was fine. We did the best that we could, but we knew that our kids needed to be around peers who were like-minded in order to thrive the best," she said.

The founders were committed to breaking free from the cookie-cutter approach to learning that traditional schools—both public and private—typically followed. They wanted to create an environment where children received individualized attention in small classes with a core curriculum that reflected a child's current mastery level and challenged them to advance at their own pace. "I think families are looking for a place for their kids to thrive," Amanda said. "We came to the table ready to create a space where kids could see their potential and where we continuously challenged them."

"I think the other thing, too, is the kids feel like they have a place that they belong," Matt added. "They know that as a faculty, we care about them. We want to know what's going on in their lives, not only at school. Our kids really feel that, and I don't know if they felt that in other educational environments," he said, noting that Refine KC students come from a variety of educational settings, including public schools, private schools, and homeschooling. Refine KC opened in August 2022 with fifteen students spanning kindergarten through high-school ages. A year later, it had grown to forty students and six teachers and was about to hit capacity on enrollment as it bulged in its leased space in a nearby church.

When the Mynatt family discovered the school in August 2023, they were able to enroll Gabe just before the school began to create a waitlist due to growing demand. Within weeks, the Mynatts noticed a transformation. Gabe was happier, more eager for learning, and more confident. He was also less anxious and disruptive. In addition to being diagnosed with and medicated for ADHD since childhood, Gabe had also been diagnosed with anxiety and had been taking anxiety medications for quite a while. When he enrolled at Refine KC, that changed. "He's currently been weaned off all medications," Cheryl said. She's noticed other positive changes too. "He loves to go to school. Before, it was always, 'Oh, I'm sick. I can't go today. I'm not going to be able to make it today.' Now it's never that way, not one day. He loves going," she said.

Perhaps the biggest change, though, was in the way Gabe was treated at school. Cheryl shared with me the story of going to Gabe's first parent-teacher conference a couple of months into his first semester at Refine KC. "It was the first time in his entire life that I heard a teacher compliment him," Cheryl recalled, holding back tears as she spoke to me. "I will never forget sitting there in every single room we went to and hearing every teacher say, 'I see potential in Gabe. One day, God's going to use this energy, this impulsivity that he has.' Mrs. Z was the last teacher we saw that day, and she said: 'I want you to know Gabe is so smart. He can do anything he wants to in this life.' When you know that somebody is speaking life and hope into your child—I don't care what they charge me. It's worth every penny," she said.

The reality is that Refine KC charges quite a bit less than other local schools, despite offering more one-on-one attention and a customized curriculum. At roughly $6,000 a year, with sibling discounts and generous financial aid, tuition at Refine KC is half that of the traditional private Christian school the Mynatts considered, and significantly less than the nearly $15,000 that the Kansas City Public Schools system spends per student each year.[13] "I don't have a fancy car. I don't have designer clothes. But you just have to make that decision of what is most important. It's an investment. The best investment you can give your children may not be college. It may just be right now," Cheryl said, adding that Gabe's future goal is to be a conservationist.

As for Refine KC's future, the founders are considering opening up additional school locations to retain the small, nurturing feel of each program while helping to accommodate growing parent interest in microschools. "I think as far as the future goes, we're going to see a huge uptick in more alternative education opportunities," Amanda said. "More and more people are recognizing, post-COVID, that the system is broken and are looking for different ways of learning."

The stories of the Elliotts and the Mynatts show what is possible as education entrepreneurs create alternatives to conventional schooling. Both families had adolescents who were struggling in a conventional classroom, were lost in the shuffle, and suffered from mental health issues. Both families stumbled upon new microschools that offered an individualized, affirming learning community and performed the specific "jobs" they needed done. Both families also had distinct values and viewpoints, and sought schools that reflected and respected those. The Elliotts wanted a space that would be supportive of nonbinary youth, while the Mynatts wanted a space that embraced a biblical worldview. Each family was able to find just what they were looking for, and each noticed a dramatic, positive transformation in their children's mental health, emotional well-being, enthusiasm for learning, and academic progress. "Being respected and accepted is so important. We all want to be accepted, with all our quirks," Cheryl said, noting that it has been that acceptance of Gabe as an individual at Refine KC that has helped him flourish most. Cheryl is especially grateful for the school's founders: "They are just ordinary people who have extraordinary gifts and love to share with others," she said.

### Chapter Reflections for Parents and Founders

Neither the Elliotts nor the Mynatts expected to choose an unconventional school, while Tim knew early on that he wanted something different for his children's education. Families and founders can both benefit from looking more closely at various motivations for educational change, and the "jobs to be done" by a school or space. Some parents may decide they want a different type of educational experience for their child well before kindergarten approaches, while other parents may not consider an unconventional school or learning environment until something goes awry in a traditional school setting. Gaining greater clarity on the underlying "why" involved in choosing a certain school or space can help parents make better decisions about their children's education and can help founders better understand what parents and students really want.

**Parents:** Look back at the JTBD framework described earlier. What is the "job" you really want done by your child's school? Are you frustrated by your child's current schooling experience and desire something else? Is your child not thriving at her current school and you want a place where she will love learning? Is your child's current school too academically oriented with limited focus on whole-child development and well-being? Or maybe you don't feel that your child is getting the academic attention he needs. Perhaps your child isn't yet enrolled in a school at all and you are thinking about the type of education you prefer. Maybe you want to find a school or similar learning space that is aligned with your personal values and parenting perspectives, fosters your child's natural curiosity and love of learning, or takes a more holistic view of education. Considering the primary "job" you want done from your child's learning environment can help you to identify the schools or spaces that would be the best fit for your family.

**Founders:** Do you know the motivations of your prospective families? While some of them may be attracted to your big, bold views on education, your top-rated curriculum, and your collection of colorful classroom manipulatives, a lot of them may simply need your help in addressing an immediate struggle. The "job" they may be hiring your school or space to do may not be as straightforward as you think. As you consider your marketing and outreach strategy to potential parents, as well as your phone conversations and school tours, how can you signal your awareness of their challenges and position your school or space as a solution? Additionally, many parents may have never before thought of an option beyond a traditional school. They may have no context for what learning can look like outside of the standard schooling model and may be scared and intimidated about doing something different. Think about ways you can reassure these parents and help them better understand what your alternative can—and cannot—offer.

## Part II

# SEEK OR BUILD

## Chapter 5
# Startups

*We elevate business through our humanity and we elevate humanity through business.*
—John Mackey (cofounder of Whole Foods Market), *Conscious Leadership: Elevating Humanity Through Business*

Many of today's education entrepreneurs are just ordinary people who take on the challenge of running a small business. They may be teachers who went into education because they love working with young people and have a knack for instructing and inspiring them. They may be parents with a range of different backgrounds and careers who couldn't find an existing school or space that suited their child or matched their vision for what education could be. Or they may be parents who are also teachers and were dually motivated to create new learning models. They could also be people working in a variety of jobs and professions who want to make a positive impact on the world through education.

Most of these founders are bold visionaries—not MBAs. They quickly discover, however, that to achieve their bold vision they must start thinking like someone with an MBA. They must adopt an enterprising mindset that fuses their role as both a dreamer and a doer. This chapter offers an initial framework for taking a school startup from vision to launch and will be helpful to both parents searching for new education options and founders hoping to get a better sense of parents' educational needs and perspectives.

## FROM VISION TO LAUNCH

"We don't super enjoy doing the business side, but we realize that if we want our school to be viable and we want it to continue on for years into the future, it has to be successful on the business side," said Todd Hepworth, cofounder of Orchard STEM School in rural Santaquin, Utah. I talked with Todd a few months ahead of the fall 2024 opening of his learner-centered K–12 microschool in a working cherry and apple orchard about sixty-five miles south of Salt Lake City. Todd was a longtime public elementary school teacher, and his cofounder had a doctorate in engineering education. They were both passionate educators eager to bring a low-cost, individualized, alternative education model to their small community. But they weren't particularly business savvy. Or at least they weren't until they began their startup journey.

Todd entered the education profession in 2007 as a kindergarten teacher in a public elementary school in Texas. The school emphasized project-based learning, or a more hands-on approach to education that involves students becoming actively immersed in individual or group projects tied to a specific theme or unit of study. He loved working at that school, where he stayed for nine years. Soon, Todd began to notice some unsettling signs of an educational shift—likely stemming, at least in part, from the federal push toward more standards-based accountability and high-stakes testing during the first decade of the new millennium.

When he began teaching, kindergarteners were only expected to be reading level B books, Todd said. These are books with a picture and a simple sentence on each page. Two years later, the kindergarten reading standard switched, and the children were expected to be reading level D books, which were much more complex. "So, two years prior, all of these kids that left my classroom prepared to go into first grade would now suddenly be identified as needing reading intervention because they weren't reading on level," Todd said. "It had me scratching my head. The kids didn't change. What changed was the expectation to push that first grade reading standard down to kindergarten. It's not developmentally appropriate for young kids."

Research confirms what Todd felt. It was the standards changing—not the kids. A study by University of Virginia professor Daphna Bassok and her colleagues found that in 1998, 31 percent of teachers thought that children should learn to read while in kindergarten. In 2010, that number rose to 80 percent.[1] Todd began to question top-down standards and became increasingly curious about alternative education models.

He went on to teach in more traditional public schools for several years before landing at a Waldorf-inspired public charter school in Utah where he worked as a teacher and eventually as the executive director. That was where his interest in learner-centered, alternative education really took hold. Influenced by the ideas of early twentieth-century Austrian philosopher Rudolph Steiner, Waldorf education prioritizes a holistic view of childhood learning that integrates intellectual and artistic pursuits. Academics aren't rushed in the early years, and creativity and artistic expression are highly valued. It was while working at the charter school in 2023 that Todd learned about the new Utah Fits All Scholarship, a universal school choice policy passed that year by the state legislature that allows each school-age student in Utah to be eligible to access approximately $8,000 in annual education funding to use on assorted educational services, including microschools and related models.

"I realized that this was an opportunity for me to take everything that I had learned as an educator, everything I knew about developmentally appropriate practice and making learning fun for kids, and create a school where that could be the reality," Todd said, adding that his students would attend his microschool nearly tuition-free through the new statewide choice program. This was a primary catalyst for starting his school, as he knew most of the families in his community wouldn't otherwise be able to pay the fees out of their own pockets. Todd connected with his cofounder over social media, and the pair began plotting their vision for Orchard STEM School, which would include a commitment to at least a thousand hours of outside education a year for each child and an integrated blend of academic and project-based learning. "We don't want kids to spend seven hours of the day in a school building. A few hours is okay, but half the time is going to be outside," Todd said.

Leaving much of the curriculum development to his cofounder, Todd assumed the bulk of the business side of the startup. A former officer in the United States Air Force, Todd registered for a small-business course offered through the Office of Veteran's Business Development. There he learned specifics about creating a business plan, determining the target market, developing a first-year budget with a three-month cash flow projection, as well as how to frame plans around school location and team development. "It was by no means on the level you would get as an MBA, but it was super helpful to do that for six months," said Todd, who pitched his school startup as part of the course's capstone project in front of judges from the local business community and the Utah Small Business Administration. Todd won the pitch competition, earning a $9,000 award that he put entirely toward launch costs, namely marketing.

In the months leading up to launch, Todd tackled other startup tasks, such as those related to organizational structure. After talking with a lawyer, Todd decided to become a registered 501(c)(3) nonprofit organization, at least partly so that his school could accept tax-deductible donations. He established a board of directors and applied for federal nonprofit status through the IRS. He also registered Orchard as a recognized private school in Utah, something that is relatively easy to do in the Beehive State.

Next, Todd began making connections, doing market research, and generating interest in his school throughout the wider community. He created a basic survey through Google Docs that he shared on social media and with his immediate contacts, asking general questions about what parents valued in their children's education and what they were looking for in a school. It included a rating scale ranging from "Strongly Agree" to "Strongly Disagree" to get a pulse on community priorities and needs. He received around two hundred survey responses, and it became clear that there was significant demand for alternatives to standard schooling. Six months prior to their school's opening day, Todd and his cofounder already had twenty registered students and were interviewing and hiring staff. Final plans were being made on their school property, curriculum was coming together, supplies were being purchased, and their vision was being realized.

"Students are the primary stakeholders in their own education," Todd said. "We spend so much time telling students what they need to learn, and we remove a lot of that choice from them. When they leave Orchard STEM School, I hope they leave with the understanding that they have a voice and a choice in their own education, and that they're really engaged in developing a good education for themselves." Looking ahead, Todd hopes to scale his model to other rural communities throughout Utah, which have historically had few education choices.

Todd's startup story provides an ideal roadmap for other prospective school founders to follow. He began with a vision of what he wanted his school to be and the beneficial impact it could have on his rural community. Then he upskilled. He realized the need for more information on how to start and run a small business, so he took a course that offered the basics and began gathering advice from trusted advisors. He conducted some simple market analysis to see what families in his area wanted for their children's education. Six months ahead of launch, he had enrollment commitments from a solid group of founding families and was able to finalize his staffing plans and his school's policies and procedures. By the time he launched, he was already thinking ahead to scalability—hoping for similar microschools across his state.

Every founder startup story will undoubtedly look different than Todd's, as one of the great features of the current alternative education movement is its diversity of people, places, and pedagogies. But following a similar, well-thought-out route to launching your own program could help set you up for both immediate and long-term success and sustainability.

## S.T.A.R.T.U.P.S. ROADMAP

In his biography of Elon Musk, Walter Isaacson describes how Reid Hoffman, Musk's PayPal cofounder who later cofounded LinkedIn, was both awed by and astonished at Musk's commitment to vision over viability when founding new businesses. According to Isaacson: "After listening to Musk describe his plan to send rockets to Mars, Hoffman was puzzled. 'How is this a business?' he asked. Later Hoffman would realize that Musk didn't think that way. 'What I didn't appreciate is that Elon starts with a mission and later finds a way to backfill in order to make it work financially,' he says. 'That's what makes him a force of nature.'"[2]

You may also be a force of nature who can backfill a business, but it's a smart idea to merge strategic vision with financial viability from the outset. To help you plot your entrepreneurial path from education idea to implementation, it may be worthwhile to use this simple, eight-step "S.T.A.R.T.U.P.S. Roadmap" that will take you from Strategic Vision all the way to Sustainability and Scale.

## STEP 1. STRATEGIC VISION

Successful startups of all sorts start with a strategic vision. For Todd, that vision is learner-centered, outdoor-based, STEM-focused alternatives to conventional schooling in rural communities. What's yours? You may only have an idea—a startup seedling—but you have a sense that it could turn into a fully formed, sustainable enterprise that could make a positive societal impact. "Develop a vision—your why—and stick to it," says Angie Wakeman, cofounder of Providence Hybrid Academy, a faith-based, Charlotte Mason–inspired hybrid homeschool program in Lehigh Valley, Pennsylvania. "You have a lot of decisions you'll have to make, so having that clear vision—why you're doing what you're doing—will help you with making those decisions."

Angie taught high school English in her community's public schools for nearly a decade. She always thought that she would send her own children to public school, and the idea of homeschooling never crossed her mind. But when her oldest of three children neared kindergarten age, her district shifted from a half-day kindergarten model to full-day kindergarten, which Angie felt was not going to be a good fit for her daughter who had been enjoying a relaxed, play-based, part-time preschool. Angie was also beginning to see, as an insider in the system, how conventional schooling can stifle curiosity. "It took until I became a parent to see that children are just naturally curious," Angie told me. "They're born that way. They're born loving to learn and know about the world around them, and I was afraid that that would be squashed in my child. I knew there wasn't going to be a lot of recess and that a lot of the time was going to be spent on tests, and I just have a real problem with that."

Angie kept her daughter in preschool for another year to delay the kindergarten decision. During that time, she became increasingly interested in the idea of homeschooling. She connected with a friend of hers, Rebecca Foley, who also had three children and was also thinking about homeschooling. There were aspects of homeschooling that appealed to them both, but neither wanted to do it full-time, all by themselves. They began envisioning a program that would blend part-time schooling and part-time homeschooling. "We kind of thought we invented the idea of part-time school," Rebecca said, laughing. "Then as we researched, we found that some people were already doing this." The pair realized that hybrid homeschooling, including with a Charlotte Mason approach, had been growing in popularity across the United States for the previous couple of decades. It seemed like their ideal educational model. They began in 2016 as an informal homeschool co-op one morning a week with a half-dozen families and with a vision of expanding. In 2017, Providence Hybrid Academy opened as a two-day-a-week hybrid homeschool program with twenty students and two teachers. Today, it runs two separate, two-day-a-week programs with 220 students in kindergarten through ninth grade, while continuing to add grades as the children grow.

"I think one thing that people are pretty attracted to is our clear vision," Angie said. "We have a hybrid model: We cater to the flexibility of homeschoolers because our families legally homeschool, but we're not reporting for them. They have the freedom to do what they want at home." Angie explained that while she and Rebecca help Providence Hybrid Academy families understand what they need to do to comply with Pennsylvania homeschooling statutes, and offer academic support through the hybrid school, it's ultimately each homeschooling family's responsibility to regularly report academic progress to the state. "We also have a clear vision with the Charlotte Mason philosophy and how that impacts our school day," Angie continued. "I think those things really made a big difference," she said, adding that when she and Rebecca hosted their first information session, they were shocked at how many strangers showed up because their program's vision resonated so strongly.

Your vision can be a simple sentence or a lengthier paragraph. It describes your aspirational dream for your key stakeholders—parents, learners, staff, business partners, advisors—and you. What is the purpose of education you are trying to unlock, the problem you are trying to solve, the people you are hoping to impact? Consider these consequential questions as you craft your startup vision.

Next, consider your mission. "In the end, a vision without the ability to execute it is probably an hallucination," said Stephen Case, former chairman and CEO of America Online (AOL).[3] Your mission statement will be your initial bridge between your strategic vision and your startup plan. Your vision statement is your picture of the future, while your mission statement is what you're offering right now to move toward that vision. Take a look at Providence Hybrid Academy's vision statement: "Our vision is to be a true hybrid program: We merge the best of homeschool with the best of private school." That vision is articulated further in the program's mission: "Students kindergarten through high school spend two days on campus with teachers covering most core academic subjects. Students spend the other three days at home with their parents completing the work recommended (or as parents choose)."

## STEP 2. TYPE OF BUSINESS

Once you confirm your strategic vision and mission, you can decide on the type of business you want to create—especially whether you'll be a for-profit or a nonprofit organization. State or local regulations may influence this decision. It's a good idea to seek professional legal and financial advice when deciding whether to operate as a for-profit or nonprofit business, and which business entity to choose, such as a corporation, a limited liability company (LLC), a sole proprietorship, a partnership, or something else. Generally speaking, for-profits ensure more ownership and control of your business, rather than sharing responsibility with a board of directors, as is required with nonprofits. For-profits can be faster and easier to establish, can be welcoming to potential investors, and can help you build personal wealth. Profit-driven companies, if successful, are able to grow quickly and potentially make an even greater impact toward positive social change.

In 2024, I interviewed John Mackey, cofounder and former CEO of Whole Foods Market, on my podcast. He explained that when he launched the natural and organic grocer in the 1970s, there were many small, nonprofit grocery cooperatives that had a mission similar to Whole Foods. Indeed, Mackey lived for a time in a natural-foods shared living community in Texas. But he came to see that being profit-driven was the primary way he could have the biggest impact on changing the way Americans produced and consumed food. "If you can make a profit, it proves that your business model is good," Mackey told me. "That's the way you could do the most good in the world. That's the beauty of capitalism... If you have a good school, we need more of them. And how are you going to do it unless you can make money and reinvest it?" This is something to consider as you determine whether to structure your business as a for-profit or a nonprofit.

Nonprofits are more explicitly focused on social purpose over profits, which is why they enjoy certain tax advantages. They also have more upfront planning steps than for-profits, such as forming a board of directors, establishing bylaws, and applying for nonprofit status, commonly as a 501(c)(3) nonprofit enterprise through the IRS. While for-profit and nonprofit businesses can each raise money from outside individuals and organizations, nonprofits typically enable donations to be tax-deductible for donors. Taxation, recordkeeping, and reporting requirements also vary between entities, so you'll want to talk with your legal and financial advisors to make sure you are complying with all local, state, and federal filings and fees. Business formation documents can be found on your state government's website and at IRS.gov. The latter is also where you will apply for your employer identification number (EIN) to begin setting up your business bank accounts. You can file this initial business formation paperwork yourself, hire a lawyer or professional advisor to do it for you, or spend a few hundred dollars to use a third-party legal website such as LegalZoom.com.

Whether you decide to run your school or learning space as a for-profit or a nonprofit, you are running a business. Just because a nonprofit is committed to a social cause doesn't make it any less of a business than a for-profit organization. Both require keen planning and financial vigilance to stay afloat and make an impact. As Amy Fass, the author of *The Business of Nonprofit-ing*, writes: "Nonprofits are indeed businesses, and to have a lasting and continued social impact, you have to have a sustainable bottom line. A healthy financial picture is what enables thriving nonprofits to do their work."[4]

Nonprofits may not be profit-driven, but that doesn't mean that these enterprises don't make money. Take Khan Academy, for example. The global, free, online educational platform is a nonprofit organization intended to make it easier and more enjoyable for anyone to learn academic content and progress at their own pace through engaging video content and mastery-based learning tools. According to data from the investigative journalism nonprofit ProPublica, Khan Academy brought in more than $53 million in revenue in 2022, and the organization's founder and CEO, Sal Khan, earned a salary that year of more than a million dollars.[5] Khan has reportedly been approached by venture capitalists to turn Khan Academy into a for-profit venture, which would result in significantly higher personal gains, but he has chosen to keep operating Khan Academy as a nonprofit, using revenue to further the organization's social mission.[6]

Iman Alleyne thinks the guilt and unease about money that founders—and especially former public school teachers like her—sometimes feel can hold them back from building successful, sustainable businesses. She is the founder of Kind Academy, a microschool in Coral Springs, Florida, that she grew from a small, nature-based homeschool co-op to a nationally-recognized model of innovative, individualized education. She also runs a separate startup-accelerator program for education entrepreneurs called

Launch Your Kind. "Educators have a lot of guilt around saying this is a service that I'm trying to provide, and I should make money from it," said Iman, who runs her microschool as a for-profit business and her accelerator program as a nonprofit business.

"We're taught as educators that we should not make money," Iman continued. "But what I like to tell my educators all the time is I want more people like you to be successful. I want more people like *us* to be successful, because we're really trying to change the world. One of the major ways we can do that is with money. Money is a tool," Iman said. The money founders earn can be reinvested into their schools or used to scale and open additional sites—or both. Founders are offering something of great value to their customers, and families are willingly choosing to enroll their children in these spaces. Money—and profit—are signals of that value. Iman coaches the educators in her accelerator program how to run financially sustainable small businesses so they can make the positive impact on their communities that they so desire.

## STEP 3. ACTION PLAN AND BUDGET

Once you've determined your organization's mission and vision and considered your preferred business type, it's time to create the action plan for your business. This is your path to launch day. It can be formal or informal, short or long, but it should contain at least these three elements: (1) a description of your school or space and the services you will offer; (2) a market analysis explaining who your likely customers are and how you plan to reach and retain them; and (3) your budget and financial projections. (See Appendix 2 for a basic budget planning worksheet.) You may also want to include information about your curriculum plan, as well as who else may be running similar schools and spaces in your area, and who potential collaborators could be.

The budget and financial analysis is often the most important, and most challenging, part of the action plan for startups of any stripe. "I just thought I'm going to take everything that I know about education, put some kids in a room, teach them, and it's going to be amazing," said Mercedes Grant, a former public school teacher who launched Path of Life Learning, a microschool in Yorktown, Virginia, in the fall of 2023. "But the first time that I heard talk about numbers, I was like, 'Oh, I don't even know what it takes to run a business.'" Mercedes decided to apply to KaiPod Catalyst, a multi-week, cohort-style microschool accelerator program run by KaiPod Learning. The Catalyst program is one of several microschool accelerator programs that founders may want to consider. Like Iman's organization, Launch Your Kind, Catalyst works with cohorts of aspiring microschool founders to provide startup business support and mentoring.

Founded in 2021 by Amar Kumar, KaiPod has its own branded network of microschools across the United States that allows parents to choose whichever curriculum they want for their children, aligned with their own personal values and preferences. Students then gather daily at a convenient microschool location to work through their curriculum in community with others—including a group of peers and an experienced educator who provides curriculum support and facilitates social and enrichment activities. Students may be homeschoolers, charter schoolers, or virtual schoolers, but they are seeking a consistent classroom and community experience with curriculum autonomy. While it was founded in Massachusetts, where Amar lives, KaiPod microschools are growing in states such as Arizona, where new universal school choice programs enable families to attend tuition-free or nearly so.

"We look at the vision of education as being much more personal, much more flexible and individualized for every family," Amar said. "We know that one-size-fits-all just doesn't work for most people, so our vision is to bring education down into smaller and smaller communities." As his microschool network grew, Amar discovered that there were many people like Mercedes who wanted to open a microschool but didn't feel confident about the business side of being an education entrepreneur. He created the KaiPod Catalyst program to serve as a startup accelerator for independent microschools and related models.

"Just like any accelerator, we want to take something that could take years and do it in months. Our vision is you'll start in February and you'll have a school live by fall," said Amar, a former teacher with an MBA from Harvard Business School who worked in both management consulting and online-school product management. Amar also went through his own startup-accelerator experience in 2021 when his new business idea for KaiPod was accepted into the prestigious Y Combinator program in Silicon Valley.

Lasting up to twenty-eight weeks, the KaiPod Catalyst accelerator enables prospective founders to get coaching from the KaiPod team, access to industry experts, and connections to possible grants and funding sources. Founders also get templates and help with setting up business processes. It costs nothing for participants to attend, but if they choose to launch a microschool, then they agree to a small revenue-sharing agreement with KaiPod, which includes ongoing coaching and startup support for three years. Founders run their microschools completely independent of KaiPod, pursuing their own vision for education, but benefit from KaiPod's back-end business support. As of 2024, over one hundred founders have participated in the Catalyst program.

"I think that it is really important to seek advice and to understand the big picture of what it looks like to be a business owner, especially on the financial end—because we know what we're doing in the classroom," Mercedes said, explaining how she initially underestimated her startup costs to be around $2,000 but soon realized they were going to be closer to $15,000 once she went through her budget-planning process with the

KaiPod Catalyst team. "They have a whole financial planning sheet that helps you account for your rent, your utilities, your curriculum and supplies, your per student income that's coming in, how much you're paying your employees, how much it costs for workman's compensation, how much you're paying in taxes—all of these things that I just didn't know," said Mercedes, who operates her microschool as a for-profit LLC. The ongoing financial coaching was especially helpful for Mercedes because she expected to open her microschool with just a handful of students in her home but ended up launching with thirty students in a rented church space because local demand was so high.

As a founder, you have several startup strategies to choose from. You can do your own research, tap into friends and professionals in your community for advice, create an action plan and budget that make sense to you, and get ready for launch. That's what Angie and Rebecca at Providence Hybrid Academy did, and it worked out well for them. You can do some personal upskilling, as Todd at Orchard STEM School did by taking a small business startup course that helped him create a solid action plan and budget. Or you can connect with a microschool network or join an accelerator program, such as the ones that Iman and Amar offer. Refer to Appendix 1 for more information and links to various school startup accelerator and incubator programs. The key is to have a full understanding of potential startup struggles and an accurate picture of your budget and financial projections.

Harvard Business School professor Tom Eisenmann says that he and his colleagues have long "defined entrepreneurship as *pursuing novel opportunity while lacking resources*."[7] Financial risk is part of the entrepreneurial equation. If you're like most of today's everyday education entrepreneurs, you're investing your own hard-earned money to get your school or space up and operating. You don't have angel investors or wealthy benefactors cutting you a check. Grants are rare and it can be difficult to get a bank loan. Fundraisers can be helpful but are often unpredictable.

You might ask friends and family members to chip in, but mostly you're the one on the hook for the initial startup investment—which can range from a few hundred dollars if you're starting in your home, to a few thousand dollars if you're launching elsewhere. You're scrappy, but you're smart and steadfast. Take care with your action plan and budget to cross your t's and count your pennies.

## STEP 4. RULES AND REGULATIONS

A common challenge for founders of innovative schools and spaces is that their programs don't fit neatly into existing regulatory boxes largely intended for traditional schools. Zoning and land-use regulations; building, occupancy, and fire codes; and certain business licensing requirements may not yet adequately reflect the evolving learning landscape. Some properties or parts of town simply may not permit unconventional educational models. Chapter 9 delves deeper into challenges school founders sometimes encounter, including regulatory roadblocks; but as you think about the form and location of your program, it's important to thoroughly investigate your local and state regulations to ensure compliance—as well as any homeowners association policies that might impact you.

"It is funny for me to say because I used to work in policy, but I just didn't know the regulations around childcare at the time," said Rida Rizvi, who in 2017 cofounded Al Hadi Learning Organization, a Muslim microschool that emphasizes holistic, student-centered, individualized learning in the Washington, DC, area. "Unfortunately, that's the reality. I just never really looked into it," Rida said. She and her cofounders met at a weekly Muslim mommy-and-me class in 2016 with their toddlers and preschoolers and began imagining a more formal space that would blend faith, family, and a focus on personalized learning. "We shared that vision of what education should look like for early childhood, and really the only thing we needed to do was secure a space. We pitched a local mosque to use their basement and went from idea to open in just a matter of a couple of weeks," Rida said.

Soon, the founders confronted childcare licensing requirements in their area that weren't agile enough to accommodate a homeschool cooperative arrangement. "We thought, 'We're a co-op, we're a bunch of parents,'" Rida recalled. "We really didn't think too much of it because to us it was like, 'We're all here and we're all doing this together.' It turns out that you actually need a license for this sort of thing, we were told." It wasn't a deal-breaker, but Rida's small homeschooling cooperative had to backtrack a bit to get licensed as a registered daycare provider and then create a distinction between their licensed early childhood program and their school-age microschool for homeschoolers—both of which they currently run in private residences.

Based on her experience, Rida recommends that new founders do their due diligence regarding state and local regulations very early in the startup planning process. "I would say step one is probably going to be to look at your local regulations," Rida said. "We used to say to each other that we're building this house while we're living in it, so if you can construct the house before you move in, I think that's always a good idea. Check out your local regulations and develop your five-year plan accordingly so you're not caught in a position of taking two steps back in order to progress," said Rida, who is now in the process of creating a new organization, Azeez Academy, to accommodate upper-elementary-age students.

While waiting for a regulatory refresh, there may be some things founders can do to stay true to their unconventional models while avoiding potentially onerous oversight. Many founders I've talked to position their programs as tutoring centers or drop-in offerings for homeschoolers, which can sometimes make them eligible for exemptions to existing childcare or related regulations. Other founders have told me that they avoid the word *school* altogether—including microschool—because using the word *school* in any way could thrust them into a regulatory labyrinth.

Using a word other than *school* when describing your program could help you stay truer to your mission and stay clear of regulations intended for more conventional conceptions of schooling.

This advice is oddly similar to advice I gave readers in my first book, published twenty years ago, about nontraditional wedding planning. The book had nothing to do with my day job at the time—which was running my own small business working with professional services firms on learning and staff development strategies. Brian and I got married barefoot on a beach back in 2001, and I decided to write a fun how-to book for couples craving an alternative to nuptial norms. One of the key tips I shared in that book is to avoid using the word *wedding* in your nontraditional wedding planning, if possible. While a couple certainly doesn't want to be deceptive, it's true that various vendors have preconceived notions of what a "wedding" looks like. It can be difficult for them to hear the term *wedding* and think of something unconventional, so they stick to their standard wedding packages, protocols, and pricing. A surprise backyard barbecue wedding, for example, looks more like a barbecue than a wedding, so I suggested that couples emphasize the term *cookout* when ordering flowers to ensure they get the floral arrangements they want.

Similarly, many of today's alternative education models don't look anything like traditional schools, so using a different term may make sense. Language matters, and sometimes language hasn't quite caught up to creative ventures of all kinds. This all varies based on state and local rules and regulations, and on what kind of program you want to be. For instance, you may want to become a recognized private school in your state for a host of reasons, including increased legitimacy in the eyes of potential parents or to participate in particular school choice programs. Some states also make it really easy to start a private school, while in other states it's more difficult. The Education Entrepreneur Freedom Index, published by the nonprofit yes. every kid. foundation., provides a cross-state comparison of regulations to show a state's particular friendliness toward unconventional learning models.[8] Additionally, in 2024, EdChoice released a "School Starter Checklist" report detailing private education regulatory requirements in all fifty states and the District of Columbia.[9] Both of these can be helpful resources for founders.

The optimal path forward, of course, is a broader cultural acceptance of unconventional undertakings in many segments of society—including education. Perhaps a group of faith-filled families gathering together in a church basement might not need to be licensed as a childcare center. Perhaps a learning pod where homeschooled teens join regularly for classes and connection shouldn't be regulated in the same way that a 1,000-student conventional high school might be. Indeed, the word *school* itself might need to evolve from its current definition as "an institution for educating children," to an interconnected, unbundled ecosystem in which children become educated.

## STEP 5. TRUSTED ADVISORS

Starting any new business requires knowledge that may be outside of your area of expertise. That's why you should seek out trusted advisors—professionals who can help you ensure a smooth startup process. These advisors could be attorneys (including those through reputable online legal websites) who can help you file your initial business creation paperwork, comply with any licensing and reporting requirements, consider various employee contracts and related policies, as well as provide guidance as you grow or scale. Your trusted advisors could also be accountants and financial professionals who can help you understand your tax obligations and advise you on basic bookkeeping strategies, such as getting you set up on QuickBooks or a similar accounting software. They could also be real estate agents or architects who can help you find a location for your school or space that meets local zoning and occupancy codes, as well as insurance professionals who can advise you on what you need to do to ensure adequate insurance coverage for yourself and your business.

Talk with your friends, family members, Facebook acquaintances, as well as other small business owners you know, to ask them about their trusted advisors. These recommendations and referrals can set you up for early and ongoing success. Additionally, check out the pro bono legal assistance offered by the yes. every kid. foundation., mentioned in Step 4. The organization has a team of attorneys at yeslegal.org who help new and aspiring education entrepreneurs identify and address various startup and operational challenges.

## STEP 6. UNDERSTANDING YOUR CUSTOMERS

You've thought about your vision and the type of business you want to run. You've created an action plan, investigated local rules and regulations for running a small school or learning space, and have some trusted advisors at your service. Now, it's time to let your potential customers—local families—know who you are and what you're offering.

When Candace Fish made the decision in the fall of 2021 to launch a new microschool the following August, she had no idea whether anyone would be interested. She was still working as a teacher in the Wichita, Kansas, public school system and decided to post in a local Facebook parenting group about her idea. "Within the next three days, I had about three hundred Facebook messages from parents saying, 'I'm interested!'" Candace told me. They wanted to know more about her vision for a low-cost, faith-based microschool with a highly personalized curriculum. As a special education teacher for about a decade, and a mother of five, Candace valued independent learning plans and customized curriculum for each child based on abilities and areas for improvement. She also had the opportunity to homeschool one of her children briefly a few years prior and loved the flexibility and personalization of homeschooling. "I wanted it to look like homeschool in a building, basically," Candace said of her vision for the school. She knew that there were a lot of families who wanted to homeschool but couldn't for a variety of reasons, and she also knew that there were elements of a typical school that were beneficial. She wanted to merge the two, offering a homeschooling experience in a classroom environment.

Once Candace saw how much early interest there was in her program, she sketched out her startup plan. "I was working by day, and evenings and weekends I spent figuring out how to make this happen." At the end of October, she mentioned her idea to Sarah McCosh, another teacher with whom she worked in the local public schools. Sarah was immediately lured by Candace's vision. They decided to become cofounders and spent their fall evenings on the phone, making plans to quit their jobs at the end of the school year and start their microschool, reminiscent of a one-room schoolhouse, which they anticipated would have about thirty mixed-age learners. They were in for a surprise.

Over the next several months, Candace and Sarah hosted several casual informational meetings at their church. At the first one, they had eighty-two people. At the second one, they had sixty-five, and at the third, they had sixty. "We were kind of like, 'Oh my gosh, this is a lot of people.' And it was new people every time," Candace recalled. They realized that their microschool might not actually be that micro. Still, no one had committed yet to enroll their kids or pay the tuition, which was set significantly below other private schools in the area. The founders established an enrollment cutoff date of May 31, 2022, for anyone interested in joining the school, which they named Freedom Preparatory. The deadline came, and when the founders tallied all their applications and deposits, they had 120 kids. "We sat here at my kitchen table and looked at each other and went, 'Wow, we need to hire some teachers,'" Candace said.

They assembled their team, including several teachers who had retired from the public schools and wanted to do something new. They found a location at what had previously been a senior center, became registered as a recognized private school—something that is relatively easy to do in

Kansas—and ended up opening the doors to Freedom Preparatory in August 2022 with 132 students in kindergarten through high school. Candace's school now has about 150 students. It graduated its first group of seniors in 2024. She continues to see growing demand for new schools and spaces in her area and is part of a grassroots group of education entrepreneurs—Wichita Innovative Schools and Educators (WISE)—that emerged in 2021 to support and encourage a diverse group of founders. "I think that parents, no matter their background, are finally going to have options that fit their family, whether they want a religious school like ours or a nonreligious one, whether they want an outdoor program or something that's more traditional," Candace said about the burst of education entrepreneurship in her community.

As you create your startup's website and begin to market your idea on various social media groups for local parents—as well as on your own social media pages—you will gain a better understanding of your potential customers. You will see what families in your area are looking for in terms of alternative education options, and what their interest level might be for a program like yours. According to a 2024 microschooling analysis by EdChoice, more parents are attracted to the idea of a small learning environment rather than a "nontraditional" educational option, so you may want to carefully consider your wording, emphasizing the nurturing, individualized aspect of your school or space rather than its unconventional approach if you are looking to reach a broader audience.[10]

Hosting information sessions in local community spaces, meeting prospective families for coffee or at a park, and responding quickly and thoroughly to questions and concerns can help you get the word out about your forthcoming program and build trust within your community. It's also worth referring back to Thomas Arnett's research, described in the previous chapter, about the various "jobs to be done" that parents are seeking. Identifying parents' points of struggle, and being able to demonstrate how your program could be a solution, can position you for a solid start with a committed group of parents and learners. Who knows? Like Candace, you may even have more demand than you anticipate, bringing you a whole new set of startup challenges.

## STEP 7. PEOPLE, PLACES, AND POLICIES

You're getting close to launch. You understand the local market demand for your new school or learning space, and you've gained verbal (and hopefully monetary) commitments from some founding families several months ahead of your proposed launch. Once you know what your startup size will likely be, you'll want to finalize plans related to space and staffing. But there could be some shocks.

Mercedes of Path of Life Learning had planned on launching her microschool inside her home in August 2023, expecting only a handful of learners and herself as the only teacher. When she opened her program for enrollment in April, Mercedes was startled to have more than twenty learners registered within two weeks. She had to pivot to find a new place and hire new people—and update her budget to reflect higher startup costs than predicted.

Like many founders, Mercedes settled on a local church space to rent. The church was an older congregation that did not use its former preschool wing and was happy to lease several classrooms to Mercedes for her microschool. She found her location relatively quickly, but for many founders, securing a suitable space that meets appropriate zoning and occupancy codes for educational offerings can be an enormous challenge. One founder I spoke with who wanted to open a secular microschool emailed or called the pastors of thirty churches before finding one who loved her vision and was happy to offer a space. Other founders visit dozens of properties, often working with a local real estate agent, to find a location that works. Still others use their own homes or another residential space, or even look for land to build on. There is also the option to use public spaces, especially in the early days of your startup. Some founders launch their programs outside in a local park a couple of days a week or meet in a public library. This can help you get started quickly and with minimal costs.

Another challenge can be staffing and training. To accommodate the thirty students she had enrolled by her summer 2023 launch date, Mercedes posted on Facebook and the online staffing site Indeed.com to recruit another full-time educator, along with a part-time instructor. Mercedes received some resumes from certified teachers like her, but she wasn't impressed. "They seemed good, but not really into or ready for alternative education. It's a whole process to wrap your mind around," said Mercedes, who explained that it can be difficult to train some conventional school teachers to think in more unconventional ways about teaching and learning. "My full-time teacher without experience has honestly been one of the best educators I've ever met," she added. The following year, as her enrollment doubled to sixty students, Mercedes added more teachers and used a similar staff recruitment strategy. "I think what attracted the qualified candidates was the potential for a position with smaller class sizes, less prep work, and more autonomy to do what's best for kids instead of state objectives," she said.

Other founders I've talked to share similar experiences. For example, Laurel Suarez from Compass Outreach and Education Center in South Florida, whom we met in Chapter 1, posted two teaching positions in the fall of 2023 on Indeed.com. She received more than three hundred resumes, the vast majority of which were from current public school teachers. According to Laurel, previous job postings would typically yield fifty to seventy-five resumes. She was shocked at the volume of candidates—especially because she posted the jobs after the academic year began and listed a salary that was lower than what traditional school teachers earn. I asked Laurel why the candidates she ultimately interviewed were attracted to her microschool. "They want a peaceful place and to be part of the development of a learning program instead of just being given something to teach," Laurel replied. She also noticed a growing acceptance of unconventional learning models among traditional teachers. "They are more open to alternatives now. They know it's okay to take chances, to do something different," Laurel said.

Linked closely with startup decisions about people and places are policies. You'll want to make sure that you look closely at your location's lease terms and any policies with which you need to comply. You'll want to set up an account with a background check website to run checks on your staff and any other adults who will interact with your learners. You'll also want to create policies and procedures for your program, including generating contracts for staff and families and producing basic forms, such as media releases, so that you can populate your program's Instagram page and website with student photos. Outline your general program expectations in a student handbook for parents, students, and teachers to acknowledge. Check out the websites of traditional public and private schools in your area, as well as microschools you may know. Many schools have their student handbooks publicly available, and those can be helpful to reference as you craft policies for your unique program.

## STEP 8. SUSTAINABILITY AND SCALE

In his bestselling book *The Lean Startup*, author and entrepreneur Eric Ries describes at length the concept of a Minimum Viable Product, or MVP. It's typically used in reference to new, experimental products or services—often in the tech sector—that are just being introduced into the market. The goal with MVPs is to launch something small and imperfect to gauge initial interest and encourage ongoing customer feedback and iteration. "The MVP is just the first step on a journey of learning," Ries writes.[11]

You may also launch with an MVP—an early, and perhaps incomplete, version of your ultimate vision for your school or space. The key is to start, and then to learn and improve from there. "I found the way to get started was to quit talking and begin doing it," Walt Disney said regarding his early startup phase.[12] Over and over again, the entrepreneurs I talk to say the same thing: Just go for it.

It could be that your MVP isn't yet a school at all. To get their feet wet and begin with a more low-risk model, some founders start by offering summer camps, afterschool programs, tutoring services, or similar "side hustles" while they continue to work another job. A 2023 survey of more than 1,300 general business owners revealed that 44 percent of their enterprises began as side projects.[13] Starting small can enable you to build a brand, create community connections, and generate initial business income before quitting your day job to jump into full-time education entrepreneurship. Families can also get a better feel of your style and approach through your side project before committing to paying a full year's tuition. The rules and regulations for establishing camps and afterschool and enrichment programs also tend to be fewer, so they can be faster and easier to get going.

Even if you decide to start as a full-time microschool or similar model, be honest with yourself and with your founding families that this will be a learning experience for all and that feedback and adaptation will be essential for continuous improvement. This openness to input will set you on a path toward business sustainability, with happy customers who re-enroll their kids and refer their friends. That is how you build a business that can have meaningful, enduring impact.

You also need to have a plan for getting paid. While it's not unusual for entrepreneurs in any sector to forgo a paycheck for the first year or more of running their startups, your business isn't likely to last if you don't have a strategy for earning an income—even a modest one—within the first three years of running your new school or space. Exceptions can include founders who have created a school that their children attend at no cost. They may trade their salary for their children's tuition, at least in the short run; but getting paid should be part of your longer-term business strategy.

"A lot of founders come into this, and they don't realize that there's not a whole lot of money," Mercedes said. "I did want to take home a salary from the get-go. I value what I'm offering, and I think that it is okay to want to have a salary," she added. Her startup costs were more than anticipated, so Mercedes earned less in her first year than she had planned, but she was on track to increase her salary in subsequent years.

Most founders I speak to are content to run a small school, earn a small salary, and enjoy a small business that brings them big personal and professional fulfillment. Some founders, though, have dreams of growing beyond a single school or space. They want to scale, but often want to do so laterally—opening several small schools rather than creating one large one. It's the small size that offers the individualization and personalization that sets these creative schooling options apart from traditional classrooms. As your first year as a founder gets underway, and you plan for financial stability, you may want to consider what scaling would look like for your school or space—should you choose to go that route. Chapter 10 offers more thoughts on scaling your startup. Some founders didn't intend on scaling but found that their enrollment was higher than expected, or they had a lot of learners on their waitlist, or they had parents asking for new schools in new places. Think carefully about your growth plan as you begin.

There's never been a better time to launch your school startup. Parents are eager for new and different education options, and learners deserve an educational setting that enables their curiosity and creativity to blossom. Approaching your educational venture as the small business that it is, and thoughtfully executing a startup plan from idea to implementation to iteration, will position you for a smooth launch of your successful, sustainable, socially impactful enterprise.

*Chapter Reflections for Parents and Founders*
This chapter provided an initial pathway for founders considering launching a new school or learning model, and Appendix 2 includes a blank

"S.T.A.R.T.U.P.S. Roadmap Worksheet" to begin to turn these ideas into action. Whether you are a founder or a parent, your first step should be to consider the vision and mission of the program you are either evaluating or designing.

**Parents:** When you are exploring new and different educational options, begin by identifying a program's vision and mission. Make sure that they align with your educational preferences and personal values. Use these organizational statements as a launching pad for further questions when talking to a school's founder and staff. For example, let's say a program's vision is to foster individualized learning within a holistic educational environment. One of your first questions could be what, practically speaking, does individualized, holistic learning look like in this school or space?

**Founders:** Invest time early in your startup process to clearly identify and articulate your program's vision and mission. This can help you clarify your purpose and goals while also helping to attract the families and learners who will most benefit from your endeavor. Consider why your program is needed, who it will serve and how, and what the result will be if your program is successful. I recommend visiting the websites of the founders featured in this book for examples of powerful educational visions and missions.

## Chapter 6
# Searches

*I had to make my own living and my own opportunity. But I made it! Don't sit down and wait for the opportunities to come. Get up and make them!*
—Madam C. J. Walker (first American self-made female millionaire)

There is no doubt that launching a startup school or space requires an entrepreneurial spirit. But if you are a parent searching for such a space, you are also entrepreneurial in your own way. Like the entrepreneurs building new learning models, you question the status quo and have a willingness to try new things. You may never have thought about an option beyond a local traditional school, but now you are curious about new possibilities. You are a problem-solver, searching for an education solution that will fit your family. You are optimistic that positive change is possible. You also likely have some fear: fear of the unknown, fear of making the wrong decision, fear of failing your child or of disappointing yourself and others. Choosing a new education option for your child can be intimidating, but just as there are steps school founders can take to ensure a successful startup, there are steps you can take to make your school search successful as well.

Melissa Shah knows what it's like to have fear and uncertainty about choosing an unconventional learning model. When she had to find a more personalized high school option for her son Kadin, she didn't expect to choose a new and untested startup. Her seventeen-year-old is considered twice-exceptional, a term sometimes used to describe individuals who are intellectually gifted with at least one special learning challenge, such as dyslexia, ADHD, or autism spectrum disorder. Kadin was diagnosed with autism when he was two years old, and Melissa spent much of her son's childhood trying to get him the services he needed in order to thrive academically, emotionally, and socially. Kadin spent his early-elementary years at various charter schools before switching to a private Montessori school where he and his two younger siblings spent most of their elementary and middle school years. As an Arizona resident, Melissa was able to take advantage of the school choice programs available for special needs students in the state, which enabled her to use education funds toward the school or space that worked best for Kadin, as well as access funding for additional educational therapies and support services.

The Montessori school was working well for Kadin through middle school, but he needed a new option for high school that would challenge him socially and academically—especially in math, where he was doing advanced-level work. "He was teaching algebra to everyone else," Melissa said, laughing. "He was the teacher, which was a great skill to develop—especially for someone on the spectrum—but his learning was being stunted," she said. Melissa and Kadin considered several conventional high school options, including public, private, and charter schools, but the large size of most of these schools was a concern, given Kadin's anxiety and sensory-processing issues.

"Then I thought: How else can we do this? What are other people doing?" Melissa recalled. She turned to Facebook, joining local parenting and homeschooling groups and asking about options. Someone mentioned the idea of an online school, so Melissa began exploring that possibility and discovered Ignite Learning Academy, an Arizona-based, private online school with a specific program for gifted students and those with special needs. It would enable Kadin to work at his own pace, quickly accelerating through math content while taking the time he needed to master other subjects in a more personalized way. Tuition would continue to be fully covered by Arizona's school choice programs, for which all the state's K–12 students became eligible in 2022.

Melissa and Kadin found the curriculum they desired, as well as online virtual interactions for Kadin with other twice-exceptional students through Ignite, but they also wanted an in-person learning experience. Melissa went back to Facebook, again seeking advice and suggestions. "I found out that Ignite was doing a collaboration with this place called KaiPod," Melissa said, referring to the new microschool network and startup-accelerator program described in the previous chapter. Melissa thought the model was fascinating, enabling families to choose whichever curriculum they wanted while allowing for daily, in-person interaction in a local community space with peers and experienced educators. Then she realized that the one KaiPod microschool in Phoenix at the time was brand new and that the company itself was a startup with only a few locations sprinkled across the United States. "I'm like, oh gosh. How am I going to sell my son on this? How am I going to sell my ex-husband on this? It was a leap," she recalled.

Melissa had a lot of questions. Would the space in a suburban strip mall in Gilbert, Arizona, just outside of Phoenix, work well? Would Kadin fit in? Would there be bullying? Would Kadin be able to concentrate on his academics at the same time as developing social skills? "I just wasn't sure they were going to get him. I just wasn't sure they were going to meet his needs. I just wasn't sure. I think that was all rooted in the fear of something new," Melissa explained. After many encouraging phone calls and conversations with the KaiPod staff and management team, as well as getting Kadin and her ex-husband on board, Melissa enrolled her son at KaiPod in the fall of 2022.

"Within two weeks, we knew we had found the winning combo. He was so happy," Melissa said, describing all of Kadin's friends at KaiPod and his ability to take on leadership responsibilities. "It's such a place of acceptance. It's a place where everybody just gets to be themselves. They get to do the academic work that fits them," she said, adding that Kadin had been attending KaiPod five days a week for the previous two years but was about to drop down to a part-time option the following semester so he could take advantage of on-campus dual enrollment classes at a local community college. After high school, Kadin plans to enroll in a four-year university to study engineering and math. Melissa couldn't be more satisfied. "KaiPod has provided a structured, calm environment for my child to thrive both socially and academically. He has finally been able to achieve true friendships and be completely accepted for his authentic self," she said.

## IS THIS SCHOOL A GOOD MATCH?

As you explore and evaluate new schools and spaces for your child, what should you be looking out for? The following questions can be helpful whether you are choosing a startup school or one that has been around for a long time, but they may be particularly useful when searching for newer, more unconventional learning settings. There are numerous benefits to enrolling in a fledgling school. You can be part of helping to shape a new program's vision and culture. You can benefit from an ambitious founder who is often highly motivated to ensure your overall satisfaction. You may enjoy lower costs and greater flexibility. But you also want to do your own due diligence. The following questions can provide a starting point:

- **Educational priorities:** What are your top priorities for your child's education, and how does the learning model you are considering reflect those priorities? Melissa wanted a rigorous but flexible curriculum for Kadin that would challenge him in math and allow for greater self-pacing and mastery in other subject areas. She also wanted a convenient, in-person microschool model that would be safe and accepting. She was able to find exactly what she was looking for through a combination of online learning and a microschool.
- **Location:** What is the space like? Does it seem clean and safe? Is the location convenient? What is the surrounding area like? Melissa had initial reservations about the location of Kadin's KaiPod. While it was tidy, safe, and code-compliant, she initially thought that the strip mall location on a busy street would be a drawback, limiting off-campus excursions. "I was hoping that there would be something like a Starbucks that Kadin could walk to or things he could do with friends," Melissa said. "Well, it turns out they never want to leave, so it doesn't make any difference," she laughed. "All they want to do is stay there and hang out with friends."
- **Founder and staff:** What are the founder and staff members like? What are their backgrounds and credentials? Are they responsive and eager to communicate with you? Have they had background checks? Melissa recalled Sunday evening calls with KaiPod's staff who patiently answered her questions and addressed her concerns before she enrolled her son. If the teachers and staff members aren't responsive, or are dismissive of your concerns and questions, it's a sign to look elsewhere.

- **Curriculum:** What is the curriculum like? Does it meet your expectations? Is it aligned with your values? With KaiPod, Melissa was able to retain full curriculum control, choosing an online school that met Kadin's specialized learning needs. You'll want to make sure that you like the curriculum used in the school you are considering, and that it reflects your personal and educational priorities and preferences. You'll also want to assess the school's extracurricular offerings and support services. Many startup schools don't have the breadth of clubs, activities, and educational supports that traditional schools do. This is one way that they keep their costs down. Kadin participates in out-of-school enrichment activities, such as piano, band, and karate, and receives supplemental educational therapies beyond KaiPod. Make sure you're okay with a school with more limited extracurricular and nonacademic options and services.
- **Schedule:** What is the schedule like? Does the rhythm of the day and week seem smooth and well-thought-out? At KaiPod, academic time is interspersed throughout the day with group enrichment opportunities and collaborative projects. How are academics and enrichment activities balanced at the school or space you are considering? KaiPod enables families to choose full- or part-time enrollment options. Does the school or space you are exploring offer scheduling flexibility? Is that important to you?
- **Policies:** What are the program's policies and procedures? You should inquire about a school's policies regarding a range of topics, such as screen time, acceptable student behaviors and responsibilities, parent involvement, attendance expectations, and so on. Make sure you agree with these policies. If the school has a student or family handbook, ask to see a copy prior to enrolling.
- **Culture:** What is the school's culture like? When you visit, do the students seem happy and engaged? Ask to talk to parents of

current students to find out more about the school's culture and to make sure that behaviors such as bullying aren't tolerated. "At KaiPod, everybody belongs," Melissa said. "Bullying doesn't exist because it is such a place of acceptance."

- **Classification:** Is the school recognized by your state or local government as a private school or is it classified as something else (e.g., tutoring center, homeschool resource center, afterschool/enrichment program, etc.)? If you need to register as a homeschooler, how does that process work in your state? Many of today's innovative learning models are not legally classified as traditional schools for a variety of reasons, ranging from founder and family preferences to regulatory parameters. KaiPod supports homeschoolers, online schoolers, charter schoolers, and traditionally schooled students and helps parents navigate their self-chosen curriculum options.
- **Cost:** Is this school or space affordable? If you live in a state with school choice policies, ask if it participates in such programs. In Arizona, parents are able to use their universal scholarship funds at both online options like Ignite and in-person microschools like KaiPod. That is not the case in all states with school choice policies. Some are limited to traditional private schools only and don't (yet) cover today's emerging learning models. Even so, these innovative programs are typically less expensive than other private education options. If cost is a concern for you, ask about private scholarship programs, sliding-scale tuition options, and other creative payment possibilities. Some nonprofit organizations, such as the Children's Scholarship Fund, offer partial scholarships for low-income students attending private schools or microschools. See if the school or space you are considering participates in this program, or may want to participate. Many founders bend over backward to make their programs as accessible as possible to any student who wishes to attend.

- **Future plans:** What are the founder's plans for the future of the school or space? Are you excited about them? Melissa saw that KaiPod was growing both locally in Arizona and elsewhere across the country. Growth can be a sign of startup strength, but make sure to ask about ongoing quality-control measures as a program grows.
- **Intuition:** What is your overall intuition regarding the school or space you are exploring? Are you wowed by what you see? Do you feel like your child will thrive there? At the end of the day, parents need to rely on their superhero "Spidey-sense." If something doesn't feel right—even if you can't put your finger on it—move along and find someplace else.
- **What-if scenarios:** Before you enroll your child, ask yourself: What is the worst thing that could happen if this space doesn't work out? Will you be out thousands of dollars in tuition that won't be refunded? If so, see if your child can do a trial week or month at the school before committing to a year-long financial agreement. If you enroll and it turns out to be a bad fit, what happens next? Would it be truly devastating? Melissa knew that if Kadin left KaiPod, he would remain with his online curriculum provider and she would return to Facebook to ask again for more advice and recommendations. That took some of the pressure off and helped her have the confidence to try something experimental.

Moreover, just because you decide to enroll your child somewhere today doesn't mean you're locked into that place for years to come. Melissa found that the private Montessori school worked well for Kadin during his elementary and middle school years, and that an online school plus KaiPod and college dual enrollment courses worked better for the high school years. One of the great benefits of today's innovative learning models is the flexibility they allow families to curate a best-fit education and make changes as needed.

## FINDING THE IDEAL SCHOOL OR SPACE FOR YOUR CHILD

Melissa is particularly fortunate to live in Phoenix, Arizona, an area rich in educational options that are also widely accessible due to the state's expansive school choice policies. When she posted in local parenting and homeschooling Facebook groups about what options were available for Kadin's high school experience, Melissa was showered with suggestions for both new and established schools and spaces. She was ultimately able to find both a curriculum provider and a microschool that matched the distinct needs and interests of her child, as well as her priorities and preferences as a parent. Facebook and similar social networks can be great resources to learn about your education options and connect with families and founders involved in the innovative education ecosystem.

You may also find local websites and resource hubs, such as LoveYourSchool.org, that can help you navigate your options. Founded by Jenny Clark, an Arizona homeschooling mom, Love Your School is a nonprofit that works with parents to identify what they want for their children's education, and then helps them consider various possibilities, including traditional public, private, and charter schools, microschools, learning pods, homeschooling programs, online learning, and more.

## HOW DID WE GET TO ONE-SIZE-FITS-ALL SCHOOLING?

As parents like Melissa seek more bespoke learning options for their children, and entrepreneurs build more alternatives to traditional schooling, it may be worth asking: How did we get here in the first place? How did we come to adopt such a uniform system of schooling?

Prior to the mid-nineteenth century, American education consisted of a decentralized patchwork of schools and schooling alternatives. There were public schools, private schools, charity schools often connected with churches, and small, low-cost "dame schools," run by entrepreneurial women out of their homes. Historian Carl Kaestle also describes the presence of "entrepreneurial private-venture teachers," similar to today's education entrepreneurs, to whom families would send their children for instruction.[1] Homeschooling and apprenticeship experiences were also ubiquitous. Sadly, women and racial and ethnic minorities were often excluded—or forbidden, in the case of American slaves—from participating in various educational pursuits; but the options that did exist represented an assortment of models—even if a top-down pedagogical approach persisted.

Beginning in the 1800s, American social reformers were attracted to the centralized, compulsory, state-regulated model of education adopted by the German state of Prussia, which emphasized standardization in classrooms as well as in teacher training. This was also a time of efficiency-focused industrial innovation that was transforming the American economy. Centralization and innovation trends blended with larger social reform efforts to give rise to a similar model of mass schooling in the United States. This was a time of rapidly increasing immigration, especially of Irish Catholics in cities like Boston. These immigrants threatened the prevailing Anglo-Saxon-Protestant cultural norms, leading to calls for more heavy-handed control of education. Poor and immigrant parents were particularly targeted. In the fall of 1851, editor William Swan echoed the sentiments of many of his contemporaries when he wrote in *The Massachusetts Teacher*:

> In too many instances the parents are unfit guardians of their own children. If left to their direction the young will be brought up in idle, dissolute, vagrant habits, which will make

them worse members of society than their parents are... Nothing can operate effectually here but stringent legislation, thoroughly carried out by an efficient police; the children must be gathered up and forced into school, and those who resist or impede this plan, whether parents or *priests*, must be held accountable and punished.[2]

Six months later, Massachusetts became the first US state to pass a compulsory school attendance law, mandating attendance under a legal threat of force. Similar laws would be passed in all US states in the coming decades, ushering in a "common school" movement undergirded by coercion. This coercion may have been considered by some reformers to be necessary or important for achieving larger social goals, such as greater literacy (even though US literacy rates were already quite high[3]), assimilation of newcomers, or cultural cohesion; but it shifted control of education away from parents and local communities and toward the state. The force of these laws continues to be felt today. In 2023, the Missouri Supreme Court upheld a high-profile case involving two separate single moms who were sentenced to jail because their elementary-age children each missed approximately fifteen days of school during the 2021/2022 academic year.[4]

Beyond coercion, many of the elements of traditional schooling that are now commonplace emerged during the dawn of the compulsory schooling era. These include a prioritization of order and compliance, age-segregated classrooms that gradually replaced one-room schoolhouses, bells regulating mobility, and standardized curriculum and assessment measures. But it wasn't just a desire for stricter social control that led to the rise of standardization in schooling that persists today. It was also the innovative thing to do.

To our modern mindset, these nineteenth-century characteristics of conventional schooling may seem outdated, or even backward. But at the time they were actually avant-garde. These ideas were revolutionizing many sectors of American society as it moved from an agrarian economy to an industrial one. It's not surprising that nineteenth-century schooling would adopt these novel ideas and cutting-edge practices. While today we use "factory-model schooling" as a pejorative, nineteenth-century education reformers were wowed by factories and related industrial processes. Stanford University educational historian David Tyack explained how these reformers drew inspiration from the technological and managerial advancements of the industrial era. He wrote: "They were impressed with the order and efficiency of the new technology and forms of organization they saw about them. The division of labor in the factory, the punctuality of the railroad, the chain of command and coordination in modern businesses—these aroused a sense of wonder and excitement in men and women seeking to systematize the schools."[5]

The problem is not so much that nineteenth-century schooling was shaped by the centralizing impulses and industrial innovations of its time. It's that mass schooling still clings to centralization and standardization even as decentralization and individualization increasingly define our contemporary culture. In fact, schooling has become even more standardized in the twenty-first century.

Beginning in 2001, with the passage of the federal No Child Left Behind Act (NCLB) under President George W. Bush, federal education policy blended with state and local policy to reinforce rigid curriculum standards and regular high-stakes testing to ensure accountability. The enactment of the Every Student Succeeds Act under President Barack Obama in 2015 replaced NCLB and sought to shift control of education back to the states, but it retained annual testing requirements for all third through eighth graders, as well as for high schoolers, along with requiring states to introduce additional accountability metrics, such as absenteeism rates. "Clearly, states are tightening standards more than ever since NCLB took effect," wrote Harvard Kennedy School's Paul Peterson and his colleagues in 2016.[6] Some might argue that the widespread embrace of curriculum standards and high-stakes testing in the new millennium is a positive trend, leading to greater accountability for schools, teachers, and students. Whatever your opinion, there is little doubt that standardized, test-driven schooling has shaped twenty-first-century learning in ways that nineteeth-century education reformers could have only imagined.

## WHAT IF YOU CAN'T FIND WHAT YOU'RE LOOKING FOR?

Today, more parents are seeking innovative education possibilities that embrace a modern vision for education—rejecting uniformity in favor of uniqueness. Sometimes a parent's search comes up short. She just can't find what she needs for her child. In that case, it may be time to build. That's what Jen Granberry had to do.

Five miles south of Kadin's KaiPod is ARROWS Christian Academy, the school Jen opened in August 2023. A stay-at-home-mom with a master's degree in soil science who worked previously for the US Department of Agriculture, Jen was frustrated that she couldn't find a school or other learning setting for her youngest child, Zane. Born with Down syndrome, and later diagnosed with autism, Zane has unique and complex learning needs. For Zane's preschool years, Jen was able to find relaxed, play-based Christian learning environments for him, but once it came time for kindergarten, she hit roadblock after roadblock trying to locate a Christian school that would accept her son. She knew that public school would be overwhelming for Zane and potentially not offer the level of parent involvement she desired. The traditional faith-based private schools she explored were not accommodating. Jen homeschooled for a year, but it still didn't feel like the right answer for Zane's education. At one point, Jen asked herself if maybe she was supposed to be part of the solution. "I wasn't seeing the invitation that God was giving me to do this," Jen said. "It took Him closing all of these doors to really see what He was wanting me to do."

Once she realized that opening a school was the path she was meant to take, Jen was able to lean into it and start slow. She didn't want to rush her school's launch, instead giving herself about eighteen months to prepare for the opening of ARROWS Christian Academy in Chandler, Arizona. One of the first things Jen did was hire an education consultant, Heather Lloyd, who founded Idaho-based Concordis Education Partners, which supports the launch and ongoing operations of classical Christian schools across the United States. Classical education is focused on the traditional liberal arts and the foundations of Western civilization dating back to ancient Greece and Rome. Since 2020, interest in classical education has surged, with more classical schools opening and expanding across the country.[7]

Heather saw immediately what Jen wanted to create: a small school with a big emphasis on individualized, Christ-centered, classical education that would fully integrate neurotypical and neurodiverse learners. According to a 2024 sector analysis conducted by the National Microschooling Center, nearly two-thirds of today's microschools serve neurodiverse learners, and Jen wanted to create a model that she hoped would work well for her son and a variety of other learners in her community.[8] Heather coached Jen through the startup process, including offering guidance on how to set up her school as a nonprofit business, create bylaws, find board members, decide on curriculum, hire teachers, find a suitable location, and recruit families.

Taking her time to open the school took some of the pressure off, but it didn't shield her entirely from the inevitable stress of entrepreneurship. "I didn't want to fail, but the stress just pushed me into Jesus more, and my faith grew immensely," she said. Her biggest challenge was being patient and letting things unfold at the right time. "The need for neurodiverse kids to have Christian education, and to be welcomed and supported in Christian education, is really great. Even for our own son, it was hard to not jump ahead in steps or try and push things into being," Jen said. She was able to find experienced teachers mostly through word of mouth. They were working in teaching jobs at the time Jen approached them about ARROWS but were eager for a change during the following academic year. Securing a location was a bit more challenging, with Jen calling or emailing all the churches in her general area. The pastor of the church she ultimately found was attracted to Jen's original, inclusive educational model.

Finding families who wanted to send their children to ARROWS proved to be easy, given the enormous demand for individualized, integrated, faith-based education around Phoenix. Many families were ecstatic that their neurotypical children could now attend the same school as their neurodiverse children, each benefiting from a curriculum tailored to meet their own individual skill level. "We group our kids based on mastery of the subject. That is another way our kids who may have learning differences or challenges can do really well. We assess them and see where they're at with different subjects, and then we place them in the learning group that's going to give them the appropriate challenge and the appropriate support—instead of just moving them along because they had a birthday," Jen said, adding that this curriculum flexibility includes the ability to accelerate or slow down as needed. "What makes it beautiful with having the neurotypical and the neurodiverse kids is that everybody is on the same playing field. It really cultivates curiosity. It cultivates that love of learning, and it helps us identify and play to the students' strengths and weaknesses," she said.

I visited ARROWS in early 2024, about six months after the school opened with twenty-three students, three teachers, and three aides. Thirty percent of the students are neurodiverse, with a range of special learning needs including autism, ADHD and behavioral challenges, and dyslexia and other language learning difficulties. Jen greeted me at a locked metal gate that led into an open, sun-filled courtyard where the children spend time moving and playing between classes, as well as for extended recess periods. Perhaps this prioritization of children's movement and play is why

Jen says that some of her neurodiverse students who entered ARROWS the previous August would be moving into the more neurotypical category the following academic year. "Just having their needs supported and being placed in the right spot, they are becoming our peer role models," Jen said of these previously labeled learners.

Jen led me into one of several classrooms surrounding an outdoor courtyard. There, the students were beginning their day together with a Bible lesson before moving on to math class. All the students were fully supported, with aides available to offer one-on-one attention to learners. Children were able to move freely at their tables while they worked on individualized math lessons using worksheets and manipulatives. There was an overall feeling of comfort and care as children worked through their quantitative content. In an adjacent room filled with exercise balls and mats and a ball-filled foam pit, Jen explained that most of her students are able to attend ARROWS because their families participate in Arizona's universal school choice program, which gives parents the ability to choose the best learning environment for their child by helping to cover the cost of tuition at schools like ARROWS.

Some students with special learning needs take advantage of different Arizona school choice programs that apply to that population and offer significantly greater funding beyond the school's tuition. This enables those families to access educational therapies at no cost. Other families may have their children's therapies covered by private insurance. Part of Jen's mission is to integrate these therapists and specialists into the school day, welcoming them to ARROWS so that they can work with students individually without disrupting family life. The therapeutic room in which Jen and I stood as we talked was intended for this purpose. She has built connections with different community clinics and tutors to offer scheduled times for therapies and related services. "We have kids who require speech or occupational therapy. We have some students who might have ABA [Applied Behavior Analysis] therapy or dyslexia, so they might want to work with a specialized tutor. We work with the family. It's hard, especially if parents are working, to get their kids to those therapies," Jen said.

My visit to ARROWS was on a Thursday, one of the school's three core academic days when students focus on typical subjects such as math, reading, writing, science, and history, as well as Bible study. Fridays are focused on enrichment activities, such as art and physical education. On Mondays, Jen opens her space to local homeschoolers who join ARROWS students for special classes taught by outside instructors, such as martial arts, music, and drama classes.

She had a nearly 100 percent re-enrollment rate for her second school year, along with a waitlist. Despite significant demand for her program, Jen is committed to growing gradually each year, with a goal of eventually reaching 125 to 150 students. If demand continues to surge, Jen says she will open additional school locations, but she doesn't want any one location to be larger than 150 learners. "We don't want to grow too fast," Jen said, explaining that it's challenging because the interest is currently there from families to expand rapidly.

Jen urges more parents to consider a school like ARROWS. "Our world is not cookie-cutter where everybody is exactly like us. When we are out in society, we are interacting with different people of different beliefs, of different thoughts, of different abilities. By being a part of a school that really integrates everything, you start to exercise a muscle that I think a lot of us don't have the opportunity to," Jen said, adding that some of the children who arrive at her school have had little or no exposure to children who learn differently, but very quickly they overcome any hesitation, gravitate toward each other, and enjoy running around and playing together. "It's almost like they don't see the difference anymore," she said.

Jen also encourages more parents to do what she did and open a new school. Even in an area like Phoenix that is increasingly brimming with education choices, many of these programs quickly fill to capacity. If your searches come up empty, you may want to follow in Jen's footsteps and create your own program, aligned with your values and vision. You may not have thought about being an education entrepreneur, but if you can't find what you're looking for, it could be time to build a solution.

*Chapter Reflections for Parents and Founders*

Melissa and Jen wouldn't settle for second-best for their kids' education. They expected better. Using local Facebook parenting and education groups, Melissa was able to gather community wisdom to curate an ideal learning experience for Kadin that met both his academic and social needs. Jen also tried to find the perfect school for her son, but her search came up short. She decided to start the school she wanted. As you search for creative schooling options in your area, or consider creating them, it may be helpful to know how financially accessible these options are. While today's microschools and related models tend to be far lower in cost than traditional private schools, that cost could be considerably lower—or even tuition-free—in states like Arizona with private school choice programs that are inclusive of alternative education options.

As of early 2025, thirty-four states plus the District of Columbia and Puerto Rico had some type of private school choice program that enables a portion of state-allocated education funding to go directly to students and families to use toward approved private education expenses. These programs can include voucher programs that apply to private school tuition; tax credits that families can take advantage of if their child is enrolled in a private school or homeschool; tax-credit scholarship programs in which individuals or businesses donate to a school scholarship-granting organization and receive a tax credit as a result; and education savings accounts (ESAs) that are similar to vouchers but enable funding to go directly to families rather than schools. ESAs typically try to disentangle education from schooling by defining a wide variety of approved educational expenses, often including innovative learning models.

**Parents:** Does your state have one of these programs? You can visit EdChoice.org, a school choice advocacy organization, to see what choice programs may be available in your state and if your child qualifies. Several states have universal-eligibility programs applying to all K–12 students, and many others have limited programs, often targeting low-income families or students with special needs. These policies are continuing to expand, so if your state doesn't currently have a school choice program, one may be coming soon. "The future of K–12 education is more choice," said Robert Enlow, president and CEO of EdChoice. "It's unbundling what you learn from where you learn. What parents want is an education that is customized to their child's unique needs in an environment that is free from bullying, anxiety, and stress. That's why educational choice will continue to grow in America, because more and more families will demand policies that allow them to find or create the education that works best for their child," he told me.

**Founders:** You may want to think about starting or scaling your school in a state with generous school choice programs that enable funding to follow students. Not only can this help make your school more financially accessible to more families, but it can also create a consistent revenue stream. If you are operating in a state with school choice programs, you'll want to find out whether or not your program is eligible to participate. For example, some states have expansive school choice policies, but they only apply to state-recognized or accredited private schools. In other states, choice programs include innovative models such as microschools, pods, and homeschooling collaboratives. You'll also want to find out what, if any, strings may be attached with these programs and decide whether or not you're willing to accept them. For instance, are you required to administer a state standardized test in order to participate? You may find such stipulations to be fair and desirable, but it will be important to know what is expected of you and your students before you agree to participate in any school choice programs.

## Chapter 7

# Solutions

*If we tried to think of a good idea, we wouldn't have been able to think of a good idea at all. You just have to have a solution for a problem in your own life.*

—Brian Chesky (cofounder of Airbnb)

The greater Phoenix area where Jen and Melissa live represents a microcosm of what is increasingly possible for families as education options become more personalized, decentralized, and accessible. Your area may not yet have the variety and abundance of education options that many Arizona families enjoy, but as education entrepreneurship and choice expand nationally, it will hopefully only be a matter of time before you have a diverse assortment of schools and spaces within a small radius of your home.

Jen's story of building a school that intentionally integrates neurodiverse and neurotypical students is one example of how entrepreneurial parents and teachers are taking the initiative to create community-based learning solutions for children whose identities, experiences, or educational needs are not being met in traditional schools. Whether it's a school especially designed for LGBTQ+ youth, a program that validates and celebrates the heritage of BIPOC families, or one that focuses on students with ADHD or dyslexia, new, niche programs are offering relevant, responsive, and often restorative educational solutions. One-size-fits-all schooling is increasingly unappealing to many parents and learners. For some, it can be downright distressing. Don't settle for subpar schooling. Find or build the solution your child or community needs.

## A NEW SCHOOL FOR LGBTQ+ YOUTH

In the heart of Phoenix, just a few miles from both KaiPod and ARROWS Christian Academy, is the inaugural location of Spark Community Schools, a partnership microschool affiliated with Goodwill of Central and Northern Arizona. Located inside the downtown one·n·ten Youth Center, a local LGBTQ+ youth organization, Spark Community Schools launched in August 2023 with a dozen middle schoolers, all of whom identify as LGBTQ+. Partnership microschools are an up-and-coming concept in which various entities—such as businesses, nonprofits, libraries, museums, churches, and so on—collaborate with an education provider to run the microschool. Goodwill of Central and Northern Arizona is one of the first nonprofit organizations to embrace partnership microschooling as part of its overall mission to uplift individuals and communities. As microschools become more popular, it is likely that more businesses and organizations will want to explore partnership microschooling, either as an employee perk or as a community resource.

In 2023, Goodwill hired Darla Baquedano to be their Director of Education and to launch their Spark Community Schools throughout Goodwill's Arizona and Maryland territories. Darla had worked as a teacher and administrator in Phoenix-area public schools for more than twenty years. She thought she would never leave, but the education disruption caused by COVID led Darla to consider other career options. She discovered the idea of microschooling and was immediately attracted to the model. When she found out about the Goodwill job, she couldn't resist. "It really is an opportunity to be very free within education, and I really enjoy that; but at the same time, to use what I know are best practices and support my staff with best practices and instruction to give each of our children what they need to succeed academically. That is feeding my soul much more than just making sure that students are supervised every day," Darla told me.

The microschool supporting LGBTQ+ youth in Phoenix is the first Spark microschool Darla helped to open through the Goodwill partnership. It has been immensely rewarding. "I've had over twenty first days of school in my public school career," Darla said, "and none of them has been as meaningful as this first day of school that we had in August because I got to stand at the door as students were coming in, and I heard the things that students and parents were saying. Parents were saying things like, 'My child is excited to come to school for the first time ever! They laid all their clothes out last night. They made their lunch. They got up early, and they're ready to come to a place where they're accepted for who they are and where everything else can be set aside and they can just focus on learning.' It was very meaningful to hear parents say that and to know that I have been a part of helping to make that happen," Darla said.

This pioneering Spark microschool is a state-recognized, full-time private school that is tuition-free for all students under Arizona's universal school choice program. Darla explained that most of the students who attend the Spark microschool at one·n·ten come from conventional public schools or have been homeschooled after being in public schools. School was largely a traumatic experience for them. "What they were experiencing in their previous school settings included a lot of bullying, a lot of misgendering, a lot of deadnaming, not being able to use the restroom of their choice," Darla said. These experiences can contribute to poor mental health. CDC data reveal that 69 percent of LGBTQ+ youth felt "persistently sad and hopeless" in 2021, compared to 35 percent of heterosexual youth.[1]

Darla's Spark students were looking to re-engage socially with other students and receive top-quality instruction, but they did not want a large or traditional educational environment. The microschool at one·n·ten was an ideal solution. During its first year in operation, Darla witnessed recovering mental health, along with soaring self-confidence. She also saw a rekindling of students' eagerness to learn and engage with others. They were excited to come to school, whereas previously they may have been chronically absent or dealt with school refusal. Some students entered Spark several grade levels behind academically, and Darla observed astounding academic growth, as measured against Arizona's state education standards. "That's because we're able to personalize their curriculum and give them exactly what they need," Darla said.

The Spark microschool at one·n·ten will be expanding its enrollment in subsequent years and adding a full high school to complement its middle school program. Darla says that more Spark microschools will be opening throughout Arizona, as well as nationally. Each one, she says, will be tied to the specific needs and wants of the learning communities it serves. For the one·n·ten location, that is a robust educational program aligned with state standards, as well as a specialized focus on LGBTQ+ history and a civics curriculum that emphasizes the experiences of BIPOC people and other marginalized groups. "That's what this community has asked us for, but if Spark was in a different setting, we are fully prepared to meet the needs of that community," said Darla, who believes that we are just at the beginning of the microschooling movement.

"We named ourselves Spark for a reason, because we're going to start off really small, a spark, and then we're just going to ignite and be able to educate as many students as possible," Darla said. She adds that she adored her time as a public school educator and still supports public education, but the one-size-fits-all structure of standard schooling doesn't work well for many kids: "The more research that we do and the more that we learn as educators about individual students and their needs, the system, in my opinion, is just not set up to support that."

## A BIPOC-CENTERED SCHOOLING ALTERNATIVE

In some cases, the system itself may be the problem. That was what Alycia Wright discovered. She planned to send her oldest daughter, Alex, to kindergarten at the local elementary school in the top-performing Virginia public school district where she'd worked as a teacher for more than a decade. Alycia and her husband had moved to this area specifically so their children could attend the same schools where Alycia taught. "I really thought it was going to be this wonderful experience," Alycia said. She imagined strolling with Alex to school each morning and then continuing on to the middle school to start her teaching day. "It turned out to be really disheartening," Alycia said with a sigh.

Testing revealed that Alex was profoundly gifted, so Alycia visited the elementary school principal before the start of kindergarten to talk about how the school might be able to accommodate Alex's accelerated learning needs. As a longtime teacher and special education department chair for the middle school, Alycia was familiar with the elementary school principal and had met her several times over the previous few years. The elementary school was a feeder school for Alycia's middle school, and Alycia did all the transition work for special education students who were progressing upward. She had had periodic conversations with the elementary school principal, but on the day Alycia arrived to talk about Alex—dressed more as a mom than a teacher—the principal didn't recognize her.

Alycia was there to talk about Alex's giftedness, but the principal immediately started talking about options for free and reduced-cost lunches and various tutoring programs. She was making false assumptions about the child's academic abilities and socioeconomic status, presumably based on race. "I remember thinking, 'I didn't mention any of this. Why is this the verbiage I'm getting?'" said Alycia, who chose not to remind the principal who she was. She also knew that her daughter would be one of only two Black children in the entire kindergarten. "If this is the conversation that's being geared toward me, what might this feel like for my daughter?" Alycia recalled. "I felt like the entire conversation was very dismissive."

After their meeting, Alycia and the principal were walking down the corridor together when several other teachers passed by. "Oh, Mrs. Wright, do we have a meeting today?" one of them probed. Alycia shook her head and said she was there about her daughter. "Then to see the lightbulb go off in the principal's mind," Alycia recalled, "it was like a whole personality switch." Alycia found the entire experience alarming but enlightening. "You always say if you could pretend to be someone else and walk in their shoes, what might that experience feel like? I felt like that's exactly what I was able to do," she said, wondering what that same conversation would have been like for other parents of color enrolling their children in that school. "Needless to say, we decided not to enroll her in public school," she said. Alycia placed Alex in a private Montessori school before switching to homeschooling for all four of her children a few years later, in 2013.

While US homeschooling rates have been climbing for years among all racial and ethnic groups, more Black families are choosing this option in response to concerns about systemic racism and persistent stereotypes about Black children and families—such as what Alycia experienced. In their 2015 book, scholars Ama Mazama and Garvey Musumunu wrote about homeschooling motivations among African Americans. They explained that many of these parents "are concerned for their children's emotional well-being, intellectual development, and knowledge of self, and have come to the conclusion that the American school system is antithetical to their children's optimal growth."[2] While certainly not the only reason why more Black parents are choosing to homeschool, a culturally dismissive or antagonistic schooling environment can be a big factor.

COVID also boosted the Black homeschooling rate. The US Census Bureau reported a doubling of the homeschooling population throughout 2020, and a fivefold increase in the number of Black homeschooled students.[3] Angela Watson is an assistant professor at the Johns Hopkins University School of Education and creator of the Hopkins Homeschool Hub, a national research center launched in 2024 that focuses on analyzing homeschooling data. Watson has been studying the homeschooling population for years, noting its growth and demographic diversification before, during, and after COVID. "Prior to the pandemic, homeschooling was growing, but it was very slow," Watson told me when we spoke soon after the introduction of the Homeschool Hub. "Within that overall growth, Black and brown homeschoolers were growing at a higher rate than white homeschoolers. During the pandemic, Black and brown homeschooling really increased. We know that homeschooling post-pandemic is even more diverse than it was pre-pandemic," Watson said.

For Alycia, homeschooling became a way to meet the advanced intellectual needs of her oldest child, Alex—who would go on to get accepted into a highly competitive early-college program, graduate with a bachelor's degree in biology at age nineteen, and enter a PhD program in bioengineering at Duke University at age twenty. It was also a way to cultivate more culturally relevant learning opportunities for her family and others. That desire is what led Alycia to become a founder, launching Cultural Roots Homeschool Cooperative in Richmond, Virginia, in 2016. What began as an informal weekly gathering of a dozen homeschooling families has grown into a suite of homeschooling programs specifically designed for BIPOC families that now serves more than 125 learners.

Even before she officially launched Cultural Roots, Alycia embraced a mindset of building what she couldn't find. After quitting her job as a teacher to be a homeschool mom, Alycia started by replicating school at home. "For the first three or four months, I sort of mimicked what I had been taught in school. Then I thought, 'Why are we doing this? Why are we punishing ourselves by creating such a rigid schedule that no one needs to follow?'" Alycia recalled. She decided to relax and branch out, exploring the larger homeschooling community to see what was available. "We dated all the homeschool co-ops," Alycia said, laughing. "We tried to find every homeschool space in our general area to see if something was a fit. We found one that worked for proximity, five minutes from our house; however, they had some core beliefs that we just weren't in line with. It's really hard to be in a community of people in which you have strong differences around life. Then I remember thinking: 'Why not just build it?'"

So she did. She started simply, finding a local instructor who was willing to lead a biology dissection class for her children while inviting other interested homeschoolers to join. From there it grew to more classes and, eventually, to a once-a-week co-op with like-minded families. It hasn't stopped growing since. "I have always taken a philosophy of figuring out what it is I need for my family and then putting that out there and hoping that people who also found that interesting would gravitate toward it," Alycia said, explaining how that is the approach she recommends to other budding entrepreneurs who are starting innovative schools or spaces. "Don't try to please everybody. Figure out what it is you want for you—what you need for your family—because that's what you're going to be the most passionate about. And the people who are also passionate about that will come to you. That way you're not doing backbends for something you really don't care about or your kids don't really care about," she said.

I visited Cultural Roots, the large co-op Alycia founded in 2016, on a Wednesday morning in mid-September 2023, seeing in action one of the two full days of weekly programming co-op members of all ages enjoy. Some homeschooling moms gathered in the open lobby area of the large, colorful community center to chat with each other while their children learned in one of several spacious classrooms along a wide corridor. Other parents worked on their laptops or tended to infants and toddlers. In one classroom, a group of middle school students participated in a literature class, while in a different classroom a group of elementary-age children engaged in a science class led by a local expert. Another class made music with a talented drummer, while still another took a mathematics test. That fall, Alycia added a drop-off microschool program for teenage homeschoolers. A more in-depth, academic program, the teen microschool meets at the community center space Monday through Wednesday each week from 10:00 to 3:30 for both core academics and enrichment classes taught by experienced community instructors and content experts.

Cultural Roots began by focusing on the culture, history, traditions, and people of the African diaspora, but as interest in the program has grown, its focus has expanded to include BIPOC families more generally, including multiracial and multiethnic families. "We really just try to celebrate the cultures and histories of all the children, all the backgrounds," Alycia said, explaining that this might involve reading authors from the Philippines, or incorporating a recipe from a child's Korean grandmother, or participating in a discussion about Senegalese holidays. For many BIPOC families, Alycia explains, stories and traditions have been lost or missed. "We're helping to bring these stories back, to affirm these cultural influences for young people." Her program also emphasizes intentional, conscious parenting that centers on respecting children. "We want to raise strong, free children," she told me. The cost of the co-op is $275 a month per family, which covers the community center rental fees and payments to the expert instructors who lead the classes. Unlike traditional homeschool co-ops, very few parents teach classes at Cultural Roots.

After COVID, the co-op program reached capacity at more than a hundred students with a waitlist, so Alycia created additional offerings. She started sponsoring Friday fields trips at least twice a month to places like the local zoo or to watch theatrical performances in downtown Richmond. These programs are open to the wider homeschooling community—not just BIPOC families. Similarly, in 2023, Alycia created a new program called Rooted Tuesdays with an additional fifty students that meets at a nearby church and is also open to all homeschoolers. It features a la carte classes with a blend of enrichment and academic content.

By 2024, Cultural Roots had nearly outgrown its community center location, and Alycia was looking for larger spaces. She sees rising demand for programs like hers—and for homeschooling collaboratives more generally. She is exploring ways to grow her program, and urges others to launch their own. "If you're an ordinary mom or dad or parent, I just say start. Really. Even if it's just you and one other family getting together to do something, share that as much as possible, including on social media, to allow others to see. You never know who you might be inspiring and what partners you might attract," Alycia said, adding that prospective founders shouldn't feel pressure to secure a large space or sign a big lease. Alycia offers this advice to new founders: "Just start small. Start renting a library room. Start at a local park and rent the shelter. Then as you grow, you'll learn and you'll build."

## ADHD STUDENTS BREAK OUT OF SCHOOL

In addition to new schools and spaces for LGBTQ+ youth and BIPOC families, young people with particular learning needs are also better able to find programs just for them. In Utah, for example, BreakOut School is intentionally designed for students with ADHD, an increasingly common neurodevelopmental disorder impacting more than 11 percent of children ages five to seventeen, according to the CDC.[4] Dallin Richardson launched the K–12 school in 2019 with a handful of students and a vision for education where most learning takes places outside, immersed within the wider community. A pharmacist for twenty years, he counseled many families with children diagnosed with ADHD and heard story after story about how difficult it was to get their needs met within the confines of conventional schooling. Dallin, whom everyone calls "Doc" because he has a doctorate degree in pharmacy, could relate. He and his two children have been diagnosed with ADHD. He knew the frustrations of getting his kids an appropriate Individualized Education Plan (IEP) in school and of helping them to succeed within a rigid classroom model.

Two decades into his career, Doc was thinking about new opportunities and felt the pull toward education entrepreneurship. He had been researching forest schools, a growing outdoor education movement where children spend most or all of their school day outside in nature while weaving in academic skills. Doc knew from his review of scientific studies that time in nature leads to significant behavioral and social-emotional improvements for children with both ADHD and autism spectrum disorder (ASD)—two conditions that are frequently found together.[5] Many BreakOut students, known as "heroes" at his school, share this combination. According to Doc, "ADHD and ASD aren't disabilities, they're superpowers." That's a main reason why he adopted an outdoor, nature-based model for BreakOut School, influenced by the Charlotte Mason educational philosophy. "She believed in very short learning periods in an outdoor environment with a rich, broad milieu of art and literature and also the hard sciences," Doc said.

In addition to seeing enhanced behavioral and emotional wellness among his students, Doc has noticed dramatic academic gains. Student entrance assessments at BreakOut School typically show widespread deficiencies, with most learners several grade levels behind in math and reading. With a smaller, more personalized learning environment and abundant time to move and be outside, Doc says that within one school year, most students are able to quickly catch up to—or even surpass—their peer group's performance.

BreakOut School is a state-recognized private school, and Doc's students now attend tuition-free through Utah's new universal school choice policies. He is eager to scale BreakOut School by opening additional locations in the coming years, while keeping enrollment capped at twenty students. "My vision is to have modular growth, so every time one fills up at twenty, we'll open up another module, in another area. We'll just keep adding those modules, but we'll keep them semi-independent. We want independence and individualized learning. Only by keeping it small, I believe, can we keep the bureaucracy out of it," Doc said.

Avoiding institutional bureaucracy by keeping operations lean is a primary way that today's microschools and related models keep their costs low and their curriculum personalized. Most founders don't want, or need, layers of school administration, such as assistant heads of school, guidance personnel, and operations, admissions, and development staff that populate many traditional private schools. For today's startup schools, the founder often takes on those roles and many others—including principal, secretary, school nurse, guidance counselor, social media manager, custodian, groundskeeper, bookkeeper, and so on.

## A MICROSCHOOL FOR DYSLEXIC STUDENTS

In Portland, Oregon, Greg Brown wears all those founder hats. Like Doc's, Greg's school, Activate, has some learners with ADHD, autism, and other special learning needs, but his program's main focus is dyslexia, or a language processing disorder that makes it difficult to learn to read. The earliest documented cases of dyslexia date back more than a century. Today, it is estimated that up to 20 percent of the US population is dyslexic.[6]

More than a decade into his work as a special education teacher in the Portland Public Schools system, Greg was drawn toward entrepreneurship. In 2017, he launched an arts-based summer camp to earn some extra income while also doing some tutoring on the side. He continued to do that for the next two years and dreamed about one day opening a school. Then in 2019, after fifteen years working in the district, Greg resigned. "I was just feeling a lot more passionate about the camp and about the tutoring," Greg said when we first spoke in 2023. "I liked the autonomy that I had, and I was growing increasingly frustrated with the way that standard schools operate." When COVID arrived in 2020, Greg shifted fully to online tutoring services.

By summer, parents of his tutoring students started asking Greg if he would create a pandemic pod for the fall. The parents wanted a small, in-person space where their kids could gather and use their Chromebooks while continuing with their remote schooling through the public school district. Greg felt that he would just be hovering over his students and not really adding value to their learning. He recalled, "I really had absolutely no interest in doing that because I just couldn't envision what that would be like for myself or for them. So I said, 'I'll just start up a school.'"

Due to COVID, businesses like Activate could sometimes register to become emergency childcare centers during the 2020/2021 school year, enabling learners to meet in person. It was a lengthy process, but it was worth it to Greg to be able to get his microschool up and running with in-person programming that fall for third and fourth graders. The following year, nearly all his students remained at Activate, even though their schools reopened for in-person learning. Greg shifted from running as an emergency childcare center to becoming a state-recognized private school. He added fifth grade that year as well, moving into a much larger storefront building in the trendy Sellwood neighborhood of Portland, which I visited in the spring of 2024.

I arrived at Activate on a sunny and warm April day, noticing how the microschool's bright branding on its wide wall of street-facing windows would immediately signal to passersby that this is no ordinary school. Colorful handmade medallions flanked Activate's large sun-framed logo, while yellow letters on the door, above the school's website address, described exactly what goes on inside, stating: "Activate is a 3rd–5th grade microschool specializing in art, hands-on learning, and comprehensive dyslexia support."

As Greg opened the door, I stepped into a large, open, immaculate room with enormous ceilings and natural light beaming in from the wall of windows. White wooden cubbyholes were on my right, filled with each learner's belongings, while opposite those was a long shoe rack overflowing with boots and sneakers. Behind the rack in front of the windows adorned with hanging plants was a library area and reading space with bean bag chairs and a soft rug.

I sat down in one of the small chairs next to a long rectangular table to observe Greg finish up a literacy lesson with four young sock-footed learners on how—and why—"Ch" sometimes sounds like "K." Etymology and linguistics are key components of Greg's curricular approach to teaching reading. In the adjacent classroom space, separated by a half-wall, a larger group of older students worked quietly on a math lesson with their teacher, who had taught previously in Montessori schools.

As the students, known here as "Activators," took a break for lunch, Greg and I sat down to talk more about his microschool. His students all attend five days a week at an annual tuition of $13,000, which includes the extended-day program from 8:30 am to 5:00 pm. While still financially out of reach for many lower- and middle-income families, Activate is about one-third the cost of traditional secular private prep schools in the area. He used his $10,000 microgrant from the VELA Education Fund toward student scholarships, adding that VELA is one of the few grant-making organizations to offer funds to for-profit schools like his, as well as to nonprofits. Even though it may constrain his eligibility for certain donations, Greg likes to run his school and camps as a for-profit LLC. "I didn't want all the paperwork that goes along with being a nonprofit, and I wanted to maintain full control over my programs," he said.

He told me that he frequently receives inquiries from interested parents looking to enroll their children at Activate, but he needs to turn them away because he is at capacity with eighteen students. Greg also runs week-long art and literacy summer camps. "They fill up in a day," he said.

He explained that most of his current families, along with those who wish to enroll their kids in the school-year program, are deeply committed to public schools. "These are families who really wanted the public schools to work for them," Greg said. Once he is able to help students gain reading proficiency, many are able to move on to the local public middle school with no problem.

I asked Greg if he has thought about expanding, given how much demand there seems to be for his programs, along with his high student retention rate. He told me that he has definitely considered adding a K–2 school in a separate location, but finding space that is zoned properly—and that can be approved for educational occupancy under local building codes—is a huge challenge. "The biggest hurdle is finding space. It's very complicated and it's hard to get straight answers," Greg said. He encourages would-be school founders to work with an architect who has established relationships with city officials and to choose newer construction whenever possible.

Greg said that finding affordable insurance can also be a challenge. "Part of that is being a school that doesn't fit into a box," he said, explaining that some providers don't know what to make of microschools. One insurance company he spoke to wouldn't provide insurance because Activate, while being a state-approved private school, is not accredited. Pursuing third-party accreditation is not something Greg is interested in, as he feels it's irrelevant and unnecessary. "I don't need an accrediting agency's stamp of approval. My stamp of approval is that my students are thriving, my school is full, and my camps fill up in a day," he said.

## WHAT DOES ACCREDITATION MEAN?

Some parents may wonder if the school or space they are selecting is accredited, while some founders may wonder if it's worth seeking accreditation. But what exactly does that mean? Accreditation for K–12 private schools is typically a voluntary process through a third-party nonprofit accrediting organization that can help to validate a school's processes, curriculum, and accountability metrics. Even for public schools, accreditation is only required in about twenty states. A 2024 analysis conducted by the National Microschooling Center found that only 16 percent of microschools are currently accredited.[7]

Accrediting agencies can be regional, such as the New England Association of Schools and Colleges, or they can be model-specific, such as those for religiously affiliated schools, some Montessori schools, or other niches such as the International Association of Learner-Driven Schools. Most states don't require a private school to be accredited in order to operate, but some may require accreditation for certain designations, such as being eligible to participate in a state's school choice programs or to access certain student scholarships.

Accreditation may offer parents an additional quality indicator, in the same way that a "green" building with a LEED (Leadership in Energy and Environmental Design) certification can do. In this way, accreditation can also be appealing to some school founders. But it's important for both parents and founders to keep in mind that the accreditation process is expensive, can sometimes take years to complete, and new schools are often not eligible for accreditation until they have been operating for a while. Additionally, many—but not all—accrediting organizations take a conventional view of education, with traditional notions of top-down curriculum and assessment. This can limit the flexibility of founders to change, add, or eliminate certain curricula during the school year or make other ad hoc adaptations to meet learners' needs. These constraints may not be appealing to founders or parents seeking a bottom-up alternative to the standard schooling model.

After lunch with Greg, I joined him, his students, and two of his teachers for their daily, hour-long afternoon recess at a sprawling city park a couple of blocks away. Activate's plentiful recess time is a far cry from the twenty-five-minute national average for US elementary schoolers.[8] Some of the children climbed on the playground equipment while others scattered to stomp in the shallow creek. "Greg, check this out!" one boy eagerly yelled, beckoning Greg to investigate the beaver-chewed bark of a tree. Like so many of the microschool students I've met during my many school visits, Greg's students are happy, relaxed, and enthusiastic about learning. Greg is happy too. "The most rewarding part of operating a microschool is having the autonomy to structure a program that is optimal for my students," he said. Everyday entrepreneurs like him are building educational solutions that show just how joyful learning can be.

## *Chapter Reflections for Parents and Founders*

The potential for personalization in education today is astonishing. Want a culturally relevant homeschool co-op prioritizing the experiences of Black, brown, and Indigenous families? Alycia has done it. Looking for a school to meet the specific needs of LGBTQ+ youth? Darla has a blueprint. Want an outdoor school for ADHD children or a literacy-intensive one for dyslexic kids? Doc and Greg show what is possible. Parents no longer need to settle for a one-size-fits-all approach to education. They should expect more. Founders should also expect more, embracing the freedom to create educational solutions that meet particular learner needs and interests. Here are some thoughts to consider.

**Parents:** If you are looking for a school or space catering to the unique needs of your child, you may want to post in Facebook groups or elsewhere on social media and state exactly what you want. You might be surprised that it already exists or that there are other parents just like you who are looking for the same thing. Together, you may be able to create a co-op or learning pod, hire a teacher to lead a microschool, or find another collaborative solution to suit the needs of your children. Your post may even inspire a lurking education entrepreneur to build the perfect school or space for your child so that you don't have to.

**Founders:** Specialization may seem limiting. After all, if you're offering a program for only LGBTQ+ or BIPOC or neurodiverse students, for example, aren't you ignoring a potentially much larger group of families who might like and benefit from your offering? This is a reasonable concern, but "niche entrepreneurship," or specializing in producing a product or service for a specific audience, can be extremely effective. You develop and display deep knowledge in a particular area that you're passionate about and become a go-to expert. Families begin to seek you out and may even want to pay more for your services, given your unique understanding of their needs. You intentionally choose not to serve everyone, but those whom you do serve become committed customers who happily tell others about your amazing program. This niche approach can also be helpful in fundraising efforts. Some founders have reported success in securing donations or grants when they intentionally serve specific student populations, such as those with special needs.

If you would like to create a learning solution for a certain population of learners, you may first want to determine the level of demand for such a program in your community. Join social media groups related to your area of interest, and pay attention to pain points and potential opportunities. You may want to begin by offering one-off programs catering to a particular group, such as a weekend workshop. A summer camp, vacation camp, or afterschool program might also be something to consider to foster relationships and trust within the community you wish to reach.

Chapter 8

# Metrics

*Too many people measure how successful they are by how much money they make or the people that they associate with. In my opinion, true success should be measured by how happy you are.*

—Richard Branson (cofounder of Virgin Group)

Greg has had a 100 percent re-enrollment rate at Activate for the past three years. Satisfied parents and happy kids who keep coming back to a new school or learning space each year are just some of the metrics by which to judge an education program's quality. Early on in the startup process, founders should identify the metrics that matter most to them and vigilantly track those metrics to monitor performance over time. Parents should also consider some of the traditional and nontraditional quality metrics they believe are important and evaluate a school or space accordingly.

"Anything that is measured and watched, improves," said Bob Parsons, founder of the web hosting company GoDaddy.[1] This chapter highlights an assortment of KPIs—Key Performance Indicators—that entrepreneurs may want to monitor and parents may want to look for when building or seeking unconventional schools and spaces. Some of these KPIs are quantitative, such as retention rates and test scores, while others are more qualitative, such as parent and student satisfaction levels. Each can be helpful in gauging quality while recognizing that "quality" is in the eye of the beholder.

## WHO DECIDES QUALITY?

Just down the block from me is a boutique coffee shop. Many of my neighbors love it, and it is my husband's go-to spot. The shop sells both retail and wholesale coffee, shipping its premier beans far and wide. The coffee "experts" around me say that this is the best coffee in the city—top quality. Everything from its beans to its brew process are vastly superior to any other cup of Joe, or so I'm told. The trouble is, I don't like it. I am a Dunkin' girl and will walk a few more blocks to the nearest Dunkin' Donuts for my preferred coffee—a medium hot with cream.

The coffee experts may frown on me, suggesting that I don't truly understand what constitutes a quality cup of coffee. They may think that I am ignorant and need more coffee education to realize that the fancy, boutique coffee is indeed the best coffee and should always be chosen over Dunkin'. They may show me charts and graphs to make their point, with detailed data on coffee bean growing and harvesting processes and the café's best-in-class brewing techniques. They may try to persuade me that all my peers think this is the best coffee so I should too. It won't work. I don't like the taste of their coffee. It's not for me. Thankfully, in a diverse, decentralized coffee market, I can consume the coffee that matches my individual preferences and needs while others can consume the coffee that matches theirs—or choose a different beverage altogether.

As the economist Thomas Sowell reminds us: "The most basic question is not what is best but *who shall decide* what is best."[2] For education, just as for coffee, that should be the consumer. We all define "quality" differently. Just as each of us may prefer one type of coffee over another, we each may prefer one type of school or learning space over another for a whole host of tangible and intangible reasons. Some parents may prefer a school or space where their children are outside for most of the day, playing, digging, and getting dirty stomping in the mud, while other parents may prefer a tidy, indoor school or space for their children, complete with uniforms and patent-leather shoes. Some parents may prefer a formulaic academic curriculum, while other parents may prefer an unschooling approach with no adult-imposed curriculum. Some parents may prefer a faith-based learning program, while other parents may prefer a nonreligious one. Some parents might place a high value on standardized test scores, while others might value portfolios of student progress. Some parents might prefer an in-home learning setting, while others might prefer a more public location. Some parents might embrace a classical education philosophy, while others might want something totally different, like a Waldorf education.

For Jennifer Kempin, a small, secular, home-based, Waldorf-inspired learning space with creative portfolios is what she values most for her own son. The parents who have enrolled their children in Jennifer's new microschool value the same. "I was one of those people who always loved being around kids," Jennifer told me when we first spoke in 2024, soon after she launched her microschool. Her passion for children led her to become a teacher. For more than a decade, Jennifer taught English and reading to both special education and general education students in urban and suburban public schools in Pennsylvania, where she lives. "I always felt like a round peg in a square hole as a teacher," Jennifer said. "I felt like I was always breaking the rules. I was always doing things that I saw were best for children, which did not always include all the test prep that we were required to do or making sure we hit all the topics that had to be taught in the order that they said we had to teach them," she told me.

Jennifer became increasingly frustrated with conventional schooling but never thought about doing anything else. She attended conventional public schools, as did all her friends and relatives. Traditional private schools or alternative education models such as homeschooling were never on her radar. Then she became a mom. At the time her son was born, Jennifer was working in the Philadelphia Public Schools system and commuting daily from her home in the suburbs, about twenty-five miles away. As her son grew older, she began to wonder about options for him other than the local public schools. "He's very sensitive and really bright, but he doesn't quite fit in the way that he's expected to fit in a regular school setting," Jennifer said. At first, she chose a small, traditional private school. "We did that because he just couldn't handle the larger groups and the really harsh expectations of public school," she recalled. "Some family members were a little surprised that we were doing private school because nobody ever really did that before. It seems silly looking back now because we've made a lot of leaps since then," Jennifer said, laughing.

The traditional private school wasn't a good fit either. Jennifer would pick up her son from kindergarten, and he would cry the whole way home. She had recently left her public school teaching job and was working from home doing operations projects for small businesses. She pulled her son out of school and started homeschooling him as a temporary fix until she could find a different private school. But as they explored other private school options, her son would shut down with fear over what Jennifer saw as school-related trauma. So she decided to commit more fully to homeschooling. "I was just taking it week by week, but that really snowballed into a year of teaching at home and watching him flourish and get back to that really amazing child who loves life," she said.

During that homeschooling year, Jennifer discovered the Waldorf philosophy that emphasizes child-centered, developmentally appropriate education that preserves childhood while cultivating curiosity and imagination. Jennifer visited an established Waldorf private school in her area that was very welcoming, but she still thought that a typical schooling environment—even an alternative one—wouldn't work well for her sensitive child. That's when the admissions officer at the Waldorf school told her that many families homeschool using a Waldorf approach. Intrigued, Jennifer began devouring everything she could find about the Waldorf philosophy and incorporating it into her homeschool. "I'm constantly learning more and have fallen so in love with it," Jennifer said.

In particular, Jennifer fell in love with Waldorf's unhurried approach to childhood literacy—especially as a former public school teacher. "One of the things that I always had a hard time with, even before I had my own son, is how much we're pushing children in the public schools to be reading by the end of kindergarten. Then your child is behind if they're not reading," Jennifer said. She continued: "I'm using reading as one example, but there are so many examples of that in our society today. That's something that has always bothered me about education, about our society, about schooling. In Waldorf, I found that it slows everything down to what is appropriate for the child's age." Jennifer explained that explicit reading instruction doesn't typically begin until first grade in Waldorf schools, and children aren't expected to be reading independently until third or fourth grade.

Studies confirm that not only does this more developmentally appropriate approach to reading instruction not put children at a disadvantage, but it may actually be beneficial. One large 2012 study in New Zealand found that students who attended Waldorf/Steiner schools and didn't have reading instruction until they were seven had the same reading skill level by age ten as a comparable group of students who attended conventional state schools and received initial reading instruction at age five. Moreover, the reading comprehension of the Waldorf students surpassed that of the conventionally schooled students.[3]

## Joyful Learning

A study of public Waldorf schools in the United States found similar results. Researchers revealed that students enrolled in Waldorf public schools had lower standardized test scores in math and reading in the early grades than their peers in traditional public schools, but higher academic achievement than their peers in eighth grade. This study reveals the disconnect between Waldorf's education philosophy of delaying early academics and the high-stakes testing environment of today's public schools, while also showing that a different, less hurried academic approach can have a longer-term positive impact on student achievement. The researchers noted how conventional metrics of academic success may be inadequate to fully assess the quality and longer-term impact of an unconventional school or space.[4]

While homeschooling her son in the spring of 2023, Jennifer was introduced to the concept of microschools. "I had been listening to your podcast and hearing about people's success one after the other," Jennifer told me, explaining how launching a microschool seemed more and more like a possibility. She enjoyed her operations work but knew that her real passion lay with teaching. By fall, her contracts were ending and she had to make a choice: take on additional contract work or start a school. She chose the latter. She paid $200 to form her business as a for-profit LLC and contacted her homeowners insurance provider to boost coverage for her business, which was roughly another $200 for the year.

The week after Thanksgiving, Jennifer posted in local parenting and homeschooling Facebook groups about her new microschool, which she named Fáilte, meaning "welcome and joy" in Gaelic. She knew she wanted to launch with only three children in first through third grades, in addition to her son, to keep the program small and intimate. Within days of posting on social media, she reached that number. Jennifer opened her microschool right after New Year's 2024. It quickly became financially sustainable for Jennifer, given her low overhead and startup costs. Fáilte runs three days a week in her home, with a fourth day spent at an outdoor education program for homeschoolers run by a local nonprofit with whom Jennifer partners. All the children at Fáilte are legally considered homeschoolers in Pennsylvania.

The parents who enrolled their children at Fáilte were delighted. They had been struggling to find the right fit for their children. One parent told her: "I can't believe my child was sad that they couldn't come to school on a snow day! My child's never been upset about school being closed." The children and parents adored Fáilte so much that Jennifer offered to run the program year-round. When she told the kids that they wouldn't stop for summer break, she said they literally squealed in delight. Reactions and testimonials like these are one way Jennifer measures her school's success. Another is the additional parents eager to enroll their children in her school. She says she'll add seats very slowly to make sure that the small, personalized, relaxed atmosphere remains intact. She knows she could grow bigger, add teachers, and find a different location, but right now she's content—personally and professionally. "I love every minute of it," Jennifer said. "I really love having it in my home because most of these children have had some school trauma, and I think having it in our house really takes away that aspect of going to school because it really isn't like school," she said.

Jennifer's advice to prospective founders is to keep it simple. She urges education entrepreneurs to start small and to not add "bells and whistles" until they're necessary. It's helpful that Waldorf education embraces simplicity. "In Waldorf, there are no textbooks. Children create their own textbooks," Jennifer said of the colorful portfolios students produce throughout the year. "They're actually writing and drawing pictures of what they've learned as they go, which is something that I love. It's really beautiful," she said. To track learner progress and keep parents informed, Jennifer hosts parent meetings every six to nine weeks where she presents an extensive, multi-page written progress report on each child. She highlights both academic and nonacademic gains, as well as areas for continued improvement, and works with the parents to set goals for the next term.

## POSSIBLE KPIS

Like so many of today's emerging innovative schools and spaces, Fáilte Microschool doesn't look anything like a traditional school. So how can models like Fáilte measure their success and share that success with others, including current and prospective families? Here are ten hypothetical KPIs by which Jennifer, as well as her current and prospective families, could measure Fáilte Microschool's quality and impact:

1. **Parent satisfaction:** What do parents think of Fáilte Microschool? The positive comments that Jennifer has received from parents about her microschool and its impact on their children are important metrics. These testimonials can be solicited and recorded more formally through regular parent surveys.
2. **Student engagement:** What do students think of their microschool? Given that Jennifer's students whine on snow days and cheer when hearing that they can attend Fáilte throughout the summertime, it's clear that they are happy with their microschool. Regular student surveys, along with parent and teacher observations, could be ways to assess student engagement and satisfaction—especially when compared to a student's experiences in prior learning environments.
3. **Retention rate:** Do Fáilte's families continue with the school into subsequent years? If not, why not? Jennifer can measure and share learner retention and re-enrollment rates as measures of success.
4. **Referral rate:** Are Fáilte's families telling their friends and acquaintances about the school and urging others to check it out?

How often? Jennifer can track referral rates and encourage current families to tell others about the program.

5. **Unmet demand:** Are there more families who are interested in Fáilte than can currently be accommodated? Is there a waitlist? Capturing the amount of unmet or growing demand for her microschool could help Jennifer demonstrate its reach and impact.

6. **Academic progress:** How does Jennifer know her students are learning? How is mastery measured? Can Jennifer compare her students' academic progress to students in traditional schools, perhaps using benchmarked assessment tools, if parents desire that? At Fáilte and similar microschools, a student's portfolio of work is an important metric of academic progress. Jennifer's regular student progress reports and parent conferences are other metrics. Currently, Jennifer's school only serves children in the lower elementary grades. She can show how her learners are academically and socially prepared to enter a new learning environment—even a traditional one—as they get older. Parents will also want to probe about this transition and ask about any challenges. Additionally, Jennifer could refer parents to peer-reviewed research about Waldorf education and outcomes, such as the studies mentioned in this chapter, while also reminding parents that traditional metrics can sometimes fail to fully capture the long-term, positive impact on student achievement of an unconventional learning environment.

7. **Social-emotional progress:** How are students progressing socially and emotionally? Student, parent, and teacher assessments of a child's social development and emotional well-being since joining the microschool can be helpful metrics. Have previously problematic behaviors been reduced? Is a child's anxiety or depression lessening? An initial student and parent intake survey when the family joins Fáilte can be compared to later surveys.

Jennifer could track this progress visually on a graph to show improved social-emotional skills and well-being over time.

8. **Teacher satisfaction:** How do teachers feel about working at Fáilte Microschool? For now, Jennifer is her school's only educator, and she finds the experience to be deeply rewarding—even more so than when she taught at a conventional school. Another KPI for today's innovative schools and spaces could be teacher satisfaction. What do teachers think about working at the school or space? What do students and parents think about the teachers at the school, as revealed through teacher evaluations? What is the teacher retention rate? If teachers are leaving, why?

9. **Alumni outcomes:** What happens to students when they leave Fáilte? Do they find success and fulfillment in whatever future endeavors they undertake? Does their transition to a new school or space go smoothly? Jennifer could track her alumni experiences and progress through surveys, ongoing communications, and alumni events.

10. **Mission alignment:** Is Fáilte meeting its stated microschool mission? Its website, WaldorfMicroschool.com, reads: "At Fáilte we believe in cultivating an educational environment that honors each child's individuality, fosters a love for learning, and educates the whole child." How can Jennifer demonstrate that she is achieving her school's mission? She could show examples of how communications, curriculum, school culture, policies, and student work products are all aligned with the microschool's guiding principles.

## EVERYTHING IS SUBJECTIVE

There is no such thing as a universally accepted measure of school quality or student outcomes. Some parents may be thrilled with a home-based,

Waldorf-inspired microschool like Jennifer's that delays explicit reading instruction and uses non-standardized measures of academic progress. Other parents—and founders—may prefer a different educational approach and more standardized measures of academic achievement. "Preferences are subjective," George Mason University economics professor Donald Boudreaux told me. I reached out to Boudreaux to learn more about the economic principle of subjective value, or the idea that a good or service doesn't inherently have value—its value depends on individual needs and preferences. "It's the essence of a truly liberal society: I don't get to impose my preferences on you, and you don't get to impose yours on me," Boudreaux said.

Even beyond the theory of subjective value, Boudreaux explained, there is another reason to embrace the idea of a decentralized, diverse assortment of education options from which families can choose. According to Boudreaux: "Even if people have the same preferences—which they don't, but even if they did—they could still have different beliefs about the effectiveness of different educational methods." Families need the freedom to choose the educational methods that they believe will produce their desired outcomes—whatever those might be.

For some families, that outcome could be getting their child into Harvard, with one group believing that a Waldorf education is the best way to get there and another group believing that a stricter, more traditional educational method is the way to achieve that outcome. They could both be right, given their assessment of their child's learning preferences and other needs. Other families might want different outcomes for their children, such as raising them to be deeply committed to their faith, or to serving others, or to becoming artists, activists, or entrepreneurs. As more innovative schools and spaces emerge across the United States, it's becoming easier than ever for parents to find just what they are looking for—schooling that is aligned with their own values, preferences, and beliefs about the effectiveness of different educational models.

This can ultimately lead to greater social harmony, as Boudreaux alluded to. An entrepreneur-driven, choice-enabled education marketplace enables families to pick the schools and spaces that are best for them without thrusting their values and viewpoints on others. There is a reason we don't see neighbors screaming at each other in local grocery store aisles the way we sometimes witness at local school board meetings. In the grocery store, we are presented with a wide assortment of products, choosing what we want to consume based on our personal preferences and needs. Take the breakfast food aisle, for example. We can each choose from a multitude of cereals and cereal bars, pastries and pancake mixes, organic and conventionally grown foods, brand names or generic. If none of those breakfast choices appeal to us, we can go to an entirely different section and buy bacon and eggs or fruit and yogurt. If we prefer to skip breakfast altogether, we can do that too. We have our own dietary druthers and don't need to force anyone else to share them. We may personally believe that the locally produced, small-batch organic granola is superior to some sugar-filled boxed cereal. We can try to persuade our neighbors that we are right and that they should follow our lead, but we can't force them to eat our granola.

That's not the case in school board meetings dictating what is or is not taught in public schools, which is why they can become so contentious. Top-down, centrally controlled school systems inevitably create winners and losers, with one dominant group's curriculum and policy preferences imposed on others who may have different preferences about what should or should not be taught. Even something as simple as whether or not cursive writing should be taught in today's schools can lead to hours of impassioned dialogue. In the end, one group's preferences regarding cursive emerges victorious and the other group is forced to comply even though they oppose the decision. This breeds resentment.

Some families may be so upset by the cursive decision that they want to pull their children out of that public school for a private option, or even move to a different city or state with different cursive protocols. Unless they have the personal financial resources to do that, or live in a state with school choice policies, they may be stuck with their compulsory school assignment—and its cursive commands. Neal McCluskey, director of the Center for Educational Freedom at the Cato Institute, maintains a Public Schooling Battle Map showcasing the ongoing ideological conflicts occurring in public schools across the United States when values clash and generate division. By encouraging variety and choice in education, just as in the grocery store breakfast aisle, each family is able to peacefully decide what is—and what is not—right for them.

## EVALUATING STUDENT PROGRESS

How are today's innovative education models measuring student success? Jennifer uses a Waldorf-inspired portfolio assessment approach that captures various academic and nonacademic outcomes, but what about other founders? A 2023 survey by VELA, the national entrepreneur network and philanthropic fund that includes more than four thousand founders who are operating unconventional learning models, revealed a wide variety of academic assessment metrics. Measuring academic growth was a top priority for most of the founders surveyed, and 85 percent of them use traditional evaluative measures, such as observations, portfolios, and periodic reviews of student progress. Nearly 60 percent of founders said they relied on various mastery-based educational software tools to measure learner progress, with Khan Academy, Lexia, Duolingo, IXL, and Zearn cited as among the most commonly used edtech platforms. Thirty-seven percent of founders reported using standardized testing, with the Iowa Test of Basic Skills and the NWEA MAP test being the most common.[5]

The history of standardized testing is closely tied to the history of standardized schooling. Horace Mann, who helped usher in the "common school" movement in Massachusetts in the mid-nineteenth century, was also instrumental in introducing the early seeds of standardized testing. Specifically, he urged replacing traditional oral exams with written exams, suggesting that these would be more equitable. Testing expanded in the subsequent decades along with compulsory schooling and, in the twentieth century, intelligence quotient (IQ) assessments and college-entrance exams like the SAT and ACT became popular.[6] In the 1960s, the federal government took on a larger role in education with the passage of the Elementary and Secondary Education Act, which laid the groundwork for No Child Left Behind in the new millennium and the advent of regular high-stakes testing in public schools.

There is nothing inherently problematic about standardized tests, and some of today's startup school founders use them as KPIs. Similarly, some parents want to see how their children's performance compares to others on nationally normed standardized assessments. Some parents and learners also embrace tests like the SAT and ACT as tools for college admissions, and data from ACT.org reveal that both homeschooled and private school students have consistently scored well above their public school peers on the ACT exam since 2001.[7]

It's worth noting that many of the colleges and universities that adopted test-optional admissions practices during the pandemic retained their testing requirements for homeschooled students. Some selective colleges that abolished testing requirements years before COVID also kept those requirements for homeschoolers as a way to gauge the academic competence of students who might otherwise have nontraditional transcripts.[8] Still, the vast majority of US four-year colleges and universities remained test-optional for those applying for admissions during the 2024/2025 academic year, with varying policies for homeschoolers.[9]

Standardized assessments have their place, but it's not surprising that those who value individualization over standardization would favor alternative assessment indicators either in place of, or in addition to, standardized metrics. Standardized tests often don't reveal a person's true intelligence or potential. Take Gregor Johann Mendel, for instance. The famous scientist whose nineteenth-century pea plant experiments led him to become widely recognized as the founder of modern genetics failed his teacher-certification standardized tests—twice.[10] Severe test anxiety was allegedly the culprit.[11] This failure ultimately benefited him—and us. Denied the opportunity to teach, Mendel was able to pursue his scientific interests and establish statistical methods that scientists still rely upon today.

It turns out, a lot of parents today don't care that much about test scores. In its 2023 "Schooling in America" survey of more than 2,500 Americans, EdChoice found that of fourteen reasons why parents chose their child's current school—including public, private, charter, and homeschool—test scores ranked near the bottom of parents' priorities. Specifically, traditional public-school parents ranked test scores second to last, private-school parents ranked test scores twelfth, charter-school parents ranked them eleventh, and homeschool parents ranked them tenth. Other factors, such as safety, morals and character development, academic quality or reputation, and convenience, ranked much higher than test scores for parents of children in all school types.[12]

## BEYOND STANDARDIZED ASSESSMENTS

"I believe that standardized testing needs to be completely redone," Nasiyah Isra-Ul said. "It's not a good indicator of intelligence or outcomes." She, like Mendel, was never a great test taker. The founder of Virginia-based Homeschool EmpowerED, Inc., Nasiyah was homeschooled from the outset. Though her parents were both public school educators, they chose homeschooling because they believed it was important to instill their values and to create a learning environment that fostered character-building and culturally affirming lessons rooted in their family's faith traditions.

While they referenced the Virginia state education standards, Nasiyah's parents focused more on content mastery and cultivating curiosity.

They also wanted to instill a sense of personal agency in Nasiyah and her younger brother. It worked. Beginning in fourth grade, Nasiyah began to take charge of her own education. She took advanced classes through online learning portals like Khan Academy, and, as a teen, enrolled in dual enrollment classes through a local college.

Dual enrollment is when high school-age students take college-level classes, accruing college credits that in many cases can be transferred to a university when a student enrolls as an undergraduate. Some high schools enable students who are enrolled in a dual enrollment program to also accumulate credits toward high school graduation, and some of these classes may take place at the high school. Dual enrollment programs are typically offered through a local community college, but some four-year universities also provide this opportunity. Dual enrollment programs are often free or relatively inexpensive and can help lessen the financial burden of later college tuition costs if credits are transferable. These programs can also signal to college admissions committees that a student is taking an advanced course load as a teenager, similar to a student taking Advanced Placement (AP) classes in high school. Homeschoolers and others who are unconventionally educated have long known the benefits of dual enrollment programs, and fortunately more students and families are now recognizing their advantages. Today, high school dual enrollment students account for about one in five community college students across the United States, and more students participate in dual enrollment programs than take AP tests.[13]

When Nasiyah was fifteen, her mother, who left the workforce to homeschool her children when they were younger, returned to work to help support her family. Nasiyah stepped up. After completing her coursework each day, the teenager started tutoring her brother. Soon, she realized that she could create a more engaging, dynamic course of study for him. She built a virtual curriculum for her brother that eventually became a full course. "When he liked that course so much, it became two courses and then three courses," Nasiyah said, detailing the origin story of what would become Homeschool EmpowerED, a personalized, interactive online learning platform for homeschoolers, as well as a charitable engine to make homeschooling more accessible to Black and brown families like hers.

Watching how her online course content and interactive approach to learning ignited her brother's interest and engagement in learning, Nasiyah knew she was on to something. In 2020, at age eighteen and while a sophomore in college, she entered and won a business plan pitch competition, catapulting her vision for Homeschool EmpowerED, originally called Canary Academy Online. Today, Nasiyah's nonprofit startup has two main priorities: provide high-quality online curriculum content and community for homeschoolers across the United States, and expand access to homeschooling to low-income and historically marginalized groups through a philanthropic initiative that provides technology and supplies to those who need them.

Nasiyah views her startup and similar unconventional models as contributing to a fundamental transformation in education. "Unconventional education is much bigger than just creating new schools and creating alternatives for some kids," Nasiyah told me when we spoke in 2024. "It's about changing the entire way we think about education and the entire way we see how and why education happens. What should education really be measuring? What is the purpose of education? Is it that we all check a box?" she asked.

Nasiyah is passionate about making sure that unconventional education models don't become ensnared in the same standardized metrics of learning that define traditional K–12 schools. "What we're currently doing in traditional schools is not working, so we can't try to impose that on a system that is working," she said, referring to today's unconventional learning models. She offered some insights on alternative metrics for unconventional education environments. "I think agency is really one of the main ways to measure," said Nasiyah, who is now in graduate school studying organizational leadership. "Give parents agency to make decisions. Then, once students are old enough and mature enough to start deciding what they would like to do in life—I would say around sixth grade—give them that collaborative agency to make their own metrics," Nasiyah said, explaining that the goal of education should be to empower young people to chart their own course in life.

Indeed, parent and youth empowerment are built into Nasiyah's business model, as she helps homeschooling families create their own metrics of success. These metrics could include traditional outcomes, such as performance on subject-specific or standardized tests and college acceptance rates, as well as other outcomes, such as improved youth mental health and happiness, greater student confidence and independence, more personal agency, the development of an entrepreneurial spirit, and a strong connection to community.

As a homeschooler herself, Nasiyah experienced these positive outcomes. Although limited, existing research on homeschoolers generally shows similarly positive trends. For example, Professor Daniel Hamlin at the University of Oklahoma found that homeschoolers have higher rates of "cultural capital," or engagement in and connection to their community, than their traditionally schooled peers. Homeschoolers are much more likely than other students to regularly visit libraries, museums, bookstores, and historic sites, as well as to participate in local community events.[14] Other research reveals that homeschoolers who chose to attend college had no difficulty adjusting to higher education expectations and were more likely to report lower levels of depression, higher academic achievement, and a more positive overall college experience than their peers who were not homeschooled.[15]

Some colleges and universities, including highly selective ones, have pages on their undergraduate admissions websites specifically geared toward homeschoolers and other students who have learned in unconventional ways. A student's unique learning experiences could help distinguish her from the larger applicant pool. A 2018 *Harvard Gazette* profile of three Harvard University students who were homeschooled showed a broad range of homeschooling backgrounds while stating that they "share a spirit of curiosity and independence that continues to shape their education."[16] Nasiyah also exhibits an enduring spirit of curiosity and independence. That's part of the reason why she is so motivated to help more families choose homeschooling. Learner curiosity and independence are two additional outcomes that could be prioritized and measured in today's creative schools and spaces.

## MEASURING WHAT MATTERS

The expanding variety of unconventional education options also means greater opportunities for original KPIs that matter most to founders and families. For instance, if a founder is creating an arts-focused school or space, then learner originality, artistic risk-taking, and level of output could be worthwhile metrics. If a founder is creating a school or space committed to social justice or climate activism, then she could track learner involvement and output in letter-writing campaigns, petitions, and protests; the development of informational and educational materials to be publicly distributed; or the number of school-specific events, guest speakers, and other activities focused around activism and outreach. If a founder is creating a school or space committed to instilling religious values in his students, then he could measure the quantity of time spent on faith-based lessons and discussions, as well as consider using learner, teacher, and parent surveys and observations to reveal how a young person's faith may be deepening. A STEM-focused school could measure the number of robotics competitions entered, while an entrepreneurship-focused school could track the number of new businesses formed by its students and alumni. If a founder wants to create a school or space centered around community service, she could measure service hours and events, while a founder committed to global citizenship could measure hours and output related to cross-cultural content or international travel.

There are endless possibilities for KPIs that reflect each unique learning environment, as well as countless combinations of traditional and nontraditional metrics that founders can use. "We see everything from caring about rigorous academic progress to academics being the furthest thing on somebody's mind and everything in between," said Ashley Soifer, who cofounded the nonprofit National Microschooling Center in 2022 with her husband, Don. Since then, the Center has become a resource hub for current and prospective microschool founders, as well as for parents and policymakers curious about the modern microschooling movement. Measuring outcomes is happening in a variety of ways in today's microschools, Ashley explained, from surveys to standardized tests to stories of lives changed for the better due to these smaller, more personalized learning environments.

In 2024, the Center released results from a comprehensive survey of four hundred current and prospective microschool founders across the United States. It showed that most founders use observation-based reporting, tracking of academic mastery, portfolios of student work, and edtech assessments included within various digital learning platforms to measure impact. About one-third of the founders use regular parent surveys, and about one-fifth use regular student surveys. Only about one-fourth of the microschools surveyed use traditional student letter grades, and slightly more than one-third use standardized tests. Moreover, the top desired outcome for today's microschool founders was academic growth, with more than 80 percent of respondents indicating that this was their main objective. Academic progress was followed by "child happiness/thriving in a new setting," with 70 percent of founders stating that this was their most important outcome.[17] "I think that in the whole conversation about measuring outcomes, we need to keep in mind that parents are choosing these microschools for a reason, and that reason matters," Ashley said, explaining that flexibility in measuring outcomes is a crucial component of today's unconventional learning models.

Ashley knows firsthand how much these new learning models matter. While in elementary school, her daughter struggled in the conventional education model—she become increasingly stressed by standardized assessment metrics. The family switched from a traditional public school to a charter school, but the struggles remained and the stress grew. Ashley's daughter felt increasingly depressed and hopeless, and her son was also unhappy in school. "He would spin in circles in the morning before school until he made himself throw up so that he could come and tell me, 'Mom, I threw up! I can't go to school today!'"

As her children's desperation grew, Ashley knew she had to make a change. She pulled her children out of school and enrolled them in new microschools that had recently opened in the Las Vegas valley—an arts-focused one for her daughter and a STEM-focused one for her son. The positive change in her children's moods, motivation, and mindset around learning was immediate. On the day Ashley retold this story to me over Zoom, she was working at home because her son was, ironically, home sick that day. "I can't tell you how many times today I've heard him say, 'I wish I felt better. I miss not being at school. Do you think I can go yet? Am I still contagious?'" Ashley said. "This is the child that would purposefully make himself sick so that he didn't have to go to school. I can't talk to his microschool founders about it without crying. It's amazing to me that this is the same child," she said.

The microschool metrics that matter most to Ashley are her children's improved mental health, their level of joy at school, their eagerness for learning, and their growing self-confidence and sense of personal agency. Some of these metrics can be captured quantitatively through surveys and observations, but they go well beyond conventional measures of educational outcomes. "As a parent, you can just see the difference," Ashley said. "You know your kid, and you know when they're growing and when they're thriving."

## A CHARLOTTE MASON APPROACH TO ASSESSMENT

Rebecca Ellis thought her child was thriving at her new school until she got a phone call from school administrators saying that the fourth grader was lying on the floor complaining of chest pains. That's when Rebecca discovered the potentially dangerous downside of traditional testing. Rebecca and her husband were both homeschooled as children and had a positive experience, so when they became parents, homeschooling seemed like the obvious path. But after having five children in a few short years, including a set of twin boys, Rebecca became overwhelmed with juggling parenting and teaching and enrolled her oldest in a traditional, private, Christian school in Chattanooga, Tennessee, for fourth grade. Her daughter enjoyed it and excelled, and Rebecca and her husband recognized some of the benefits of schooling that they missed out on as homeschoolers, especially the consistent social interactions with other children and the exposure to additional adult educators. The drawbacks were the hefty tuition costs and long school days with nightly homework that eroded family time. The Ellises were considering what to do about the following school year when Rebecca got that phone call.

She drove to pick up her daughter from school. "I was like, 'Oh my gosh, what is wrong with my child?' I had never seen her like this," Rebecca recalled. She then drove straight to the doctor, who said the girl was having a panic attack. "This was just absolutely shocking," Rebecca said, explaining that her ten-year-old had always been a very calm and carefree child. Rebecca probed to find out what could have triggered such a strong emotional and physical reaction and discovered that her daughter was extremely anxious about the multi-day standardized testing that was happening at school that week. "She was so stressed and anxious about these tests that she had sent herself into this panic attack," Rebecca told me. Her daughter is far from alone. The National Institutes of Health reports that up to 40 percent of students contend with test-related anxiety.[18]

I met Rebecca in early 2024, about halfway through her second year of running Canyon Creek Christian Academy in Chattanooga. I pulled into the driveway of what I thought was the main church building where her hybrid homeschool program meets three days a week, but when I texted Rebecca to say I had arrived, she told me that I was actually in the parking area of a second church next door where Rebecca had recently added space, as her program grew from about thirty students in 2022/2023 to more than fifty students and five full-time teachers the following academic year. I drove to the other church building next door and was greeted by Rebecca walking up a grassy hill holding her toddler's hand. Behind her, children walked casually back to the church building from a wooded area in the distance. They were returning from their morning outdoor meeting and preparing for math class.

Rebecca, who originally planned to earn her college undergraduate degree in education before switching to an English major in her junior year, opened Canyon Creek Christian Academy in August 2022 as a Charlotte Mason–inspired hybrid homeschool program for elementary- and middle-school-age homeschooled students. She had begun contemplating the idea of opening a hybrid homeschool when her daughter experienced the panic attack, but it was the sudden death of her mother from cancer that really propelled her entrepreneurial journey. "When my mom passed away, I was inspired to not wait to do things that are really important, because you never know how much time you have left," she said.

Rebecca told me that a key tenet of the Charlotte Mason philosophy is a focus on treating each child as an individual and not subjecting them to a standardized approach to learning. "It's all about meeting the child where they're at and working with them, knowing that each child is going to develop at a different pace. Each child is going to be interested in different things," Rebecca said. Within a Charlotte Mason environment, most learning is acquired and assessed through oral and written narration coinciding with deep study of classic literature. For example, Rebecca described how her sixth and seventh graders are reading the book *Robinson Crusoe* and sharing what they've learned orally and in writing each week.

Math and spelling are the exceptions, where Rebecca uses the well-known Saxon math curriculum focused on mastery-based skill development, as well as a common spelling textbook. Math and spelling are assessed regularly throughout the term and are the only subjects that are graded. Even then, the grades are used to help students, parents, and teachers measure growth areas and identify gaps until each child masters the content in his own time. Rebecca said she has students who were failing math in the traditional schooling system but are now math whizzes and love math because they have been able to build confidence and work at their own pace.

Three times a year, Canyon Creek holds formal "assessment weeks," marked by individual student narration, both orally and in writing, in all the content areas covered over the previous twelve weeks of the term. Parents are given a recording of their child's oral assessment, as well as the child's written essays. The students, including those like Rebecca's daughter who confronted so much anxiety around testing, adore Canyon Creek's assessment weeks. "They say it's their favorite week of the school term, which is great! I absolutely love how we're changing the tide on that," Rebecca said, explaining that her students now see assessment times as enjoyable, low-pressure opportunities to showcase what they've learned.

In addition to her Charlotte Mason–style assessments of learner progress, and tracking of math and spelling gains, Rebecca notes her strong re-enrollment rates and growing waitlist as two additional metrics of her program's success. Powerful parent testimonials are another. "I never imagined the families that are coming here in tears saying, 'This has literally changed our lives.' That has been a really unexpected joy out of this whole journey," Rebecca said. She adds that being an education entrepreneur "is definitely not for the faint of heart," with many hours and much stress—especially during the startup year—but it's been worth it. The children in her school—including her own—are happy and thriving. And so is she. "Seeing my kids' own personal growth, and then all the other students' growth, it's just been amazing," Rebecca said.

*Chapter Reflections for Parents and Founders*
After observing a potential downside of standardized testing in her daughter's traditional private school, Rebecca knew that she wanted to create a learning environment that would be committed to core academics and student progress without stress-inducing assessments. She also valued other schooling qualities, such as ample outside time for children and a strong school-family partnership. As a parent or a founder, you will want to take stock of your own values and preferences and how you define educational quality and effectiveness. If you're a parent, know that not every school will be aligned with your educational preferences or meet your specific needs—and that's okay. If you're a founder, know that you can't satisfy everyone. Below are some additional thoughts to consider as you evaluate a potential school as a parent, or as you establish and monitor metrics as an entrepreneur.

**Parents:** You'll want to think carefully about the type of learning environment you want for your child and make sure that you understand—and agree with—the curriculum and culture of a particular school or space. If you want your child to learn cursive, and the founder has no interest in introducing that skill, then you'll need to keep shopping around. If standardized test scores are important to you, ask about standardized assessments and results at the school or space you are considering, including how the school approaches test preparation and administration of college entrance exams, such as the SAT and ACT, if applicable. If other types of metrics, such as level of learner agency and engagement in learning, matter most to you, be sure the school you are considering prioritizes and monitors them.

As you assess the quality of a particular school or space, think about how you assess quality in your other consumer decisions. When you are looking to buy a car, what do you do to determine if that car is a good value and the right fit for you and your family? You might consult *Consumer Reports* to read evaluations of different car brands, or refer to automotive industry resources, such as Kelley Blue Book, to gain more information. It's very likely that you'll ask your friends, family members, and Facebook acquaintances about their cars, and then test-drive a few different models to see what you like and what you don't. You might prefer a Prius, while your neighbor prefers a pickup truck—and that's totally fine. You can each choose the vehicle that's right for you. Take a similar approach when evaluating and choosing a new school or learning environment. Gather information, including from some of the resources shared in these pages and in Appendix 1. Ask around, visit schools, inquire about having your child do a trial day or trial week, and make the best decision you can with the information you have. While car purchases and school decisions are both large and consequential, they are not permanent. If a school does not meet your expectations or your educational needs change, you can leave and choose a different option.

**Founders:** As an education entrepreneur, you can't be all things to all people. If you prioritize cursive writing, own that. The families who think cursive is passé will know that your school is probably not a good fit for them. Like those families, you have your own values, preferences, and beliefs about educational models and methods. You should be clear about what those are and transparent with potential families about how those values, preferences, and beliefs will be integrated into your school or space, including the type of curriculum you will use and the type of assessment you will, or will not, include. If none of your prospective families want cursive in the curriculum, then you may need to pivot or consider a different approach to attract and retain students and families. Or maybe you will ultimately decide that you can't run a school without a cursive curriculum, and instead choose to move on to a new endeavor.

## Chapter 9

# Challenges

> *I'm convinced that about half of what separates the successful entrepreneurs from the non-successful ones is pure perseverance. It is so hard.*
>
> —Steve Jobs (Apple cofounder)

Entrepreneurship is hard. If it wasn't, everyone would do it. It's difficult to take on the personal and financial risks of launching and running a small business, knowing full well that, statistically speaking, it has about a one-in-five chance of failing within the first couple of years and a roughly 50 percent chance of failure within the first five. It's not surprising that "fear of failure" was the #2 barrier cited in a 2022 poll of Americans who wanted to start a small business but ultimately didn't. The top barrier was "inadequate capital."[1]

Fear of failure and lack of funding are just two of the big challenges today's founders face. In the workshops I've led since 2022 with current and prospective education entrepreneurs through my fellowship role at State

Policy Network, a national nonprofit focused on encouraging state-based, free-market policy solutions, founders reveal a litany of challenges. From a culture largely shaped by traditional schooling expectations, to a complicated and hazy regulatory landscape, to difficulty finding suitable spaces in which to operate, to occupational licensing barriers, to increased competition, it's often not easy to start or scale a new school or learning model. As a "parentpreneur," James Lomax confronted all these challenges.

## FACING FAILURE

I first met James in December 2022 when I visited his Las Vegas–based microschool, Life Skills Academy, which he opened that previous August. James grew up in Maryland, just outside of Washington, DC. When he was seven years old, the original *Top Gun* movie was released, and he decided then that he wanted to be a fighter jet pilot. Around the same time, he read an article in a Boy Scouts magazine about an F-14 pilot who said he went to the United States Naval Academy for college. "So that's what I set my sights on and didn't look back from there," James said. He graduated from the US Naval Academy and worked as a Navy Weapon Systems Officer, later earning an MBA. After retiring from active duty, James became an engineer, working on electronic warfare system testing for military aircraft. That's when he discovered alternative education.

"The alternative school space is not something that people would expect from my pedigree, I guess," James said, laughing. He had taken a very conventional schooling path through his K–12 years and beyond and had felt that despite some flaws, it was a fairly decent system. That began to change as he worked with new engineers fresh out of college. "A lot of these engineers went to very top universities with perfect grades," James told me when he appeared on my podcast in early 2023. "We get them on the job, and it's very clear, very soon, that the only thing they really learned how to do in their education was to take tests. So, they can't think critically, they can't solve a problem without being given the exact path to solve the problem. They don't have basic life skills."

At the same time, James's daughter was enrolled in a pricey private preschool in Las Vegas because James and his wife thought that was the best pathway for success. As he increasingly observed what that "success" looked like in his young employees, and the cost to their critical thinking, curiosity, and creativity, he started wondering about other educational options for his daughter. James recalled several occasions in which, visiting with the preschool teachers and administrators, he found them fixated on "kindergarten readiness." James wanted to know how his daughter was getting along with others, how she was resolving conflicts and collaborating through play. Yet, the preschool educators were focused on making sure she was counting to 150 and that her Spanish language comprehension skills were improving. "Around this time, it's starting to click with me that maybe these aren't the important things," James said, adding, "I started to think this is not the path I want for my daughter, because the skills we need are different skills than what's being taught in school."

James began researching alternative education options and stumbled upon Acton Academy, the learner-driven microschool network described in Chapter 4. It was everything he wanted for his young daughters. "I discovered that anybody could open an Acton as long as they were really committed, had some business background, and had children that they were willing to put in their school," James said. He felt strongly that an Acton Academy needed to exist in Las Vegas and that he needed it for his children. James remembered thinking: "If nobody else is going to do it, then I'm going to do it." It would be easier said than done.

Nevada is one of the most difficult states in which to open a secular private school, ranking toward the bottom in the 2024 Education Entrepreneur Freedom Index.[2] State occupational licensing requirements prevent anyone without a state teacher or administrator license from opening a secular private school. Church-based schools are exempt from this requirement. These Nevada occupational licensing requirements for non-religious K–12 school founders are a national outlier. Other states do not have these barriers to entry that favor certain types of educators over others and prevent competition.

Many states have occupational licensing requirements for teachers in public schools, requiring that they have a state-issued teaching certificate to be a public school educator; but these requirements typically do not apply to teachers in private schools. In most states, an educator who has a PhD, is a renowned expert in her field, and has taught as a university professor for years would not be able to teach in a public school without some type of exemption, but this scholar is usually able to teach in a private school. State teaching certificates are clearly not a universal measure of subject-matter expertise or educator quality.

Similarly, most states don't require state teaching credentials for founders who want to open a private school, but Nevada is an exception, barring accomplished individuals like James from opening the school he envisioned. Like occupational licensing restrictions in all sectors, these barriers constrain entrepreneurship and innovation. Cato Institute economist Chris Edwards explains that occupational "licensing restrictions are restrictions on entrepreneurship, particularly for disadvantaged individuals."[3] They can prevent new enterprises from even getting off the ground.

The occupational licensing barriers alone would have prompted many aspiring school founders to give up, but James persevered, determined to find a way to open Life Skills Academy. He wanted his program to be a state-recognized private school so that low-income students could attend with tuition help through a limited Nevada tax-credit scholarship school choice program that only applied to private schools. Microschools for homeschoolers were not eligible to participate in this school choice program, but opening a microschool seemed to be James's only option given occupational licensing restrictions. So he pivoted. It was 2021, and James connected with Don and Ashley Soifer who are based in Las Vegas and were about to launch the National Microschooling Center. They pointed James to Sarah Tavernetti and Yamila De Leon, the founders of Bloom Academy, another microschool in Las Vegas that had just opened that year.

Even though Sarah was a licensed teacher in Nevada who taught in the state's public schools and could have opened a state-recognized private school, she and Yamila, a former Montessori educator, wanted to launch a different kind of learning space. They were inspired by Kenneth Danford, whose North Star model of self-directed learning for homeschoolers we explored in Chapter 2. Sarah and Yamila sought to create their region's first self-directed learning center for homeschoolers, enabling young people to have maximum autonomy and flexibility over their education. Unlike its private school regulations, Nevada's homeschooling regulations are much less restrictive, and homeschooling is a popular option in the state. Homeschooling may have been comparatively easy to do in Nevada, but opening a small business to serve homeschoolers was not.

"It was challenging for us to get up and running on the business side of things," Sarah told me. She recalled how she and Yamila went to the library to research zoning and building codes to figure out what, where, and how they could operate. They took the information they gathered with them to city hall to apply for a business license. "Unfortunately, because what we're doing had never been created in Vegas, they couldn't really figure out what box we fit into," Sarah recalled. She and Yamila described their learning center to city officials. "Oh, so you're a daycare," the officials responded. "No," the founders said, they weren't a daycare because the box for daycare didn't describe what they were doing or who they were serving, which were school-age children who were legally registered as homeschoolers. "Okay, so you're a tutoring center," the city officials then said. "Not really," one of the founders said, because the tutoring center option required a ratio of two children to one adult, and that wasn't the kind of environment Sarah and Yamila were trying to create. It seemed like it might be their only option, though. They were considering going through with an application to be a tutoring center with a special use permit, but they were told it would take several months for the permit to go through.

The founders began looking around for different properties in different areas, stumbling upon an ideal location in a small strip mall in unincorporated Clark County, just outside the Las Vegas city limits. Sarah and Yamila discovered that the county had much easier business licensing and zoning restrictions than the city. All they needed to do was show that they were operating at the headquarters of their nonprofit organization and they got their business license immediately, opening Bloom Academy in the summer of 2021.

"They were telling me about the trials they were having with getting a location and zoning," James said, describing his first conversation with Sarah and Yamila in 2021. "I'm military," James remembered smugly thinking, "so regulation and figuring out how things work just comes naturally to me as a military officer." He didn't think it would be a big deal to navigate the regulatory maze and open his microschool. James researched building occupancy and zoning codes and visited city hall in another suburb of Las Vegas to apply for his business license. Like the Bloom Academy cofounders, James planned to operate as a learning center for homeschoolers, given that he was prohibited from opening a private school due to the occupational licensing restrictions.

Despite his optimism that he would be able to handle the regulatory requirements with aplomb, James encountered the same challenges at his city hall that had plagued Sarah and Yamila in Vegas proper. City officials wanted to put James's program into existing boxes, such as daycare centers and tutoring facilities, that didn't apply to his microschool. He was bounced around to different municipal offices over the course of several weeks until he finally discovered a category for miscellaneous business licenses that he thought might work. It did, and James got his business license, but his challenges were far from over.

It took James almost a year to find a properly zoned location that had the characteristics he was seeking, including room for growth and plentiful outdoor space where the children could play. He finally found a classroom space connected to a Jewish temple that worked perfectly, and James opened Life Skills Academy as a full-time, secular microschool for homeschoolers in August 2022 with ten mixed-age students in kindergarten through sixth grade. He expected to triple his enrollment the following year, with plans to grow steadily, up to 150 K–12 students in subsequent years.

It seemed like a success story. James had been able to find a workaround to onerous occupational licensing requirements. He jumped through the necessary business licensing and zoning hoops. He signed a lease at an ideal location with abundant outdoor space, and he was up and running with promising growth projections. He'd persevered in the face of significant entrepreneurial challenges and prevailed.

Sixteen months later, his school closed. I talked to James again in February 2024, exactly one year after our podcast conversation aired and two months after he shuttered Life Skills Academy. What happened? "In the spring of 2023, I thought I was going to have to find a bigger space for fall," James told me. He was giving dozens of tours to prospective families and thought for sure he would be busting at the seams of his space heading into his second academic year. He was able to add an additional classroom to his existing lease with the temple in preparation for rising enrollment. But the tours weren't converting into registrations. Upon reflection, he thinks he was probably ignoring the parents' "jobs to be done." "I was focused on the nuts and bolts of how everything works instead of really focusing on the big picture: Why are you here? What do you want out of your journey?" James said. He also only gave tours after the school day because he didn't want to interrupt his learners or expose families to the often unpredictable nature of learner-driven education. This was a mistake, James admitted. He should have let prospective families see his microschool in action.

While not the growth he anticipated, James increased his enrollment from ten to fifteen students for the start of his second school year. Soon, though, there were signs of trouble. One of his founding families left, and he accepted some students who, in hindsight, weren't a good fit for his program. Another family left, and by October he was down to eleven students. More families unenrolled to create their own separate microschool, and by November 2023, James had only eight students remaining. He had to let a staff member go. Additional microschooling options were sprouting in Las Vegas, with more expected to open, and some of James's families wanted different options.

In December, another family left and James was down to six children, including his daughter. Things were precarious. The remaining families really wanted to remain together and create some kind of co-op, and the temple didn't want to see James go. "We just couldn't pull it together. We didn't quite know what it was going to look like, and financially it wasn't going to work," said James, who had taken on personal debt to launch Life Skills Academy. By Christmas break, he closed the microschool and referred the remaining families to another microschool in the valley that James admired. James's daughter finished off the academic year at a local public school with plans to enroll in Acton Academy Red Rock, another new Acton-affiliated microschool about forty-five minutes away, as soon as James can pay off his founder debt. He's still deeply committed to the Acton Academy educational model and remains active in Acton's supportive founder network.

James has had more time to reflect on the failure of Life Skills Academy, which he says is the first real failure he's experienced. He admits, "I've lived a pretty charmed life." Failure stung, but he has no regrets about opening an Acton Academy. Looking back, James thinks a big reason his microschool failed was due to him opening and running the program while still working full-time as an engineer—something he felt he had to do to financially support his family, which shrank to one income when his younger daughter was born the same year that he launched. He is fairly certain that if he had left his regular job and devoted his time fully to the microschool and to building relationships with families in the community, his enterprise would have flourished. But he also suspects that one of the reasons he didn't make that full-time commitment was that he wasn't truly passionate about being a school founder. "I don't think that running a microschool was my calling," James confessed. "I think it was an intermediary step, because my goal was to get to a point where I could step away to do other things in the educational space." He is particularly interested in education policy.

James isn't exactly sure what the next step will be along his own "hero's journey," to use Acton Academy vernacular, but he's certain that entrepreneurship will be part of it. Failure has only fueled his entrepreneurial spirit. James hopes to create a nonprofit organization to advocate for expanded education options in Nevada and is already working to draft legislation to make it easier for microschools to operate in the state. While it is personally painful, James knows that failure is part of the startup process and is a signal of a robust, responsive educational marketplace. "I am a big believer that everything happens for a reason. I am also a big believer in the free market. So, honestly, this 'failure' is exactly how it should be allowed to work in all of education."

James's school closure was disappointing for him and the families he served, but this isn't a situation that is unique to microschools or other emerging school models. There are no guarantees that *any* school today may be around tomorrow. For example, more public schools are closing due to under-enrollment, with students transferred to other schools in the district. A 2024 analysis of data collected by the Brookings Institution and reported by The 74 revealed plummeting public school enrollment since 2020 in many school districts across the United States, leading to scattered school closures.[4] In 2024, the Broward County Public Schools system in Florida announced plans to close forty-two schools in the district due to low enrollment.[5] In 2013, fifty public schools closed in Chicago. Long-running Catholic schools have also seen an uptick in unexpected school closures.[6] In higher education, colleges were shutting down at a rate of one per week in 2024.[7] Whether your child is at a school that has been around for days or decades—public or private—there are no longer any assurances that it will remain open. As a parent, this can feel unsettling, but it's a sign of a healthier, more dynamic education ecosystem. Just as restaurants close when they fail to attract and retain enough customers, schools will also close if they fail to do the same.

The good news is that when today's unconventional schools and spaces shut down, they typically do so with care and concern for the students and families they serve. Like James, founders that close their doors often help relocate their students by making introductions to nearby schools that might be a good fit. Some founders even accompany their students and families on tours of these other spaces, and remain closely connected over time. While entrepreneurship can be risky, the rewards for founders and families often far outweigh those risks.

## REGULATORY ROADBLOCKS

Sometimes an innovative school could be growing and thriving but confront unexpected regulatory roadblocks that could threaten its closure. While the lack of regulatory clarity around microschools and other creative learning models can support "permissionless innovation," it can also lead to some of the challenges that entrepreneurs like James, Sarah, and Yamila confronted. Regulatory agencies and authorizers often don't know what to do with new schools and spaces that don't resemble traditional education models. There is frequently no box for them to fall into. Sometimes this can be beneficial, enabling experimental models to fly under the regulatory radar, but sometimes it can prevent such models from starting and scaling.

Georgia was a leader in trying to tackle the regulatory roadblocks that today's innovative education entrepreneurs encounter. In the early days of the COVID pandemic, as schools remained closed and "pandemic pods" proliferated, Georgia became the first state to pass a Learning Pod Protection Act preventing the regulation of these "pods," which were broadly defined. Texas soon followed suit. Sharon Masinelli didn't think much about the new Georgia law when it first made headlines. A mom of eight, Sharon had been running her successful hybrid homeschool program at a church in Kennesaw, Georgia, since 2019 and had never encountered any issues. Homeschooling was widespread in Georgia, and hybrid homeschools had been around for decades. You'll recall the story of Laura George from Chapter 2, who launched her Georgia hybrid homeschool, Compass Prep, in 2005. Sharon didn't think her program, called St. John the Baptist Hybrid School, was in any danger and therefore didn't need any additional protection from pandemic-era pod legislation.

Before Sharon founded her own hybrid school, which today serves more than 120 K–12 students with up to three days a week of full-time instruction by certified teachers, she had been driving an hour each way for her children to attend a different hybrid homeschool program. She loved the hybrid model, which she felt provided the ideal blend of structure and flexibility. It also enabled her to continue working part-time as a physician associate, something she had been doing professionally since 2003. But the drive was wearing on her, and Sharon began noodling over the idea of starting her own program that would be both more convenient and more aligned with her Catholic faith.

"I just decided, why not go ahead and give it a try," Sharon told me. She found a church that would accommodate her program, hosted some open houses, and discovered widespread interest. She launched with forty-seven kids. "I really didn't feel like I was doing something novel because my kids had gone to a hybrid school for seven years by the time I started ours. It seemed normal to me. I figured if it took off, that would be great. If not, then I'd just move on to something else," Sharon recalled. It did take off, growing gradually that first year and then surging during 2020 and 2021. Sharon moved to a larger church space to accommodate her rising student roster.

Beginning in 2020, Sharon said that families with students who had attended traditional public schools started enrolling in her hybrid school. Some of that was due to school shutdowns from COVID, but some of it was because of a mounting desire by parents to be more connected to their children's education. Families had been suddenly thrust together at home in the spring of 2020, and parents got a glance at their children's classrooms through remote learning. They began to explore other learning options, including Sharon's hybrid homeschool. "The primary motivation is usually that they want more time with their children and they would like to be more involved in their education, knowing the curriculum, knowing what's being taught to them," Sharon said of the parents who have enrolled their children at St. John the Baptist Hybrid School. Her program is also a much more affordable option for families than traditional private schools in her area, including both religious and secular ones.

Sharon's program was flourishing. In the summer of 2021, just before the start of her program's third academic year, she was running a small camp at the church location. There were about seven children participating, along with two adults, when the fire marshal arrived unexpectedly. Sharon said that someone had anonymously reported her program to the fire department, claiming that she was running an illegal school. Several other hybrid homeschools in the area were also reported. The fire marshal then cited the pastor of the church where Sharon's hybrid school operated, stating that the church didn't have a county certificate of occupancy for education. Sharon's program would need to close immediately. She was stunned. The church building had an appropriate certificate of occupancy for its operations, including its Sunday School. As an accredited program, St. John the Baptist Hybrid School had had to provide a certificate of occupancy to Sharon's accrediting agency, and it was also deemed valid. "However, our certificate of occupancy was missing the little word that said 'education'," Sharon said.

The church worked with the fire department to attain the necessary education occupancy certificate, which it eventually received. In the meantime, the Institute for Justice, a national nonprofit public interest law firm, stepped in to push back on the fire marshal's shut-down orders and enable Sharon's hybrid school to continue to operate under the state's new Learning Pod Protection Act. The attorneys argued that innovative educational programs like Sharon's could be considered learning pods and therefore were exempt from some of the occupancy rules intended for traditional schools. "That Learning Pod Protection Act was very important," Sharon said, "and the Institute for Justice was also key to keeping us open when we were able to go back to school in August, because otherwise it was a close call." Another local hybrid homeschool that was cited by the fire marshal that summer ended up shutting down, displacing the roughly 120 students it had been serving. Sharon's hybrid school took in some of them.

For her part, Sharon is sympathetic to building and occupancy codes. "I understand the idea behind it. The idea is to keep all of us safe," she said, explaining that it makes sense to not have overcrowded buildings that could be difficult to evacuate in the event of an emergency. She said that her program complies with all fire-safety codes, performs monthly fire drills, and reports that information publicly. "We're trying to follow all the same rules," Sharon said, "but sometimes it just does not make sense when it's a microschool, when it's a hybrid school."

As "pandemic pods" fade from memory, the protective legislation they prompted in some states remains today, with additional states weighing the benefits and potential drawbacks of adopting such policies. These protective policies can help remove regulatory ambiguity around innovative education models and enable them to have their own legal box. However, it's important to make sure that these new boxes don't box in new models. By defining in statute what exactly constitutes a pod, microschool, learning center, or hybrid homeschool program, states could unintentionally limit creative variations of each of these models and prevent new models from being invented. These definitions could also open the door to future regulations that pull innovative models back toward the current schooling status quo, with the potential for top-down curriculum and testing mandates that could compromise their creativity. Finally, there is the very real possibility that these protective policies just might not help.

"I was forced with the decision: Do I fight this or do I pivot?" said Amber Okolo-Ebube, founder of Leading Little Arrows, a homeschool collaborative in the Fort Worth area of Texas. A longtime homeschooling mom of five children, Amber saw a growing need in her community for homeschooling spaces that were more racially and ethnically diverse, as well as more welcoming of neurodiverse learners. As a Black homeschooling mom with an autistic child, Amber knew options were limited. During COVID, the number of Black families choosing homeschooling swelled in the Dallas–Fort Worth area, as it did across the country. Amber offered free homeschooling consultations and was inundated with messages from parents of color who were seeking guidance and support on their new homeschooling journey.

"I really feel that when COVID happened and parents got a little peek of what was going on in the school system, they started to say, 'Wait a minute, this is something that I can do myself and I can do it better,'" Amber said. In particular, Amber said more parents were seeing how their Black and brown children were being treated in school and were concerned about the school-to-prison pipeline. Other parents expressed different concerns about traditional schooling, including increased anxiety levels in their children, too much testing, and concerns about their children getting into trouble for things like wiggling in their seats. "Parents are fed up with their children not having the ability to just be themselves," Amber said.

In the spring of 2022, while recognizing rising demand for more diverse, inclusive homeschooling options in her area, Amber began hosting a homeschool co-op that met outside once a week at a state park. She called it Leading Little Arrows. It was enormously popular, so that fall Amber subleased a space from another local microschool to host her program indoors. As Amber's co-op expanded, and interest in additional offerings grew, she moved to her own dedicated space in early 2023. "I love that little building," she said of the spacious, ranch-style home located across from the University of Texas at Arlington campus. I first met Amber soon after she had moved into her new space, which featured multiple rooms for classes, a small kitchen, and a large backyard space. It even had a small, stand-alone building out back that Amber intended to use as her office. She leased the entire building for her weekly co-op, enabling homeschooling parents to gather together for some respite time while hired educators led academic and enrichment classes for thirty-five students, approximately 85 percent of whom are neurodiverse. Amber also added a part-time microschool option for about a dozen learners and was continuing to expand enrollment and offer new programs in the fall of 2023. She was also in the planning stages of opening a second location in a church in Irving, about twenty-five miles northeast of Fort Worth.

"Then we ran into our good old friends, the fire marshal and zoning issues," Amber sighed when we spoke by Zoom in early 2024. "They were trying to make me follow rules as if I were either a childcare facility or a traditional school, and those laws should not have applied. We were, by definition, a learning pod, but they were like, 'No, there are children here. You are a school,'" Amber said. She spoke with some attorneys who told her that she could push back using Texas's learning pod protection guidelines and likely prevail. Amber wondered what to do. She asked herself: "Do I choose to be right and go and put all my energy into 'I am right, you are wrong,' or do I keep my main focus and my main goal at my forefront?' That has always been the families and the children and the mission to provide a place for them to have rest and rejuvenation. I decided to go with the latter," she told me, soon after packing up and moving Leading Little Arrows out of its Arlington building.

Fortunately, Amber had already planned to open her second site in Irving, so she asked the pastor of that church location if she could push up the move-in date. The pastor agreed, and Amber continued to run Leading Little Arrows at the new location. It was inconvenient for many of her families, including some who now had to drive more than an hour to participate, but it didn't deter them. "I had 100 percent recommitment from my families," Amber said. "I didn't lose a single one because of our location change. We had two weeks to leave and get ready to go, but it has been beautiful to see the impact. I had one person tell me, 'I don't care if you go two hours away. I will drive wherever you are because this is a place where my grandson feels supported, and we've seen such growth.'"

Over the past several years of leading workshops with current and aspiring school founders across the United States, I've seen that zoning issues, like those Amber encountered, are always at the top of the list of startup challenges. Local zoning and land use ordinances often limit the number and type of properties that founders can consider, and can relegate new schools and learning spaces to less desirable locations, such as commercial properties on busy streets with no outdoor space. They can also prevent founders from opening new locations as their enrollment grows, constraining the supply of these innovative options. In 2024, Utah took on this issue, specifically as it relates to microschools. With advocacy from the Libertas Institute, a Utah free-market think tank, the state legislature passed a land use and zoning bill that enables microschools and similar small educational businesses to operate in all zones—including residential and agricultural zones. The new law defines a "home-based microschool" as serving sixteen or fewer students, and a community-based "micro-education entity" as serving one hundred or fewer students.

## Challenges

Utah's new law is already helping school founders. Todd Hepworth, the cofounder of Orchard STEM School in rural Utah described in Chapter 5, said that this new zoning law will make it easier for microschools like his to operate and grow, granting microschools the same zoning considerations as public schools. "Now, microschools can be located in the same residential zones as public schools, and that's much better for students and families," Todd said.

JeVonne Tanner is a former public high school biology teacher who cofounded CHOICE: An Acton Academy microschool in Bountiful, Utah, just outside of Salt Lake City. She agrees with Todd that the new microschool legislation is helpful for founders. JeVonne and her husband Paul opened their school in 2020 and encountered frustrating and costly zoning-related burdens. JeVonne says that those hassles would have been avoided if the new law had been in place then. "We wish we had this when we started because cities didn't know how to classify us, zoning was always an issue, and landlords didn't want to change the type of occupancy to be a school to meet the additional requirements typical of a larger school."

West Virginia also created new legislation specifically defining microschools and exempting microschoolers from state compulsory school attendance laws, in the same way that homeschoolers are exempt from these laws. Several West Virginia founders told me that the microschooling carve-out made it simpler and more straightforward for them to launch their desired programs, which are more structured than independent, parent-directed homeschooling and more flexible and personalized than traditional private schooling. Additional zoning-related legislation passed in Florida in 2024 to make it easier for microschools and similar models to operate in more locations, such as churches, theaters, museums, and libraries.[8] While new legislation around emerging schooling models may be helpful, the reality is that education entrepreneurs are moving ahead to create these models with or without it.

## FUNDING

Jockeying for the top spot among the challenges that new school founders face is funding. In my workshops, entrepreneurs share two main funding-related obstacles: access to startup capital and affordability for families. In addition to addressing zoning constraints for microschools, Utah is again among the states tackling the latter. In 2023, Utah implemented a universal school choice policy that makes each K–12 student eligible to access about $8,000 each year to use on various education options, including microschools, pods, and homeschooling collaboratives. Already low-cost, these programs become even more so with these new school choice policies.

While innovative schools and spaces are starting and spreading across the United States, including in states without school choice policies, they may have a higher likelihood of long-term success in places where education funding follows the student. This was a lesson learned from the failed "free school" movement of the 1960s that I discussed in Chapter 2. In his 1972 paper on the decline of the free schools, Allen Graubard foreshadowed where we are today: "It is obvious that if there were some arrangement such as a voucher plan where parents were given a choice as to where their tax money for education went, there would be much more participation in free schools than there is now. Many people are still involved in public schools only because there isn't a free school in their locality or because they can't afford to pay tuition," he wrote.[9] The ability for innovative schools to participate in emerging school choice programs can help ensure their longer-term viability.

While school choice programs can help make new schools and spaces more accessible for families, they can also motivate more parents and teachers to become founders. This was true for Kanesha Adams, a former public school teacher in Arkansas. She had been intrigued by the idea of education entrepreneurship for several years, but it wasn't until Arkansas passed a universal school choice policy in 2023 that she took the leap.

Kanesha launched The Learning Lounge, a tutoring center and microschool in Pine Bluff, Arkansas, that serves mostly low-income, Black and brown students—including many who are neurodiverse and have few other education options beyond a local public school. Kanesha grew up in Pine Bluff, which is considered to be one of the most dangerous cities in the United States according to violent crime statistics.[10] A quarter of its residents live in poverty, according to the US Census Bureau. She graduated from the city's public high school and taught in the district's schools, but she wanted to create a more individualized, learner-centered space that would be safe and nurturing for local youth.

All of Kanesha's students are legally considered homeschoolers who attend her faith-based microschool five days a week at no cost. "One hundred percent of our movement was because the funding became available," Kanesha told me regarding her decision to launch The Learning Lounge. "Without that, we wouldn't have been able to even think about how to make this vision happen for our students because we know our families at this time can't fund a private, tuition-based opportunity. But it does not mean that they don't deserve it. They definitely deserve it," said Kanesha, who plans to scale her program by opening additional Learning Lounge locations throughout Arkansas in the coming years.

As for the other startup funding challenge—access to capital—this is a big barrier for founders in general, as the 2022 polling of would-be entrepreneurs cited at the beginning of this chapter revealed. Entrepreneurs display a willingness to assume a significant financial risk, often by tapping into their own personal savings or taking loans from family and friends, knowing that their endeavor could very well fail. Kanesha, for instance, traded in two small retirement accounts and used her savings to launch The Learning Lounge in October 2023. Most of those funds went toward renting a space—a small, stand-alone building near the University of Arkansas at Pine Bluff—and bringing it up to code. Later, she received a $10,000 microgrant from VELA, the philanthropic nonprofit and education entrepreneur network.

Kanesha also applied for additional grant and recognition programs during her launch year, including from State Policy Network's Ed-Prize, and the Yass Prize for sustainable, transformational, outstanding, and permissionless (S.T.O.P.) education, which has awarded $1 million to one innovative education organization annually through 2024, along with significant monetary awards for roughly forty finalists and semifinalists. In 2023, the Yass Prize organization issued awards to founders totaling more than $20 million. While it's great to see philanthropic interest in supporting education entrepreneurs, founders shouldn't rely on philanthropic funding in either the startup or growth phases of their enterprise—with an occasional exception.

"This is too good to be true," Imani Jackson said when she first stumbled upon the website for the Wildflower Montessori microschool network in 2020. "Nobody's just going to give me money to help me start a school. That's got to be a scam," she thought. Imani had worked as a public school teacher in Maryland and Pennsylvania before shifting to teaching second grade at an established private school in Philadelphia during the 2019/2020 school year. When COVID descended during the spring semester, her school closed and Imani began teaching her students remotely from home, alongside her two-year-old daughter. Imani had always been curious about homeschooling but knew she wouldn't have the time to do it for her own child. COVID's school closures provided the time and the opportunity for her to give it a try.

Imani began researching different homeschool approaches and initially gravitated toward Charlotte Mason. "I loved Charlotte Mason because of the emphasis on beautiful books, but she also suggests that you be outside four to six hours a day, and my daughter was not having that," Imani said, prompting her to move on to the Montessori method. COVID pushed many educational organizations to begin putting materials online and offering various webinars, which is how Imani fell in love with Montessori. "Really what hooked me was a webinar about Montessori herself and her story. I was like, 'Why do more people not know that this is amazing?'" said Imani, who was particularly captivated by Maria Montessori's path as a physician turned educator.

Imani began contemplating the idea of opening a Montessori school and started googling. The Wildflower Montessori website was the top hit. Certain that it was a scam, Imani dismissed it, eventually returning to in-person teaching at the private school and forgetting about Wildflower until about two years later when she again ran her Google search and again spotted Wildflower at the top of the list. She saw that Wildflower's number of member schools had grown since her previous search. Imani wondered if the network was legitimate after all. She sent a web inquiry, but it was Presidents' Day weekend 2022, and she didn't expect to hear back from anyone for a few days. Instead, she got a note back within a few hours from Sunny Greenberg, a longtime educator who supports Wildflower teacher-entrepreneurs in the Philadelphia area.

Over the next two years, Imani worked closely with Sunny and the Wildflower team to sketch out what her school startup would look like, as well as begin her training to become a Montessori-certified teacher. Her goal was to bring an accessible K–8, African-centered, Montessori microschool to the children of Philadelphia's Germantown neighborhood. She wanted this for her own daughter and for others in the neighborhood, which lacked education options beyond traditional public schools.

Since launching its first microschool in Massachusetts in 2014, the Wildflower network has grown to include more than sixty teacher-founded, independently operated microschools across the United States, including Puerto Rico. Most are private schools, but the network also supports teacher-entrepreneurs who have launched public charter microschools in Minneapolis, New York City, and Washington, DC, as well as throughout Colorado. Imani discovered that the Wildflower startup funding was not, in fact, a scam. The nonprofit Wildflower Foundation provides a school incubator program to guide founders toward launch, as well as operational support and startup capital for teacher-entrepreneurs within their network, including grants and loans. These are primarily available to founders seeking to launch their microschools in low-income and underserved communities.

Since the pandemic, and especially since 2022, interest in Wildflower's model has surged. For example, during the 2018/2019 school year, about seventeen prospective teacher-entrepreneurs completed a "start a school" form on the Wildflower website each month. During the 2022/2023 school year, that number jumped to an average of twenty-two submissions each month, and rose even higher the following academic year to a monthly average of twenty-eight. Toward the end of the 2023/2024 school year, Wildflower received more than forty monthly submissions from aspiring founders. As these numbers show, microschooling's momentum continues to build and accelerate.

Imani was able to secure initial grant funding as well as take on a low-interest loan available through the Wildflower Foundation. "You have to show that your school can be profitable by year three and that you can pay the loan off in seven years," Imani said regarding loan eligibility, adding that, as a founder, she is also expected to personally contribute at least 10 percent of the startup costs. The average loan amount for Wildflower microschools is between $100,000 and $200,000. As of 2024, Wildflower had provided more than $5 million in loans with zero defaults.

Beyond its financial resources, Imani says some of the biggest support from Wildflower comes in the form of encouragement and knowledge offered by the network's community of founders and mentors. That support is what enabled her to quit her teaching job and launch Poinciana Montessori in the fall of 2024. It's also why she recommends founders seek out similar network affiliations or founder communities to help overcome the inevitable challenges of education entrepreneurship. "There will be ups and downs along the way," Imani said, adding: "Take a deep breath and get through it—and try and get support any way that you can."

*Chapter Reflections for Parents and Founders*
Entrepreneurship in any sector is filled with challenges. Founders often confront funding limitations and location headaches, regulatory barriers, competition, and shifting customer preferences. Developing an awareness of these challenges early in the process of finding or building a school can help you to anticipate and better navigate them if they occur. Following are some recommendations to consider.

**Parents:** If you are a parent who is interested in choosing an innovative school or space for your children, you are entrepreneurial too. You recognize the limitations of the standard schooling model and are willing to try something new and different. You are okay with uncertainty and comfortable with the unfamiliar. It's important to remember that if you are choosing a startup school for your child, the entrepreneur is running a small business—perhaps the first one she has ever run. The more help and support you can give her, the better equipped she will be to create a flourishing and sustainable program. It's also important to remember that many small businesses fail within the first few years of operation, and the startup school you have chosen could, unfortunately, be one of them.

Still, there are some things parents can do to minimize risk and spot potential challenges when evaluating various schools and spaces prior to enrolling. Here is a list of questions to ask a founder when scoping out schools and spaces:

- Why did you decide to create this school?
- How long has your school been operating?
- How has enrollment changed since your launch? Have you gained or lost students? (Declining enrollment could be a warning sign.)
- How has staffing changed since your launch? Are you hiring?
- Are you running this school full-time or do you have another job? How often are you onsite at the school? If the school has multiple locations, how much time do you spend at each?

- Do you expect to retire or shift away from day-to-day school operations sometime soon? If so, what is your succession plan?
- Are your children or family members enrolled at this school? If not, why not?
- What are your plans for this location? Do you expect to remain here or move to a different space? (A founder's plans for her location can help you assess a program's financial stability. For instance, if the founder is investing in renovations or expansion, or moving to a larger location, it can be a sign of operational strength. If the founder is planning to move to a less convenient location, it's good to know sooner than later.)
- Is your school financially sustainable? Are you able to take a paycheck from the school? (A founder may not tell you the answer, but it could be worth asking anyway.)
- How many of your students are attending with the help of financial aid? (While it's commendable that schools want to make their programs more accessible through scholarships and financial aid, an imbalance between the number of reduced-tuition and full-pay students could signal financial instability. This is less of an issue in states that have private school choice programs that enable taxpayer-subsidized tuition, but in states without these policies, too many students on financial aid could be a fiscal warning sign.)
- If something unexpected were to happen and you had to close down, what other schools or spaces would you recommend to your current families?

**Founders:** You will most definitely encounter challenges on your school startup journey. Here are five thoughts to consider before you begin:

1. **Determine your commitment level.** Make sure that being a school founder is truly your passion. Is this something you feel

ready and eager to take on? Are you willing and able to quit your day job to give it a go? Some founders are able to work full-time or part-time at another job while launching a new school, but it can be very difficult and can sometimes prevent your new school culture from coalescing the way you hope. Making sure you're fully committed to being a founder can help you navigate the ups and downs of entrepreneurship.

2. **Do your research.** Gaining an upfront understanding of some of the regulatory obstacles you may encounter could help you determine the type of program you want to open, such as a private school or a homeschool learning center, as well as give you a better sense of which cities or counties in your area may be most welcoming to your idea.

3. **Understand the financial burdens and barriers.** Most school founders have to bootstrap their business idea, often dipping into savings or borrowing money from family and friends to get started. While there are some philanthropic funding sources, they are few and far between and likely won't cover all your initial expenses. Make sure you're ready for the financial commitment of being a founder, and that you fully understand the statistically strong likelihood of business failure.

4. **Gather support.** Being an entrepreneur can feel lonely. Connect with a community of founders and mentors to gain support and encouragement before and during your launch. Choosing to launch your school or space as an affiliate member of a national network, such as Acton Academy or Wildflower, can give you immediate access to peer resources and reassurance. You can also seek out support from national entrepreneur networks, such as VELA or the National Microschooling Center, or find— or create—grassroots education entrepreneur communities in your local area. Building community with other founders will

make your startup experience more enjoyable and less stressful, and may increase your odds of long-term success.

5. **Advocate policy changes.** Work to remove regulatory barriers to education entrepreneurship, including burdensome zoning, occupancy, and licensing rules that prevent innovative schools and spaces from starting or scaling. Support school choice efforts that enable education funding to follow families to microschools, pods, hybrid homeschools, and similar programs to make these models more accessible to those who want them.

# Part III
# TRANSFORM

## Chapter 10

# Expansions

*There is no one straight path to scale. It's deeply personal to each company's experience.*

—Donna Levin (cofounder of Care.com)

Today's new alternative education models are sometimes dismissed as insignificant due to their small size and decentralized nature. After all, how could microschools, pods, or homeschooling collectives really make a meaningful difference in the larger, better-resourced, well-established K–12 education system? In the early 2000s, the cofounders of a scrappy startup wondered the same thing about a different, seemingly unshakable industry. They approached the dominant market leader with a proposal to collaborate on a new model that promised to propel the entire industry toward greater personalization and convenience. The incumbent CEO allegedly tried hard to contain his laughter, rejecting the startup as nothing but a "very small niche business." It wouldn't make a dent.

Less than a decade later, that industry leader—Blockbuster—filed for bankruptcy. By 2014, the video rental behemoth had shuttered all its corporate stores across the country, as startup Netflix gained market share through its pioneering mail-order and online streaming video services. By 2023, Netflix was worth an estimated $150 billion, and there was only one remaining independent store operating under the Blockbuster brand.[1] Now, who is the very small, niche business?

Small is scalable. While most of the entrepreneurial parents and teachers who are currently launching their small schools and similar learning programs have no plans to build billion-dollar companies and upend the entire education sector, in aggregate these low-cost, lean schools and spaces promise to be just as disruptive. Like Netflix's founders, these education entrepreneurs recognize the growing market demand for more personalized, responsive, and relevant offerings. They are building learning environments to meet that demand. Together, these small businesses are having a transformational impact on how parents, teachers, students, and policymakers view education and the future of learning.

Remember that small businesses led by everyday entrepreneurs form the backbone of the American economy. Likewise, small schools and spaces run by ordinary entrepreneurs are gradually forming America's education backbone as well. We see this trend reflected in mounting data showing a decline in traditional public school enrollment that is separate from anticipated enrollment declines due to falling US birth rates. A 2024 NBC News analysis of US Census Bureau data attributed a 4 percent decline in public school enrollment to increases in various alternatives to traditional schooling, including microschooling, homeschooling, and charter schooling. While acknowledging that new school choice policies in some states could be accelerating the decline in public school enrollment, NBC found that the dip is occurring even in states without school choice policies. Kentucky, for example, has no private school choice programs and no charter schools, yet it had the largest decline in public school enrollment between 2012 and 2022.[2] Parents want something different for their children's education, and entrepreneurs are creating it.

Most of these entrepreneurs are content to run one program in one location that serves one community of learners. The growth of today's creative schooling options will be defined by the continued emergence of these small schools and spaces across the United States. Some founders, however, want to scale their individual businesses to reach more families and learners. Scaling has its own set of challenges that both families and founders will want to look out for. If you are an education entrepreneur, it can be helpful to think about potential scalability early on. According to PayPal cofounder Peter Thiel: "A good startup should have the potential for great scale built into its first design."[3] Even if you decide to stay small and niche, exploring what scalability could look like, as well as the potential rewards and drawbacks of growth, can help strengthen your startup. If you are a parent considering enrolling your child in a growing school network, this chapter can help you spot potential pitfalls.

The founders I've talked to who decide to expand beyond a single location or service offering typically do so for one (or all) of the following reasons:

Superior offering—The founder knows that she has built something stellar and wants to spread her model far and wide, often by helping other founders get started.

Unmet demand—The founder recognizes growing demand for her program that can't be adequately met in one location.

Wealth creation—The founder wants to create a successful education business that enables her to build and pass on wealth.

## FRANCHISING

For Shiren Rattigan, each of these reasons contributed to her decision to scale her single microschool into a franchise model, but wealth creation was a top motivator. "My dad's a truck driver with a third-grade education," Shiren said, explaining that the idea of building and passing on wealth through entrepreneurship has been largely absent in her family until now. "I want to be able to accumulate and alchemize all the ancestral knowledge so that my lineage doesn't have to continue to start from scratch every generation. I want something that is more permanent and will continue to feed, clothe, and house my great-great-great-grandchildren. My calling is to be an educator, and I could not do that within the system," she told me.

Shiren didn't start off thinking about scale. She hadn't even considered being an education entrepreneur until 2020's school closures. She is, first and foremost, a teacher—a fifth-generation one at that. Her great-great Aunt Florence was a teacher, followed by her great-grandmother who taught in a one-room schoolhouse on an Illinois farm. Her grandmother and mother then taught in schools throughout the Midwest. She always knew that teaching was her life's purpose. "I think it's in my blood," Shiren said. She began her career as a public middle school teacher in a poor suburb of Chicago where more than 80 percent of the students qualified for free and reduced-cost lunch, but quit when she was expecting her second child. "I was eight months pregnant with my middle child, and I was restraining a kid on the floor trying to break up a fight," she recalled. It wasn't the first time that Shiren had broken up fights at school, but it was the first time that it occurred to her that the fights were not only dangerous to students but also dangerous to her and her unborn child. "That was it for me," said Shiren, who left the public schools, lived internationally, and ultimately moved to Florida to teach at an established private Montessori school.

That's where she was working in March 2020. Like everyone, Shiren sheltered at home that spring, juggling remote learning with her students as well as her three young daughters. By summer, Shiren was approached by a few families from the Montessori school who asked if she would lead an independent "pandemic pod" for them during the upcoming school year. She eagerly agreed, leaving her job at the Montessori school to become an education entrepreneur. Her pod with five learners began with boxes of Montessori materials and manipulatives that she dropped off at her students' homes on Sunday nights. The pod worked through these boxes together over Zoom throughout the week, and Shiren gradually began adding in-person days. "It evolved from there and we decided we wanted to meet once a week, then twice a week, and then three times a week," said Shiren, whose Montessori-inspired pod continued long after local schools reopened for in-person learning.

Shiren realized that she liked being an education entrepreneur, appreciating the freedom to lead her own program untethered by a school's set curriculum and practices. Families liked it too, with more seeking to join. "I wanted to offer this to more people, and I wanted it to be accessible. Accessibility is so important to me," Shiren said. Even though her program's tuition was below that of many traditional private schools in the area, Shiren knew it was still financially out of reach for a lot of families. She decided to transform her pod into a recognized private school in Florida so that low-income families would be able to attend her program through the state's school choice scholarship program.

In the fall of 2021, Shiren launched her full-time secular microschool, Colossal Academy, with seven learners, growing to twelve by the end of the academic year. She soon outgrew the space she was subletting and moved into a 1,000-square-foot, butterfly-painted building in Fort Lauderdale in August 2022. I first met Shiren just two months after Colossal moved to its new space, where it serves about thirty-five middle and high school students. When I arrived, the tweens and teens were making homemade ravioli with hands-on instruction from an accomplished local chef who teaches culinary classes. Shiren is intent on utilizing the talent in her community to curate a relevant, engaging learning experience for her students. While core academics are accessed through a mastery-based online learning platform, much of the students' time is spent engaging with local people and programs and connecting student interests with available resources. Entrepreneurship is a key curriculum priority at Colossal, with students learning how to launch their own businesses and create value for themselves and others.

In 2023, Shiren decided to scale her business by creating a franchise model for Colossal Academy, helping other aspiring founders to launch microschools. Like most franchise networks, Colossal franchise operators, or "franchisees," purchase a license from the parent company, or "franchisor," to operate the business independently while adhering to all network branding, policies, and protocols. McDonald's is an example of a vast franchise network where franchisees follow the restaurant chain's uniform procedures and pay a royalty to the broader McDonald's Corporation while independently running their own restaurant locations.

Like many franchises, Colossal provides startup help to franchisees. This involves assistance with scoping and securing a location, utilizing Colossal curriculum and following the Colossal education model, recruiting students, and managing enrollment. "We thought that it would minimize the amount of stress and time that people are spending on starting," said Shiren, who charges a one-time franchise fee of $14,500 and 4 percent of the franchisee's annual revenue. New Colossal franchises have opened in Miami and Jacksonville, with others coming soon. "There are sixty-seven counties in Florida. In five years, I want to have a Colossal Academy operating in each one of them," said Shiren, who also plans to grow her microschool franchise network beyond Florida.

Priti Gandhi opened Colossal Miami in 2024. She had been a homeschooling mom to her two children, ages ten and twelve, since her oldest was two years old. Homeschooling emerged out of a desire for maximum flexibility and mobility, as Priti's family is based in Chicago while her husband's family lives in Miami and the couple wanted to split their time between both cities. Gradually, they began spending more of their time in Miami, building connections with the area's large homeschooling community and caring for Priti's mother-in-law, who was battling Alzheimer's disease. Her children attended a homeschool nature school in Miami two days a week while doing their academics at home and participating in other local homeschooling classes and field trips. When COVID came, all the in-person activities ended and nature school went online. In-person homeschooling programming resumed in her area in the fall of 2020, but Priti was hesitant about these meetups given her mother-in-law's failing health and compromised immune system. "We were very, very locked down as a family in 2020," Priti told me.

In 2021, the family began reconnecting with others and eventually Priti was approached by a few families to create her own small homeschool co-op as a spinoff from a much larger homeschooling group. She hosted the co-op, which included her two children and three other homeschoolers, at her home once a week. Everyone loved the co-op, including Priti, who valued its student-centered, hands-on, community-based approach. In the spring of 2023, Priti mentioned to one of the other co-op parents how great it would be if there was a microschool in Miami like those that were spreading quickly around Fort Lauderdale and elsewhere in Florida. The parent suggested that Priti connect with Shiren to see if she had any advice on how to launch a microschool.

"I wasn't thinking of opening a Colossal microschool at first. I was just thinking of a microschool," Priti said, but when she met Shiren that summer and learned more about her franchise vision, Priti was inspired. As a director of operations for a division of Kaplan, the national tutoring company, for ten years, Priti was comfortable with the idea of running a franchise business where she would have the autonomy to lead her own school while staying tied to Colossal's overall brand, processes, and pedagogy. "Shiren has already done so much of the legwork in terms of figuring everything out," Priti said. "The alignment is there. Colossal is everything that we've been doing for the last ten years in our homeschool. The Colossal model just really spoke to me."

Priti launched with ten students in her home in 2024. Several of her students came from local public schools because their parents were frustrated by a lack of outside time and individualized attention. Many are able to attend her program tuition-free through Florida's school choice programs. Priti's students have found her primarily through word-of-mouth referrals, but as she plans a move to a larger space and expand enrollment, she expects to do more marketing. She doesn't think it will be difficult to attract additional families. "In Miami, there's a real need for this type of model," Priti said, adding that some parents want an alternative to traditional public schools, and the nearby traditional private school costs a whopping $50,000 a year in tuition. "That's not really feasible for many people that I know," Priti said. "People are looking for a nontraditional, progressive, nature-based, project-based learning environment that is affordable, and Colossal offers all of that."

## GRASSROOTS ENTREPRENEUR NETWORKS

Shiren doesn't only want to expand her Colossal microschool model. She yearns to see the growth and diversification of creative, accessible education options throughout South Florida and beyond. Shiren talks about the "educational renaissance" occurring in the greater Fort Lauderdale area. Like the European Renaissance of the fifteenth and sixteenth centuries, this educational renaissance is defined by a shift from the outdated to the innovative, while reviving and adapting forgotten historical concepts such as the one-room schoolhouse.

In 2021, Shiren and fellow Fort Lauderdale founder Toni Frallicciardi joined forces to establish the Innovative Educators Network (InEd), a nonprofit organization designed to encourage and support education entrepreneurs in South Florida. The pair had already seen how collaboration could propel learning. Shiren's Colossal students spent every Friday learning STEM concepts through surfboarding and skateboarding in the classes that Toni and her husband Uli taught through their company, Surf Skate Science. As homeschooling parents, Toni and Uli decided to blend their passions for action sports and education to create an organization that today serves more than five hundred students a year—mostly homeschoolers and microschoolers from the surrounding counties.

Shiren and Toni wanted to facilitate greater connection and cooperation among new and established schools and spaces in their area. They began hosting regular meet-ups, growing from a handful of founders to now more than 120 innovative education organizations that collectively serve more than ten thousand learners each year. Founders in the InEd network meet and communicate frequently, sharing advice on everything from complying with local zoning regulations and where to find the best insurance quotes to curriculum suggestions and grant opportunities. They also refer families to each other's programs, helping to find the best educational fit for each child. "It is a space of noncompetitiveness, collaboration, and fellowship," Shiren said of InEd's appeal to founders. The network's efforts are helping to expand the availability of new learning options in South Florida, as well as support founders through the highs and lows of entrepreneurship. In early 2024, Shiren and Toni hosted their first InEd conference, which drew several hundred parents and founders seeking and building new schools and spaces. They have also overseen the expansion of InEd to include two additional chapters in Florida, each with more than thirty founders.

Fort Lauderdale may be this educational renaissance's Florence, but the movement is spreading. Grassroots organizations like InEd are emerging across the United States. Around the same time that Shiren and Toni were plotting the creation of their collaborative nonprofit, Dalena Wallace was doing the same thing in Wichita, Kansas. A homeschooling mom of six children who ran a small co-op, Dalena started connecting with other local parents and educators who were running small schools and homeschooling programs. Like Shiren and Toni, Dalena discovered many of these founders through VELA's online entrepreneur network; she was amazed that there were so many people doing so many creative things in education right in her own backyard. A handful of founders began meeting together in 2021 to create Wichita Innovative Schools and Educators (WISE), a small nonprofit like InEd that supports and encourages local education entrepreneurs while also serving as a resource for parents to learn about their education options in the area. Today, WISE has twenty-five member schools and spaces in its network, serving one thousand learners.

## SCALING SMART

Like Shiren and so many other founders, Elmarie Hyman's path to education entrepreneurship began with a small homeschool program that scaled into something far bigger. Born and raised in South Africa, Elmarie had never heard about homeschooling until she moved to the United States and settled in Southern California. She discovered homeschooling when the first of her four children was just a baby. "I said, 'Oh my gosh, there's a space where you could actually have fun learning? That sounds like a paradox,'" recalled Elmarie, who had attended traditional schools and pursued a career as an accountant. She knew she wanted a more unconventional, enjoyable learning path for her children.

In her early days of homeschooling, Elmarie joined various homeschooling co-ops and participated in local homeschooling activities. She noticed that once homeschoolers in her area reached high school age, many of them swapped homeschooling for traditional schooling—often because they were seeking a larger cohort of kids with whom to learn and interact. Elmarie decided that if she wanted homeschooling to remain appealing to her children and their homeschooled friends well into adolescence, then she would need to create a compelling co-learning community to compete with traditional high schools.

She opened Learn Beyond the Book LLC in 2012 as a secular homeschooling resource center just outside of Los Angeles. It started with more than twenty homeschoolers in a single location in Santa Clarita Valley and has scaled to more than four hundred in-person K–12 learners and forty-five paid teachers in three locations, with more growth on the horizon. Assorted low-cost, a la carte classes in a variety of core academic and enrichment areas are offered from 9:30 a.m. to 4:00 p.m. every day, running in sixteen-week semester increments. Some students attend classes all day every day, but most attend two days a week to complement their other homeschooling activities.

While California does not have private school choice programs, it has long had public charter schools that cater to homeschooling families with either a home-based independent study option or a hybrid option that blends at-home and school-based learning. In 2017, the roughly 125,000 students enrolled in home-based independent study charter schools in California represented more than 20 percent of all charter school students in the state.[4] Students in these programs—often known as "public homeschooling" or "homeschool charter schools"—are technically enrolled in a tuition-free public charter school, but their learning looks more like homeschooling, with flexible, individualized curriculum and family-centered learning.

Students in these homeschool charter school programs are expected to meet regularly with a certified teacher, use a curriculum that is aligned with state standards (albeit usually with many curriculum options from which to choose), and participate in state-standardized testing. Learn Beyond the Book is an approved vendor for more than two dozen homeschool-focused charter schools in California, enabling homeschoolers to take several classes each semester at no cost while paying out-of-pocket for additional courses if they choose. About 80 percent of Elmarie's students are enrolled in one of the California homeschool charter schools.

Elmarie's enrollment at her flagship Santa Clarita location grew gradually in its first three years of operating, mostly through word-of-mouth referrals from current families. She wasn't planning on scaling to new locations but, in 2015, a mom of a student was growing tired of the 30-minute daily drive from her home in the San Fernando Valley and asked if Elmarie would launch a second location in that area, which she did. As that second location neared enrollment capacity, she saw gathering interest for a third location in Woodland Hills, so she took the chance on opening a third site in 2024. Elmarie also began offering live, virtual classes over Zoom for students who wanted a remote option. She currently has one hundred additional students enrolled in her online program.

Now, Elmarie is considering her first out-of-state location in the Phoenix area, where students would be able to attend tuition-free using Arizona's universal school choice programs. "I've always had this dream about a school that is full-time, but that is also a hybrid for homeschoolers. I want to do it in a different state than California because of all the rules here," Elmarie said. She is collaborating with three teachers in Arizona, including one who previously worked for Elmarie in California, to potentially open a pilot school. "It will start as something small and then hopefully continue growing," said Elmarie, who has some concerns about scaling to new, far-off locations. "I wouldn't be able to just drive there if there's a problem," she said, explaining that her decision to open more out-of-state locations will depend on how confident she is that her local on-site teachers can retain the vision and quality of Learn Beyond the Book. "The problem is if you get somebody who doesn't really represent your vision, then it is a mess."

## WHEN SCALING GOES SOUTH

Scaling seems to be working well so far for Shiren and Elmarie, but it's not always a success. Ada Salie learned this the hard way. In 2020, the homeschooling mom of three young children began hosting regular activities for the ballooning number of families who flocked to homeschooling during the first pandemic year. In her state of Massachusetts, more than seven thousand students statewide transferred from public schools into homeschooling in 2020, compared to only eight hundred homeschooling transfers the previous year.[5]

Word of Ada's homeschool gatherings grew. When it became increasingly clear that school disruptions and virus-mitigation policies would continue into a second school year, Ada was hearing the frustrations of many parents who were looking for alternatives to a traditional school. In August of 2021, she decided to take a chance and launch Life Rediscovered, a full-time K–6 microschool for homeschoolers, committing herself to a three-year lease on a stand-alone commercial building in the town of Westborough, about thirty-five miles west of Boston.

The first year was rough, with Ada thinking several times about giving up. She dealt with staff and student turnover, lack of funding, and regulatory uncertainty. Yet, she persevered. "As an entrepreneur, the road gets really hard sometimes and sometimes you just want to quit, but you can't," Ada told me when I had her on my podcast about six months after her microschool opened. For Ada, signing the lengthy lease kept her committed to entrepreneurship whether she liked it or not. "I think that if I knew everything that was involved in starting this business, I wouldn't have started it because it's been way harder than I ever could have imagined," Ada said.

This is a sentiment echoed over and over by entrepreneurs. They say that if they had overthought the startup process, or spent years planning a launch, it never would have happened. It's the fearless drive to act that separates entrepreneurs from the rest of the pack. "If we realized the pain and suffering, just how vulnerable you're going to feel, and the challenges that you're going to endure, the embarrassment and the shame, and the list of all the things that go wrong, I don't think anyone would start a company.

Nobody in their right mind would do it," said Jensen Huang, cofounder and CEO of the technology company NVIDIA, which in March 2024 became only the third company in US history to reach a $2 trillion market capitalization. In an interview on the *Acquired* podcast, Huang said that if he had to do it all over again, knowing what he knows now about being an entrepreneur, he probably wouldn't have launched at all. It's that hard. Luckily, this ignorance can be an entrepreneur's best friend. "I think that's kind of the superpower of an entrepreneur," Huang said of founders being blissfully unaware of how hard it is to start a new business.[6]

That same entrepreneurial bliss led Ada to decide to scale her Montessori-inspired homeschool program in 2023. She kept hearing from families north and south of Boston who said they desperately wanted their kids to attend Life Rediscovered, but the location was too far away. Ada decided to launch a second location in the spring of 2023 and a third that fall. It didn't go well. By December, both satellite sites closed. "Honestly, I just bit off more than I could chew," Ada told me. She didn't anticipate how much direct involvement she would need to have in those two additional locations. "In hindsight, I should have hired another me to be in each of those new locations," she said.

A 2011 report by Startup Genome of more than three thousand internet tech startups found that nearly three-quarters of them failed due to premature scaling, or growing too fast.[7] Quickly scaling the startup team was highlighted as a key vulnerability, as it can be difficult to maintain quality and vision across the organization in a startup's early days. Similarly, Ada felt the need to grow her team but wasn't able to ensure the staff quality and commitment needed to maintain successful satellite locations. It's one of the key things Elmarie worries about when considering a possible out-of-state expansion.

I checked in with Ada in early 2024, soon after she closed her satellite locations. She was coming up on the end of her three-year lease agreement at her original location. That site was running sustainably, but it was still a lot of work on top of a very busy year that included the birth of her fourth child. "I could walk away," Ada told me, acknowledging that it was that hefty lease agreement that had motivated her to keep going through all the previous ups and downs. "I could let go of all the stress, all the responsibilities, and just homeschool my kids at home," she said. That would be the easy path, but Ada doesn't feel it's the right path for her. She has gained so much, both personally and professionally, from the community of families she serves and believes that running Life Rediscovered is one way she can make a positive impact. "I really feel like the way I can serve the world and serve my community and make the world a better place is by running this program. So, I'm choosing to continue finding ways forward," she told me.

Ada moved her main microschool from its original commercial building to a local gymnastics space nearby. She continues to feel the pull to open additional locations, including in some of the areas where she launched her early satellite programs. In May 2024, Life Rediscovered was approved as a recognized private school in her Massachusetts town, but zoning and building code issues for the location she wanted prevented Ada from operating as such for the 2024/2025 academic year. Running as a private school is her plan for the future. For now, Ada is focused on steadying rather than scaling her business, and on securing its long-term financial and operational durability. "We have awesome families and awesome staff, and we're going into our fourth year as a happy homeschool program," Ada said, adding that if she can make it to year five without shutting down, as nearly half of US small businesses do by that time, she will be even more proud of what she has built.

Whether through franchising, helping other founders start similar schools, opening additional locations, or creating hyperlocal education networks, entrepreneurial parents and teachers are showing how their tiny programs can transform education in titanic ways. Can the ongoing expansion of innovation occurring outside the conventional classroom make its way inside traditional schools and systems? The next chapter explores some answers.

*Chapter Reflections for Parents and Founders*

Today's creative schooling options are expanding, which offers more opportunities for families to find what they want, as well as more possibilities for founders to scale their own programs. Below are some suggestions for parents to consider when analyzing a school or space that is in an expansion phase, as well as for founders wondering if and how to grow.

**Parents:** You may be thrilled to find that an education entrepreneur with an established program is opening an additional site in your community, but be aware of some of the potential perils of new startup locations. Talk with the founder about how often she expects to be onsite at the new location and how much attention she will be able to dedicate to it. Learn more about the staff members who will be working at the new location. What are their backgrounds and how aligned do they seem with the founder's vision?

If you are considering a school or space that is part of a franchise or an established network of schools, you may feel more reassured about the program's operations and outlook for long-term success. Still, just because a school or space might be part of a broader network or franchise, you will want to make sure it meets your expectations and reflects the brand as you understand it.

**Founders:** Be careful about growing too quickly and scaling to new locations. The desire to meet mounting parent demand for your offerings is understandable, but make sure you're not spreading yourself too thin. How often will you be able to be present at each new location? How strong are your staff members there? Do they fully get your vision and do they share your passion for quality and responsiveness? Scaling slowly and with a strong team in place can improve your odds of a successful expansion.

If you are a current founder who believes that you have an educational model that works and that families flock toward, then you may want to consider creating your own franchise network. This will involve getting additional legal, financial, and business advisory help, along with putting proper policies in place for your franchisees, but it could be a worthwhile path to scale your business and achieve greater financial security.

If you are an aspiring founder, you may want to ask yourself whether or not you really have to recreate the wheel. If you are feeling the tug toward entrepreneurship but are not as excited about crafting a curriculum or creating all the school's branding and business procedures from scratch, you might want to consider a franchise or similar licensing model. The Colossal Academy franchise network, along with other microschool networks that operate in related ways such as Acton Academy, Wildflower Montessori, and Prenda (discussed more in the following chapter), could be worth exploring. Today's pioneering education entrepreneurs are creating pathways that make it much easier for future founders to get started.

## Chapter 11

# Intrapreneurs

*When people start saying you're crazy, you just might be on to the most important innovation of your life.*
—Larry Ellison (founder of Oracle)

In the spring of 2019, just a handful of weeks before my book *Unschooled* appeared on bookstore shelves, a new district high school was preparing to open in the city of Somerville, Massachusetts, just outside of Boston. Called Powderhouse Studios, it was the brainchild of Alec Resnick, an MIT graduate who had long been interested in alternative education models—specifically those focused on noncoercive, self-directed learning. He and his collaborators had been planning for Powderhouse's opening for seven years, gaining layers of bureaucratic approval for a truly innovative, in-district (non-charter) public school.

The idea emerged while Alec was running an afterschool program that embraced alternative education principles. He was encouraged by the city's mayor at the time to consider launching an innovative district school based on his afterschool program's model. Alec initially resisted, but the mayor's insistence eventually convinced him to give it a try. The vision was for Powderhouse to run more like a research and development lab than a school, with students working on elaborate, multi-month projects in partnership with peers and mentors while tying learning to state core curriculum standards. Students would decide what they would learn—and how. The school would run year-round, with students taking vacations or time off when they wanted—much like most adults do in their jobs. The Powderhouse vision was so innovative that in 2016 it was one of only ten US high school plans that won a $10 million innovation grant from the XQ Super School Project, an initiative supported by Laurene Powell Jobs, widow of Apple cofounder Steve Jobs.

Over the years of planning Powderhouse, Alec gained slow but steady green lights from the city and the school district, including the superintendent of schools who helped maintain momentum for the idea. Additionally, he was approved by the state to open Powderhouse as a designated "Innovation School," leveraging Massachusetts legislation enacted in 2010 to encourage in-district public-school experimentation. It enabled Alec to have more freedom and flexibility around hiring and firing decisions, attendance and scheduling policies, curriculum frameworks, and assessment measures. The Innovation School designation also enabled Alec to be exempt from collective bargaining agreements with the teachers' union, and to be able to hire noncertified teachers.

Despite the exemption, in January 2019, Alec was able to secure the blessing of the teachers' union for his school. It seemed like Powderhouse really was going to open that fall, using a lottery system for interested students to ensure a student body that mirrored the diversity of Somerville's public schools of roughly 42 percent Latino, 10 percent Black, and 43 percent low-income students. This would be sure to usher in a new era of in-district innovation for more public school systems to emulate. "Powderhouse could become a leading model for conventional schools hoping to reinvent themselves to become free and open community spaces committed to self-directed learning," I wrote in *Unschooled*, signaling that—hallelujah—unconventional education could indeed be successfully adopted by traditional public school systems.[1]

Then came the March 18 Somerville school committee meeting. Stunningly, the Powderhouse proposal was shot down. The school would not open at all. Boston's local *NPR* affiliate ran a story covering the decision. "I can't look at Powderhouse in isolation," the school committee chairwoman told the reporter. "I have a responsibility to the 5,000 students currently in our system. If we approve the school, some of them will go there, but what does it mean for everybody?"[2] Powderhouse was only projected to serve about 160 high school students. Because not everybody would be able to participate, then nobody should, or so the school committee said. Even the mayor, who persuaded Alec to create Powderhouse in the first place, refused to support the school during the school committee meeting, stating: "We need to evaluate all investments through an equity lens. We are striving to close equity gaps, and I'm worried that this could inadvertently grow inequities."[3]

This is not only the wrong way to approach innovation, but it also highlights the difficulty of adopting alternative education models within conventional public schools. Imagine if Motorola had the same attitude when it invented the first cell phone in 1973. Imagine if company executives said, yes, this is a great product and can be truly transformative, but because not everyone can have one right away, then no one can. Innovation often happens on the edges. It takes experimentation and iteration. It takes time and investment. If new products and services prove worthy, then they spread into the mainstream, becoming more widespread and accessible. Today, there are more cell phone subscriptions globally than there are people on Earth.[4] If Powderhouse had been allowed to take off—and if it had succeeded—it could have quickly spread to any student or school system that wanted it. We'll never know how successful and scalable that in-district innovation could have been.

For his part, Alec says there is more to the story. While concerns around equity and access were clearly part of the reason for Powderhouse's demise, he believes there were other contributing factors. "It was really about money and control," Alec told me after the Powderhouse project stalled. The superintendent, who had been continuously supportive, withdrew her endorsement of Powderhouse just before the crucial school committee meeting, making it difficult for others to continue to champion the project. She wanted the grant money Powderhouse had raised to go to the district, not just to Powderhouse, and also had concerns about the future operating costs of the new school when and if the grant money dried up. Additionally, there was growing discomfort about how autonomous Powderhouse would be, and how rigidly Alec was holding to his vision of a fully self-directed, noncoercive public school.

I caught up with Alec five years after that March 2019 debacle. He has pivoted the Powderhouse model to a new program focused on older teenagers and young adults. Through private philanthropy, this new version of Powderhouse operates as a tuition-free private school retaining the original educational vision but with the goal of operating with legal and financial parity to public schools. In the 2023/2024 academic year, it served fourteen students ages sixteen to twenty-four, including traditionally schooled students looking for an alternative, homeschoolers, post-high school students pursuing a gap year, and other young adults interested in support for their self-directed learning endeavors. "We decided to start older and grow younger," Alec said. He plans to expand Powderhouse downward in the coming years to serve younger students who reflect the demographic and socioeconomic diversity of Somerville, ultimately becoming a K–16 program serving students into young adulthood.

Alec still clings to the hope that someday Powderhouse and similar initiatives can be publicly supported—including within traditional school districts. He sees Powderhouse as part laboratory, part demonstration project, and is working on tools and resources to hopefully make it easier for founders to start similarly innovative schools. Alec believes that the combination of invention and advocacy, or introducing new educational designs while promoting public investment in educational innovation, is the path forward.

Can out-of-system, innovative educational models be incorporated into traditional public schools and prompt positive, systemic change? The Powderhouse story reveals how difficult this can be. Money and control are enormous obstacles to overcome, but there are visionary educators working within traditional public school systems who are showing how it can be done. They are education "intrapreneurs," or teachers and administrators with an entrepreneurial spirit who are committed to in-system innovation. Like their out-of-system counterparts, these intrapreneurs confront many challenges and barriers as they help bring forth more individualized, flexible, student-centered learning experiences in their schools and districts. They are also learning from, and inspired by, out-of-system entrepreneurs and what they are building.

## SCHOOL-BASED MICROSCHOOLS

Robby Meldau is one of these intrapreneurs. For the past eight years, he has been the principal of the Eisenhower Center for Innovation, a K–6 Title 1 public elementary school in Mesa, Arizona, serving predominantly low-income students of color. Robby began his career in education with Teach for America, teaching at a public charter school in South Phoenix that regularly displayed a willingness to try new things. He began thinking about ways to innovate traditional schools from within and later accepted the principal job at Eisenhower on the heels of a multiyear effort to improve learning outcomes at the school. "To go from that charter school to what I would say is a very standard district neighborhood elementary school was an abrupt transition," Robby told me. Nevertheless, he was eager for the challenge of promoting in-system innovation. In 2019, Robby heard about a new microschool model that was being pioneered by entrepreneur and Mesa resident Kelly Smith.

A mild-mannered father of four with a master's degree in nuclear engineering from MIT, Kelly had recently created Prenda, a microschool network. After selling a small software company focused on green energy in 2013, Kelly had begun leading informal, afterschool coding clubs for kids at the nearby public library. That experience was eye-opening. He watched children who were completely disengaged at school come alive in the coding club, where they were empowered to work on projects that most mattered to them. Lethargic learners became passionate programmers. Soon, his Prenda Code Clubs began launching in libraries across Arizona and nationwide. Kelly began to wonder: Why can't schooling be more like these coding clubs? Ever the entrepreneur, he decided to build the school he imagined was possible—one in which young people would be granted respect and autonomy and encouraged to drive their own learning while being supported by a personalized curriculum and caring adults.

In January 2018, Kelly piloted the first Prenda Microschool in his living room with his fifth-grade son and six other neighborhood children spanning fifth through eighth grade. A mix between homeschooling and traditional schooling, Prenda aims to support tiny learning communities that meet daily and tailor education to each child's needs and interests while utilizing a variety of widely available educational technology tools. Leveraging a proprietary software platform that Kelly built, Prenda helps learners set and track academic and personal goals, with adult guidance. Each day is separated into four primary learning modes focusing on core academic content as well as social-emotional learning and collaborative and individual projects.

The pilot program was a success, and that fall, Kelly expanded Prenda beyond his living room, helping other parents run Prenda microschools out of their homes for their children and others in their community. Each

Prenda microschool typically has ten or fewer mixed-age K–8 learners. Over its first eighteen months, eighty Prenda microschools opened throughout Arizona, serving about 550 students. Kelly was accepted into Silicon Valley's Y Combinator startup-accelerator program and secured significant venture capital funding for Prenda, helping to propel the business forward.

Kelly wanted the individualized, learner-driven microschool model to be available to more students, and he wanted to equip entrepreneurial parents and teachers with the tools and confidence to open their own Prenda microschools. Prenda became an approved vendor for certain Arizona virtual charter schools, which are tuition-free, taxpayer-funded online public schools. He began introducing Prenda into states with expanding school choice policies that would allow more students to attend a microschool tuition-free. With the rapid expansion of universal school choice policies in Arizona and elsewhere, along with the massive education disruption brought on by COVID, Prenda has helped more than a thousand founders create microschools since that first living-room pod in 2018, reaching some ten thousand students.

Tapping into school choice policies was one strategy to expand microschooling's accessibility, but Kelly also thought Prenda could work well within traditional public schools. "My hope was to be as inclusive as possible. I think that education should be a great leveler for society, and I wasn't interested in building something just for upper-middle-class white kids," Kelly told me. He got connected to Robby at Eisenhower and set up a meeting. "It was one of those meetings I'll remember forever because he immediately understood what I was doing and why. He just got excited about it," Kelly recalled.

Robby also remembers that meeting. "Kelly and I sat down in a room and connected right away. He got specific about how Prenda was set up, and for me there was an immediate appeal," Robby said. He believed that Prenda would be ideal for two types of Eisenhower students: those who are introverts for whom a classroom of thirty students is overwhelming, and those who become distracted and disobedient in large groups. With the crucial support of the district superintendent, who was intent on spurring in-district innovation, Robby and Kelly hosted an open house in the school gymnasium to let the community know about Prenda. Families liked the idea of a Prenda microschool being embedded at Eisenhower, where a small group of selected students would be able to work through Prenda's learning model with an adult guide each day, under the peripheral supervision of an experienced classroom teacher. Kelly donated the Prenda platform to Eisenhower at no cost, eager to see how a pilot program in a public school could work.

I met Robby and visited Eisenhower's Prenda microschool in 2024, halfway through its fifth year operating there. Tucked into a cozy, carpeted space next door to the main sixth grade classroom, ten students, ranging from fourth to sixth grade, sat at small tables with their computers. Clear LED lights rimmed a whiteboard and a colorful bulletin board on one side of the room, while a door on the other side led directly to the school's outdoor interior courtyard. The microschoolers were in "Conquer Mode," Prenda's core academic content block, working on math and language arts lessons geared toward their individual mastery levels. Maritza Rodriguez was their Prenda guide. In college studying to be a teacher, Maritza was hoping to follow in the footsteps of Eisenhower's first Prenda guide who, like her, was a teacher-in-training and is now a full-time classroom teacher at Eisenhower. "I wish I would have had this when I was in elementary school," Maritza told me. "The smaller group means actually being able to connect with the guide and with each other. The children are able to learn at their own pace," she said, adding that she recalls how hard it was for her to learn in large, loud classrooms.

The students I spoke to agreed that the small size and one-on-one attention made a big difference in their learning. "It turned my life upside down for me," one eleven-year-old boy said. "In the other class, I was always being funny and the kids were copying me and I was getting into trouble," he said. In the Prenda microschool, the boy was able to focus on his coursework without the social pressure to perform in front of his peers. Both his academics and his behavior dramatically improved. Robby told me that Prenda has played a crucial role in lowering student disciplinary incidents and avoiding out-of-classroom placements for students with significant academic or behavioral challenges.

"I'd rather be in a classroom with ten kids than thirty," a ten-year-old boy told me. "I like it way better here. I like working in small groups," he said. Another student heard that I had a degree from Harvard. "That's my plan. I want to go to Harvard too," she said. In addition to doing their core academic work in the Prenda microschool, and working together on fun projects like slime-making, the students interact with the larger elementary school community for all their other classes, such as art, music, and physical education. They also join their other classmates for breakfast, lunch, and recess, and take the bus with them to school.

As I was walking out the door at the end of my visit, I asked Maritza, the guide, if she had anything else to add. "We need more of Prenda!" she declared enthusiastically. It seemed to me like a no-brainer. Why wouldn't every elementary school want something like this for their students? Kelly joined me for my visit to Eisenhower. In the school parking lot, I asked him how many other Prenda microschools were operating inside traditional public schools. "None," he responded.

I sat across the table from Kelly over a taco lunch after leaving Eisenhower. Tall with blond hair, blue eyes, and a ceaseless smile, he is both soft-spoken and strongly zealous about supporting each learner's unique path toward self-actualization and success. He explained how hopeful he was when Eisenhower introduced its Prenda program in 2019, and how optimistic he felt that in-school microschooling would spread to other public schools in Arizona and beyond. Then, when COVID hit just a few months later, it seemed obvious to Kelly and others that microschools would be an ideal solution for ensuring small, safe, in-person learning communities to prevent learning loss and social isolation.

"I brought this idea to the district leadership, saying that we could do lots of microschools right away and it could be a big help to the kids and the families," Kelly said. "Robby and other administrators in the district were fully supportive of the idea. Even some of the school board members that I talked to really saw what was possible here and how this could be not only a temporary good thing to do for the families of Mesa, but also that it's a way to innovate and show the world something different."

Support grew districtwide, and it seemed like Mesa was going to move ahead with Prenda's pandemic microschools. Then, at a school board meeting that Kelly thought would approve the plan, it died. "What happened?" I asked Kelly in disbelief. "The teachers' union heard about it," he replied, explaining that while he can't say for certain that teacher union opposition is ultimately what buried the microschool proposal, it was likely a main factor. An October 2020 article about Prenda in the *Wall Street Journal* reinforced the claim, pointing to an "opposition report" released by the National Education Association, the country's largest teachers' union, naming Prenda and other microschool providers as groups to defeat.[5] The teachers' union didn't want microschool models like Prenda and similar programs in public schools. "It still hurts," Kelly said, his voice trembling. "Even just the retelling of that story. It hurts because I know these families and I know these kids and we could be doing so much more and it would be easy."

Robby explained that the resistance to expanding Prenda microschools during COVID was largely driven by fear. Some teachers and their unions were afraid of microschool models like Prenda operating in traditional public schools. "One Prenda pod at one school doesn't feel like a threat or doesn't confuse or frighten teachers. But I think the proposal, when it felt more widespread, raised some hackles," Robby said. He thinks that these fears could prevent ongoing innovation as well, but it's not a lost cause. "At the moment we're at in education, there is a lot of fear from a variety of angles. There's also a lot of momentum for parent voice and parent choice. I think in a district that has the right mix of those factors, microschools and similar innovations could really take hold and be incredibly successful," Robby said, adding that he's not naive to think this process will be easy or straightforward.

Robby has no plans to abandon traditional district schools. He believes in public schooling and wants to do the best he can to serve students in these schools—especially poor and historically marginalized students. Despite the aggravations and frequent resistance to innovation, Robby believes that there are opportunities for education intrapreneurs like him to introduce new ideas and change the system from within. Robby urges current traditional educators to seek schools and districts that support intrapreneurs. If an educator's current school or district isn't supportive, find another one that is. Teachers don't need to leave the traditional school system to innovate, Robby said, but they may need to leave a particular school or district if it doesn't support its intrapreneurs.

Teachers can look to the education entrepreneurs working outside the system for inspiration along their intrapreneurial path. "While I'm not going to go found a microschool or do something like that, I feel each day deeply indebted to the work of those individuals because it has shown that education can and should be done differently," Robby said. "We have to show those individuals in the system what's possible. I think that systems are responding. Large ships take a long time to turn, but I do believe that public education is shifting, especially in places like Arizona where things have really been opened up for competition."

## NEW DISTRICT SCHOOLS

Like Robby, Sherrilynn Bair also sees how increased competition in the form of new and different education options can lead to sustained innovations within traditional school districts. She believes that intrapreneurial educators can use this competition to their advantage to introduce positive change.

Sherrilynn had a varied background as an educator, beginning her career teaching at a Bureau of Indian Affairs school in Idaho and then working for the Idaho Virtual School, a statewide virtual public charter school. Later, Sherrilynn earned a graduate degree in curriculum and worked as a school librarian and curriculum director for the Snake River School District in rural Blackfoot, Idaho. That's where she was working when she became determined to find a way to create a new type of school within her traditional district that would better serve students.

The idea came to her years earlier when she was working at the virtual charter school. She had an eight-year-old student who was on grade level for every subject except math, where he was far ahead of his peers. He would devour any math content he was given, quickly progressing through multiplication, division, long division, decimals and fractions, and even exponents. "His mom had taken him out of the traditional building because he was ready for and hungry to learn math. He just loved it, and he was sitting in a classroom all day long practicing times tables, because that's what you do in third grade," said Sherrilynn, who described the experience as a pivotal moment when she realized that there were many families who wanted or needed something different than a one-size-fits-all conventional classroom.

I met Sherrilynn at an education conference in the fall of 2023. There, she told me that she began planting seeds years earlier with her district superintendent about offering a new, online school within her district that would create opportunities for individualized learning and curriculum choice. Those seeds didn't sprout until COVID hit. "My superintendent said be careful what you wish for," Sherrilynn recalled. The pandemic upheaval created the opportunity Sherrilynn needed to get the superintendent to sign off on creating a new school "building" in her district, even though that "building" was a virtual school. In 2020, Snake River Online opened as a K–8 virtual school within a traditional public school district. In its first year, three hundred students enrolled in the school. Enrollment doubled the following year, and today Snake River Online has more than 1,300 K–12 students enrolled across Idaho, with a lengthy waiting list. Sherrilynn is the principal.

I asked Sherrilynn why she was so committed to creating Snake River Online as a new school within an existing school district rather than opening a new virtual charter school, such as Idaho Virtual Academy. I was under the impression that charter schools—especially virtual charter schools—offered more opportunities for experimentation than district schools. But Sherrilynn knew otherwise. She sits on the state's charter commission and sees all the paperwork and bureaucratic hoops founders need to jump through to open a charter school. "I knew how much work it was, and I just didn't have the bandwidth at the time," she recalled, adding that to open a new school within an existing school district in Idaho is much simpler. "It's one form and the superintendent's signature. I filled out the form. It said: I'm opening a new building, Snake River Online. The superintendent signed it," she said.

Families who enroll their children at Snake River Online are able to choose the curriculum that works best for them and their children. They work with certified teachers to craft a flexible yet comprehensive learning plan that is aligned with state standards. Most of the student's per pupil state funding allocation goes to the district to pay teachers, but families are given some funds directly to purchase curriculum, supplies, and materials. Students and parents meet regularly with their teachers over Zoom to track progress. Students who are local to Blackfoot sometimes meet with their teachers in person at the public library, which is also the school district's library. I spoke with teachers at Snake River Online who told me that they appreciate the freedom, flexibility, and opportunity to customize learning for each of their students. The families appreciate these qualities as well, which Sherrilynn says is why the school's enrollment continues to rise.

She is energized by the amount of innovation occurring outside of conventional schools and told me how much she enjoys hearing the stories on my podcast of school founders who are building new, nontraditional learning models. But she is equally energized by the possibilities to innovate inside the system as an intrapreneur. "I love the fact that we can step out of the traditional system to make a difference if we need to—and I have hope that we can make a difference within the traditional system," Sherrilynn said.

## OVERHAULING AN ENTIRE SCHOOL DISTRICT

Sherrilynn's new district school creates a blueprint for traditional school systems to follow. As post-pandemic enrollment in traditional public schools continues to decline, school districts that create the kinds of learning options that families want—especially those with curriculum and scheduling flexibility—will not only retain existing students but attract new ones.

That's what Cory Steiner is finding. A 2024 report on public school enrollment trends published by the Brookings Institution found that rural schools have had among the most significant enrollment declines in recent years.[6] Yet, the Northern Cass School District in rural North Dakota, where Cory serves as the Superintendent of Schools, is experiencing the opposite. Families are flocking to his district due in large part to its innovative, individualized approach to learning that upends traditional notions of schooling. When Cory started with the district a decade ago, there were 575 students enrolled in the Northern Cass School District. Now there are more than seven hundred students, with 35 percent of them coming from outside district lines, some up to thirty miles away. "We're growing, which in rural North Dakota is a complete anomaly," Cory told me when we spoke in 2024. "We think it's because we've created lots of big-school opportunities in a very small learning environment."

In 2018, Cory spearheaded the launch of an entirely new public schooling model focused on helping each student to uncover their interests and talents and create a customized pathway to adulthood. The idea came to him about three years into his tenure at Northern Cass when he noticed the audience's reactions during Commencement. During the ceremony, each graduate's future plans would be projected onto a screen. When a student was heading off to college, the audience reaction was loud and exuberant, but when a student was forgoing college to enter the workforce instead, the reactions were tepid. "In that moment, I started to recognize that people thought those kids were failures. They had been through our system for thirteen years, had done everything we asked, had played school enough to get to the point where they got a diploma. They were going to be contributing members in society, paying taxes, paying bills, doing everything we want adults to be able to do. They were just going to do it at an earlier age—and we thought that was a disappointment," said Cory, who began collaborating with colleagues and the wider community to design a new school system that would support, nurture, and celebrate each student's enthusiasms and goals, whatever those might be.

Leveraging existing state education legislation focused on fostering in-district innovation, Cory was able to secure waivers that freed Northern Cass from some standard schooling policies and practices. It took a lot of work, persistence, and persuasion, but Cory re-engineered his school district to focus more on individualized learning. For elementary students, that means retaining some direct instruction but adding small-group coaching and more one-on-one attention to learner needs and interests. For middle school, Northern Cass adopted a "studio" model with deep inquiry into various topics, as well as collaborative and individual projects. High schoolers build on those projects and begin to set and accomplish goals based on their own ambitions, culminating in a senior capstone experience of their own choosing.

Some students participate in dual enrollment programs with local colleges that enable teens for whom college is a goal to accumulate enough credits to earn an Associate's degree by high school graduation, and transfer those credits to a four-year university if they choose, making the college price tag much more affordable. Other students for whom college isn't their desired path participate in robust internships and apprenticeship programs, accumulating high school credit for these activities. Cory told me of a current student who spends his mornings in the high school studio, and the rest of the day working as a farrier who shoes horses. The student plans to start his own business and is gaining high school credits in areas such as math and science related to his real-life experiences. Another student has been taking piano lessons for the past ten years. "He should get school credit for that," Cory said.

To allow for that credit, Cory partnered with Mastery Transcript Consortium (MTC), a membership-based nonprofit organization that is working to support more personalized learning models, including microschools. MTC helps member schools shift away from traditional credits toward competencies, while capturing students' immersive learning experiences. It translates these experiences and competencies into a tailored transcript that displays a much more authentic, holistic learning experience connected to a student's interests and achievements. These MTC transcripts are increasingly being embraced by colleges and universities across the United States—including some of the most selective ones. "We are the only school district in North Dakota that I know of that has passed a policy to allow competencies instead of credits for graduation," Cory said.

So how has this district-wide shift toward more personalized, competency-based, holistic learning turned out? Cory downplays the value of standardized test scores but notes that his district's scores have actually improved since making the shift and are above the state average. Northern Cass has a 92 percent high school graduation rate, higher than the national average, and a 70 percent college acceptance rate, with some students choosing to enter the workforce or enlist in the military.

The high school capstone ceremony is, however, Cory's most important metric of success. "It's a celebration," he said, explaining that in addition to parents and teachers, the audience includes mentors and employers and military recruiters and other adults who have had a significant impact on a graduate's high school learning experiences. They listen eagerly as the graduates present their capstone experiences and share their future plans. "There's nothing more powerful," Cory said. "These are red-eye days. Every one of us leaves weeping," he continued, adding that nobody looks at any kid now as a failure. "They look at them as kids who made a choice that is the right choice for them."

He believes that change is possible within the conventional schooling system, and hopes more schools follow in the footsteps of Northern Cass. Every June, Cory and his leadership team host the Personalized Learning Institute, a conference that brings together teachers and administrators from across the country who are interested in reimagining their schools and districts to be more innovative and individualized. During the gathering, there is so much hope and optimism about what is possible, but Cory says that to date no other school district has been able to make the shift toward personalized learning the way Northern Cass has done. "They come to our Institute and are so excited," Cory said of his conference participants. "Then we'll check in with them later, and they'll say it was really hard and that they couldn't get consensus." Cory tells them that commitment is more important than consensus in moving forward: get colleagues and community members to commit to change and put in the long hours of work to make that change happen within the system.

*Chapter Reflections for Parents and Founders*
This is an ideal time for intrapreneurs to suggest and spearhead innovative changes within conventional schools. I hear from a growing number

of new school founders that traditional schools and school districts are more eager to collaborate with and learn from them in a variety of creative ways. This will most certainly continue, especially as education is becoming increasingly unbundled from traditional schooling, whether through statewide policy or community preference—or both. While barriers discouraging to in-system innovation remain, education intrapreneurs should feel emboldened to recommend new ideas that will attract and retain students and families. I am optimistic that we will see more schools and districts innovate in the coming years as competitive pressures build from outside the system. This is one of several trends that will transform US K–12 education, infusing a stagnant sector with entrepreneurial vibrancy.

**Parents:** What can you do to encourage more innovation within your local school or district? Try to find the teachers, administrators, and parents in your school or district who are eager to see conventional schools adopt creative educational practices, such as in-system microschools. Build a grassroots coalition for change while sharing examples of schools like Robby's that are trying new things and seeing positive results.

**Founders:** Are you an intrapreneur? Robby, Sherrilynn, and Cory show that in-district innovation inspired by out-of-system models is possible, whether it's introducing a small learning pod or restructuring an entire district. If you want to try to make change within your school or district, here are some questions to ask yourself:

1. **What innovations would you like to see within your school or district?** Consider your top priorities for change and what impact you believe would result from these changes.
2. **What are some examples of these innovations, either within or outside of conventional classrooms, that most inspire you?** Gather examples of the places where these innovations are being implemented, and of people spearheading these initiatives.

Reach out to these changemakers to build relationships and seek advice. Collect as much information as you can about outcomes, including both academic and nonacademic metrics, to begin to build a case for change within your school setting.

3. **What policies and pathways for innovation currently exist?** Both Alec and Cory leveraged existing state education policies around "innovation schools" to introduce new educational models and methods within the traditional schooling system. Does your state or school district have similar policies? If so, lean on those existing policies to encourage change. If not, consider proposing such policies.

4. **Who shares your vision?** Find others in your school or district who share your passion for in-system innovation. These could include parents, teachers, students, staff members, administrators, school board officials, teachers' union representatives, and community leaders. Communicate your idea and together begin brainstorming an action plan.

5. **What are your first five steps?** With your group of supporters, consider the initial steps of an action plan to realize your vision of in-system innovation. What can you do this week and this month to move ahead on your goal?

6. **What is your minimum viable product (MVP)?** Entrepreneurs often launch a new product or service with an MVP—a barebones version of something to show that it works and to gauge the level of interest in their offering. In Chapter 5, I described how a founder's MVP could involve initially launching a new school in one's home or at a park, or running a summer camp, to begin to bring their idea to others. As an intrapreneur, you can do the same thing. What would an MVP related to your vision look like? For example, if your goal is to introduce in-system microschools, a possible MVP might involve creating a microschool

community that meets at your school building before or after school hours or during a school vacation week.

7. **How can you demonstrate success?** From your MVP experience, you can begin to collect and share data with other stakeholders in your school or district. For example, if you run a microschool during spring school vacation week, create and track some Key Performance Indicators (KPIs). Refer to Chapter 8 for possible KPI examples. You can then use these metrics to show the positive impact of your program, including academic and social-emotional growth, parent and student satisfaction levels, learner engagement, and so on. Share these results far and wide so more people will know what you have accomplished.

8. **What's next?** Once you have an initial prototype of your idea and some (hopefully positive) data on pilot implementation, work with your group of supporters to think about ways to expand your MVP into a full-fledged program. If you feel strongly about in-system innovation but find that your colleagues and community aren't on board, or that there are too many barriers to change, then consider working in a different school or district that may be more eager for innovation and experimentation. If you still can't find what you're looking for, you may need to build it yourself, outside the conventional education system.

## Chapter 12
# Trends

*The most valuable businesses of coming decades will be built by entrepreneurs who seek to empower people rather than try to make them obsolete.*
—Peter Thiel (cofounder of PayPal, Palantir Technologies, and Founders Fund), *Zero to One*

In 2019, I gave a keynote presentation at the Alternative Education Resource Organization's (AERO) annual conference in Portland, Oregon. Founded in 1989 by Jerry Mintz, AERO has long supported entrepreneurial educators in launching new schools and spaces, with a particular focus on learner-centered educational models. It was about a month after *Unschooled* was published, and I was talking about the gathering interest in unconventional education. Homeschooling numbers were gradually rising, and more microschools and microschooling networks were surfacing. I predicted that these trends would continue, but I said they would remain largely on the edge—as alternative education had for decades. They would offer more choices to some families who were willing to try new things, similar to those of us who eagerly embraced Netflix's mailed DVDs when they first appeared. But I didn't think these unconventional models would upend the entire education sector the way Netflix ultimately did with entertainment. I thought they would remain small and niche. I was wrong.

The COVID crisis catapulted peripheral educational trends into the mainstream, not only creating the opportunity for new schools and spaces to emerge but, more importantly, permanently altering the way parents, teachers, and kids think about schooling and learning. The pre-pandemic tilt toward homeschooling and microschooling has converged with several post-pandemic trends that are profoundly reshaping American education for families and founders. Together, these trends are shifting the K–12 education sector from being an innovation laggard to an innovation leader.

## FIVE TRENDS SHAPING THE FUTURE OF LEARNING

Chris Turner is a father and a founder. A tech entrepreneur, Chris sold his mobile application development startup and was pulled toward education entrepreneurship after being dissatisfied with the available school options for his rising kindergartener. Coming from the tech sector, Chris expected to find K–12 classrooms that reflected the innovation occurring all around him. But when he toured local public, private, and charter schools, he was surprised to see classrooms for his child that looked largely the same as they did when he attended public schools years earlier. From his desk at a coworking space outside of Atlanta, Chris created a prototype for a new kind of learning environment for kids: a low-cost, membership-based, in-person, tech-enabled learning environment that would support self-directed learning. It would be like coworking for kids. He called it Moonrise.

I visited Moonrise's spacious flagship location in a Decatur, Georgia, storefront in the fall of 2023, two years after writing about its opening in my Forbes.com column. In that time, it had grown from a small startup serving a handful of students, called "Risers," into a vibrant learning space with 150 homeschoolers, ages five to fourteen. From the climbing wall to the professional digital recording studio to the fully-stocked makerspace, Moonrise encourages children to explore their self-chosen interests in community with peers and adults. Chris's nine-year-old son and five-year-old daughter both attend.

Using Georgia's Learning Pod Protection Act legislation, Moonrise legally functions as a homeschool resource center and offers families up to twenty hours a week of drop-off programming. In his early startup months, Chris experimented with different membership models, but he has found that focusing specifically on homeschoolers is the ideal market. "I see Moonrise as the future of learning," Chris said, explaining that he wants to serve families who are interested in an entirely new educational vision beyond schooling that cultivates curiosity and creativity. "I think the best thing that we can do for humanity, for progress, is to empower human creativity. Humans are inherently creative. Everybody who deals with kids sees this all the time. You don't have to create creativity. You just have to not stand in the way of it."

Chris is right that models like Moonrise are fast becoming the future of learning. They provide the freedom and flexibility in education that more families want, and reflect broader changes in US education, including many that are just beginning. The intersection of five major trends—the growth in homeschooling and microschooling, the adoption of flexible work arrangements for parents, the expansion of school choice policies, the advent of new technologies and artificial intelligence (AI), and the openness to new institutions—will dramatically change the way young people in America learn over the next decade. The successful schools and spaces of the coming years will both shape and be shaped by these overlapping trends. Let's explore them further.

### Trend #1—The growth of homeschooling and microschooling

"I think homeschooling itself is changing," Chris said, referring to the evolving motivations and methods of today's homeschoolers. Not only have homeschooling numbers surged more than 50 percent between 2017 and 2023, according to data analyzed by the *Washington Post*, but the homeschooling population has also become more demographically, geographically, and ideologically diverse—closely mirroring the overall diversity of the American population.[1] While the cartoonish portrayal of homeschoolers as isolated ideologues sitting around the kitchen table with their textbooks was always overblown, contemporary homeschoolers bear even less resemblance to that stereotype.

In the fall of 2024, Professor Angela Watson at Johns Hopkins University revealed that homeschooling numbers continued to grow during the 2023/2024 academic year compared to the prior year in 90 percent of the states that reported homeschooling data, shattering assumptions that homeschooling's pandemic-era rise was just a blip. This rise occurred in states across the US, with North Dakota seeing a 24 percent increase in homeschoolers and Rhode Island seeing a 67 percent increase, between the 2022/2023 and 2023/2024 school years. Moreover, Watson found that as the overall US school-age student population declines due to falling birth rates, the number of homeschooled students is actually growing.[2] Many of these homeschoolers are attending microschools and other traditional schooling alternatives, which have experienced a similar jump in recent years.

The nearby microschool for homeschoolers that my children attended before COVID was one of only a sprinkling of schooling alternatives in our area. Now, it's part of a wide, fast-growing ecosystem of creative schooling options—both locally and nationally—representing an array of different educational philosophies and approaches. Families today are better able to find an education option that aligns with their preferences. From Maine to Miami to Missouri to Montana, the majority of the innovative schools and spaces I've visited have emerged since 2020, and many already have lengthy waitlists, inspiring more would-be founders. The demand for these options will grow and accelerate over the next ten years, as will the number of homeschooling families, many of whom will be attracted to homeschooling as a direct result of these microschools and related learning models. Parents that otherwise wouldn't have considered a homeschooling option will do so because homeschooling enables them to enroll at their preferred school or space.

Similarly, more low-cost, personalized private schools will sprout, offering a wider variety of educational choices. In Florida, for example, *Politico* reports that private school enrollment increased by nearly 12 percent between the 2019/2020 and 2022/2023 school years. Florida's school choice policies became universal in the summer of 2023, likely accelerating private school enrollment in the coming years.[3]

One particularly striking and consistent theme revealed in my conversations with founders as I've crisscrossed the country is that their kindergarten classes are filling with students whose parents chose an unconventional education option from the start. These parents aren't removing their child from a traditional school because of an unpleasant experience or a failure of a school to meet a child's particular needs. They are opting out of conventional schooling from the get-go, gravitating toward homeschooling and microschooling before their child even reaches school age. This trend is also likely to accelerate, as younger parents become even more receptive to educational innovation and change.

## Trend #2—The adoption of flexible work arrangements

Today's generation of new parents grew up with a gleeful acceptance of digital technologies and the breakthroughs they have facilitated in everything from healthcare to home entertainment. These parents see the ways in which technology and innovation enable greater personalization and efficiency, and expect these qualities in all their consumer choices. It's no wonder, then, that parents of young children today are generally more curious about homeschooling and other schooling alternatives. Like Chris, they are perplexed that traditional education seems so sluggish.

The response to COVID gave these parents license to consider other options for their children's education. The school closures and extended remote learning during the pandemic empowered parents to take a more active role in their children's education. That trend persists, as does the remaking of Americans' work habits. The number of employees working remotely from home rather than at their workplace has more than tripled since 2019. While no longer at peak-pandemic levels, it's estimated that at least 20 percent of US workers are remote.[4] Hybrid work arrangements, in which employees spend part of the time on-site at their workplace and part of the time working remotely, have also become increasingly common and popular since 2020, according to Gallup polling.[5]

As more parents enjoy more flexibility in their work schedules, they will seek similar flexibility in their children's learning schedules. Spaces like Moonrise offer that flexibility. While remote and hybrid work generally remain privileges of the so-called "laptop class" of higher-income employees, the growing adoption of flexible work and school arrangements is driving demand for more of these alternative learning models, including many of the ones featured in this book that offer full-time, affordable programming options for parents who don't have job flexibility. Remote and hybrid work patterns are here to stay, and so is the trend toward more nimble educational models for all.

Chris is jumping on that trend. He is in the process of creating a profit-sharing ownership model for Moonrise so that entrepreneurial parents and educators can open their own Moonrises across the United States. He is also refining his Moonrise mobile app, which works as the operating system for Moonrise, easing scheduling and communication among members while also facilitating partnerships with local community organizations to offer programs such as sports leagues, clubs, and field trips.

As Moonrise locations spread, families will have reciprocal memberships at all Moonrises, creating a national network of Risers. "My goal is to have one hundred Moonrise locations by the end of 2028," said Chris, who is in the process of raising early-stage venture capital. Chris is also eyeing expansion in the growing number of states with school choice policies that apply to creative schooling models like Moonrise, so that whoever wants to be a Riser can be one.

### Trend #3—The expansion of school choice policies

The burst of creative schooling options since 2020 is now occurring all across the United States, in small towns and big cities, in both politically progressive and conservative areas, and in states with and without school choice policies that enable education funding to follow students. Take Massachusetts and Mississippi, for example. In my populous, progressive Bay State, which has no private school choice policies, a wide variety of microschools, private schools, and related learning models have emerged or expanded since 2020. In my city of Cambridge, for instance, the number of school-age children who attend a private school jumped from 16 percent in 2014 to 23 percent in 2023.[6] Similarly, in the less dense, more politically conservative Magnolia State, which has only very limited private school choice programs for some special needs students, education entrepreneurship is also flourishing. All the microschools I visited there, from those sprouting around the city of Jackson to others in tucked-away towns like Pontotoc, have emerged since the pandemic. They are being championed by both state-based nonprofits such as Embark Mississippi, which supports school founders as they launch, as well as national nonprofits like the National Microschooling Center. Education entrepreneurs aren't waiting around for politicians or public policy to green-light their ventures or provide greater financial access. They are building their schools and spaces today to meet the mounting needs of families in their communities.

That said, there is little doubt that expansive school choice policies in many states are accelerating entrepreneurial trends. Founders like Chris, who are developing national networks of creative schooling options, are intentional about locating in states with generous school choice policies that enable more parents to choose these new learning models. Other entrepreneurs are moving to these states specifically so that they can open their schools in places that enable greater financial accessibility and encourage choice and variety. Jack Johnson Pannell is one example.

The founder of a public charter school for boys in Baltimore, Maryland, that primarily serves low-income students of color, Jack grew discouraged that the experimentation that defined the early charter school movement in the 1990s steadily disappeared, replaced by an emphasis on standardization and testing that can make many—but certainly not all—of today's charter schools indistinguishable from traditional public schools. He saw in the choice-enabled microschooling movement the opportunity for ingenuity and accessibility that was a hallmark of the charter sector's infancy. In 2023, Jack moved to Phoenix, Arizona, to launch Trinity Arch Preparatory School for Boys, a middle school microschool that families are able to access through Arizona's universal school choice policies. In addition to utilizing funds from Arizona's universal school choice program, three-quarters of Jack's students receive financial aid.

It's not just founders who are moving to these states. It's families too. "I know a parent who moved from the Midwest to Arizona because it's a 'free-to-educate' state," said Michael Strong, a longtime educator, author, and founder of The Socratic Experience, a highly personalized and interactive online school based in Austin, Texas, that he launched in the wake of the pandemic. Arizona students who enroll in The Socratic Experience are able to use their school choice dollars to attend the program at low or no cost. Michael sees Arizona as the leader in these choice policies, not only because it was the first state to introduce universal choice in 2022, but also because the policy enables education to be fully separated from traditional schooling, allowing families to pick and choose among different learning models and methods. In Arizona, families can use their school choice funds for traditional private school tuition if they want, but they can also use these funds for other educational expenses such as homeschooling curriculum, educational therapies, music lessons, tutoring services, as well as a host of microschooling and homeschooling programs. For school founders like Michael, who considers himself and others like him to be "entrepreneurs of happiness and well-being," this uncoupling of education from standard schooling is crucial.

Michael believes that the education system needs a monumental overhaul to foster happier, healthier, more humane learning environments in which young people can thrive. Entrepreneurs are critical to that overhaul. "Many of the great entrepreneurs of the twenty-first century will be entrepreneurs who create exceptional enterprises that are preeminent producers of beauty and grace, culture and experience, happiness and well-being," he wrote in his book, *Be the Solution: How Entrepreneurs and Conscious Capitalists Can Solve All the World's Problems*.[7] In education, Michael sees the burst of more learner-directed approaches, or what he refers to as "agency-based models," as the key to improving youth mental health and overall human flourishing. When people of any age have more control over their lives and learning, they often find greater happiness and fulfillment.

### Trend #4—The advent of new technologies and AI

New technologies are accelerating the rise of these agency-based educational models, while also making it harder to ignore the inadequacies of one-size-fits-all schooling. The ability to differentiate learning, personalizing it to each student's present competency level and preferred learning style, has never been easier or more straightforward. It no longer makes sense to say that all second graders or all seventh graders should be doing the same thing, at the same time, in the same way—and failing them if they don't measure up. Today's new educational technologies, including free ones such as Khan Academy, ensure that students are progressing through core content on their own timetables, moving ahead once they have gained proficiency. Eventual subject mastery is expected of everyone.

Emerging and maturing technologies help prioritize students over schools and systems, but the widespread introduction of artificial intelligence (AI) tools, and bots like ChatGPT, will hasten this repositioning. New AI bots can act as personal tutors for students, helping them navigate through their set curriculum. The real promise, according to founders focused more on agency-based or learner-directed education, is for AI tools to work for the students themselves, helping them to control their own curriculum.

"We don't have a set pathway for our learners. It's personalized," said Tobin Slaven, cofounder of Acton Academy Fort Lauderdale, which he launched with his wife Martina in 2021. Part of the global Acton Academy microschool network first described in Chapter 4, Tobin's school prioritizes student-driven education in which young people set and achieve individual goals in both academic and nonacademic areas, participate in frequent Socratic group discussions, engage in collaborative problem-solving and shared decision-making, and embark on their own "hero's journey" of personal discovery and achievement. "The ability to set smart goals, do hard things, and be a person who says what they're going to do and then does it may be the most important thing that we're doing in our school," Tobin told me.

When we spoke in 2024, Tobin had recently founded an educational technology startup building AI companion tools that act as a personal tutor, life coach, and mentor all in one. He sees AI tools like his as being instrumental in helping learners have more independence and autonomy over their learning. Rather than AI bots guiding a student through a pre-established curriculum, Tobin thinks the truly transformative potential of AI lies in tools that help students lead their own learning—answering their own questions and pursuing their own academic and nonacademic goals.

"When I hear the visions of some other folks in the education space, their visions are very different from mine," Tobin said, referring to many of today's emerging AI-enabled educational technologies. He offered the example of a device known as a jig, used often in carpentry, to further illustrate his point. "The jig tells you exactly where the curves should be, where the cut should be. It's like a template. The template that most of the AI folks are using is traditional education. It was broken from the start. It's a bad jig," Tobin said.

Instead, he sees the potential of AI to help reimagine education rather than reinforce a top-down, traditional model. While recognizing the limitations and legitimate concerns about emerging AI technology, particularly related to its use by children, Tobin views the benefits of these technologies as outweighing their drawbacks. As part of the lively South Florida cluster of innovative education models, his school is one of several in the area that focus more on learner-centered and learner-driven education. Tobin is collaborating with these neighboring schools and spaces to beta-test new AI tools that put learners in charge. He is helping create a new and better educational jig.

### Trend #5—Openness to new institutions

The final trend that is merging with the others to transform American education is the shift away from established institutions toward newer, more decentralized ones. Some of this is undoubtedly due to emerging technologies that can disrupt entrenched power structures and lead to greater awareness of, and openness to, new ideas, but the trend goes beyond technology. Annual polling by Gallup reveals that Americans' confidence in a variety of institutions has fallen, with their confidence in public schools at a historic low. Only 26 percent of survey respondents in 2023 indicated that they had a "Great deal/Quite a lot" of confidence in that institution.

Public schools weren't alone in their declining reputation. They joined the police, large technology companies, and big business as being at or tied with their record lows. Public schools and the US presidency were among the two most politically polarizing institutions in the nation, according to Gallup.[8]

The good news is that confidence in small business remains high, topping Gallup's list with 65 percent of Americans expressing a "Great deal/Quite a lot" of confidence in that institution in 2023. The falling favor of public schools occurring at the same time that small businesses continue to be well-liked creates ideal conditions for today's education entrepreneurs. Families who are dissatisfied with public schooling may be much more interested in a small school or space operating or opening within their community. For founders, this can be a reminder to lean into your role as a small business owner and build relationships with your neighbors.

For another signal of the shift away from older, more centralized institutions toward newer, more customized options, look at what the *Wall Street Journal* calls the "power shift underway in the entertainment industry," as YouTube increasingly draws viewers away from traditional television networks.[9] Individual YouTube content creators, such as the world's top YouTuber, MrBeast, who has some 300 million subscribers, appeal to more viewers than the legacy media networks with their more curated content. New content creators are particularly attractive to younger generational cohorts like Gen Z, who prefer decentralized, user-generated content over traditional, top-down media models.[10] Consumers today are looking for more modern, responsive, personalized products and services, especially those being developed by individual entrepreneurs who bear little resemblance to legacy institutions. This is as true in education as it is in entertainment and will be an ongoing, indefinite, and transformational trend in both sectors.

## WATCHING OUT FOR COUNTERTRENDS

What could slow the above trends? The two biggest threats are regulation and standardization. These are likely to come from the established institutions that have the most to lose from smaller, more innovative competitors. It's no surprise, for example, that big technology companies are among the most vocal advocates for more government regulation of emerging AI technologies. They want to retain control of those technologies, not compete with ambitious upstarts.[11]

Similarly, as new schools and spaces disrupt traditional educational models, we could see mounting efforts to regulate them or push them toward standardization at the expense of innovation. This is what happened with the charter school sector. When charter schools emerged more than three decades ago, they were designed to offer more freedom and autonomy for entrepreneurial educators to experiment with new learning models through tuition-free public schools. In exchange for this freedom to innovate there would be more oversight and accountability by charter school authorizers, or those entities appointed to oversee charter school operations and outcomes. "I don't think the authorizers really care very much about the innovation at their charter schools," said Jack Johnson Pannell, the founder mentioned earlier who left the charter sector to launch a microschool in Arizona.

He explained that authorizers are generally more focused on standardized test scores and similar metrics that limit experimentation and can prevent charter schools from achieving their original vision. "If you have to build your curriculum, your academic program, your teaching culture around that test, it's kind of hard to move away into something that's innovative," Jack said. He was out hiking one day with a friend who was an early charter school pioneer when she mentioned the term *microschool*. Jack was intrigued. As she described the idea to him of a smaller, more personalized, more flexible learning environment, Jack became increasingly interested in the possibility of opening his own school, aligned with his own creative vision for education. "I didn't have to spend time thinking about how to contort my vision for education into a system," said Jack, whose microschool enrollment tripled in its second year.

Jack launched his microschool with a commitment to academic excellence and student diversity, along with a highly individualized curriculum, hours of outdoor recess time, and a close partnership with families. "We are proving that the traditional school with mandated 'seat time' is a relic of the past," Jack said, referring to emerging models like his that prioritize student content mastery over outdated instructional time requirements dictating how long children need to be sitting in classrooms.

The experiences of charter school refugees like Jack remind us that innovation in education is fragile and that new models that attempt to disrupt old methods can have their creative edge crushed under the weight of regulation and standardization—even if unintentionally. For example, when Coi Morefield opened The Lab School of Memphis, described in this book's Introduction, she was able to launch her small private school with six students, quickly growing her enrollment over the subsequent months. A short time later, the Tennessee State Board of Education changed its private school approval rules for the category of schools like Coi's, now requiring those schools to have at least ten students enrolled.[12] What seems like a tiny, insignificant rule change can have a huge impact. Under these new rules, Coi wouldn't have been able to start her school, which today serves dozens of learners.

Proponents of greater regulation and standardization of unconventional education models might argue that they are necessary to ensure public accountability and strong academic outcomes. Some of these proponents could even be well-meaning founders of, or advocates for, new schools or schooling networks who think their particular model is best and should be applied more universally to all other emerging schools and spaces. Yet regulation and standardization frequently don't lead to greater accountability or higher academic achievement. Take Tennessee, where Coi runs her microschool, as just one example. In the Memphis-Shelby County Public Schools system, the largest district in the state, fewer than a quarter of students were proficient in either reading or math in 2024.[13]

Traditional public schools are among the most highly regulated and standardized spaces in contemporary society, yet they often fail to provide a high-quality education to a good number of their students. Regulation and standardization don't ensure educational quality, and creative schools and spaces should not be required to meet uniform benchmarks that many public schools frequently fail to meet. More families and founders are seeking or building unconventional education options as a direct response to the standardized curriculum and testing occurring in many conventional schools. They want new and different options. Adding layers of regulation and standardization will suppress the ingenuity that defines today's novel schools and spaces. They should become the templates for traditional schools to follow—not the other way around.

While founders and families building and seeking unconventional learning models need to be vigilant and push back against attempts to constrain education innovation, I am confident that they will prevail. A promising sign is that as homeschooling numbers have climbed over the past two decades, and private school choice policies have expanded, homeschooling has actually become more deregulated across the United States.[14] It's not a coincidence, then, that many of the most creative schooling models today began as homeschooling programs or are serving homeschooling families in a variety of ways. Innovation flourishes with freedom.

We are witnessing education veer from rigidity toward agility, from directives toward choices, and from passivity toward agency. That could raise eyebrows among purveyors of the schooling status quo, but the demand for unconventional education options is high and the number of entrepreneurs eager to build these options is growing. Traditional schooling models aren't going to disappear as new schooling models emerge, just as taxis haven't disappeared with the introduction of Uber and Lyft, but they are going to need to compete with newer educational models, adopting some of their personalized approaches. This competition will improve the overall education sector just as Uber and Lyft have improved today's traditional taxi-riding experience. Research suggests that this is already happening. In 2024, economists from the University of Rochester, the University of California, Davis, and Northwestern University published a paper finding that competition from charter schools in several Florida school districts raised the reading scores and lowered the absenteeism rates of students in the area's traditional public schools. With more educational competition in the coming years, everyone will need to up their game.[15] Pupils, like passengers, will be the real winners.

## WHAT'S NEXT?

Shortly before completing this manuscript, I spoke again at the annual AERO conference, this time in Minneapolis. Gone was my measured optimism of 2019. In its place was a mountain of evidence showing how popular alternative education models have become since 2020, and how steadily that popularity continues to grow. This isn't a pandemic-era fad or an educational niche destined for the edges. This is a diverse, decentralized, choice-filled entrepreneurial movement that is shifting American education from standardization and stagnation toward individualization and innovation.

In the Twin Cities area surrounding the conference site, I visited a variety of these schools and spaces, from microschools, to hybrid homeschool programs, to low-cost private schools. Many just recently emerged, and most have experienced ballooning enrollment since 2020. For example, the Minneapolis-based Wildflower Montessori microschool network launched a decade ago but has seen unprecedented recent demand from prospective founders looking to open new schools. The network currently has its largest-ever group of participants in its School Startup Journey incubator program, with more than forty Wildflower-affiliated schools set to open in 2025 and 2026. Research conducted by VELA, the national philanthropic nonprofit organization and education entrepreneur network, reveals rising demand for today's unconventional education options. According to the report, more than "90 percent of programs served more learners in fall 2023 than they did at their origins," with these programs growing rapidly each year.[16]

We are only at the very early stages of a fundamental change in how, where, what, and with whom young people learn. Over the next decade, homeschooling and microschooling numbers will continue to grow, work flexibility will trigger greater demand for schooling flexibility, expanding education choice policies will make creative schooling options more accessible to all, AI and emerging technologies will help create a new "educational jig" fit for the innovation era, and declining confidence in old institutions will enable fresh ones to arise. The future of learning is brighter than ever. Families and founders are finding freedom, happiness, and success beyond conventional schooling, inspiring the growth of today's joyful learning models and the invention of new ones yet to be imagined.

# Afterword

As copies of this book were being boxed up and sent to retailers, my eighteen-year-old daughter Molly was packing up to leave home and begin her freshman year of college to study mathematics and data science. A lifelong self-directed homeschooler who never attended a traditional school and didn't take a formal class or test until she was thirteen, Molly knew that she was in charge of her own learning and could direct her education however she chose. For her, that meant lots of time playing and pursuing her varied interests in childhood, and later taking a host of online high school and in-person dual enrollment courses as a teen while uncovering her talents and ambitions.

When Brian and I chose a different type of K–12 education for our children than the one we experienced, we took a leap. We rejected the one-size-fits-all standardized schooling model in which we both grew up and instead embraced the simple idea that learning should be joyful and young people should be free to chart their own educational journeys, with adult support. They don't need to be forced to learn. They can become curious and well-educated outside the conventional classroom.

As Molly heads off to college, my younger children are continuing on their own self-directed learning paths. Jack and Sam remain at Sudbury Valley School, with Jack (age sixteen) taking dual-enrollment courses through a local community college and deepening his interest in business and technology, and Sam (age eleven) spending much of his time playing outside with friends in between reading novels, watching YouTube videos, and studying geography. Abby (age fourteen) adores Sudbury Valley but wants to see what a conventional classroom is like. She is about to begin her freshman year at our city's public high school, knowing that she has the freedom to stay through graduation or to leave to do something else should she choose.

Today, there are so many more educational choices for parents, teachers, and kids, including a growing panoply of new ones created by everyday entrepreneurs. Families are finally starting to experience the personalization, variety, and abundance in education that they enjoy in other areas of their lives. It's truly an exciting time.

My parting message for parents, teachers, and learners is: keep searching for your joyful school or space, and make changes as needed.

For entrepreneurs: keep building.

# ACKNOWLEDGMENTS

Thank you to my amazing husband, Brian, who is my biggest cheerleader, and to our children, Molly, Jack, Abby, and Sam, who show me what it truly means to live and learn joyfully.

A special thanks to my agent, Jill Marsal, who was enthusiastic about this book idea from the beginning; to Kimberly Meilun, who spotted its potential; and to Colleen Lawrie, Roger Labrie, Ashley Casteel, Melissa Veronesi, and the exceptional team at PublicAffairs for helping to shape and shepherd it into being.

With gratitude to my mother, Joanne McDonald, who read countless drafts, and to my father, Robert McDonald, who applauded every update. To my friends and colleagues at the Foundation for Economic Education and State Policy Network, especially Dan Sanchez and Jane McEnaney; to Lisa Snell, Adam Peshek, Keri Hunter, and Raphael Gang at Stand Together Trust; and to Meredith Olson, Beth Seling, and the team at VELA—thank you for your encouragement and your commitment to championing education entrepreneurs.

Thank you to Ed Jonson, Warren Lammert, Xiaohong Sang, Jeff and Laura Sandefer, Dan Peters, George Pearson, Cynthia Bader, Larry Reed,

## Acknowledgments

Scot Miller, Colleen Hroncich, Jon England, Peter Gray, Courtney Franklin, Alex Webb, Elisa Bishop, Patrick Carroll, Katrina Gulliver, Wayne Olson, and Diogo Costa for your leadership, friendship, and support.

Finally, to the entrepreneurs, parents, teachers, and young people spotlighted in these pages, I am so grateful for the honor of sharing your stories and so inspired by your quest to find and build joyful learning spaces.

# APPENDICES

## Appendix 1

**For Parents: Creative Schooling Options**

If you want to explore a creative schooling option for your child, here are some resources to get you started.

*General Resources*

- **Homeschooling Groups:** If you are looking for an alternative education environment—even if you're not interested in homeschooling—you should join some local homeschooling Facebook groups in your area. These can be found by searching the term "homeschooling" and your city and/or state. Once you have joined a group, post that you are looking for microschools and related alternative education programs and ask for suggestions or referrals to other Facebook groups. You may be surprised to discover what's available close to you.
- **Parenting Groups:** Similarly, you can search online for local parenting groups in your area or find Facebook groups for parents in your city/county and ask the same question there. When seeking recommendations from these groups, you may want to be more specific about what you are looking for so that you don't just get a list of conventional schools (unless that's what you want). Say that you are

looking for alternative, affordable education options that put children first, and see what kind of responses you get. I can't emphasize enough how helpful social media can be in directing you to schools and spaces in your community that you may not know exist.

- **School-Finder Networks:** As alternative education models spread, more organizations are creating directories of learning options. Some of these are local, while others are national. Here are several resources to explore:

  **Microschool Florida** (FL)—www.microschoolflorida.com
  **Wichita Innovative Schools and Educators** (KS)—www.wisetogether.org
  **Love Your School** (AZ and WV)—www.loveyourschool.org
  **Options for Education** (OR)—www.optionsforeducation.com
  **HUMA Collaborative** (TN)— https://humacollab.org
  **Ed Navigate MT** (MT)—https://ednavigatemt.com
  **EdOpt** (NH)—https://edopt.org
  **Schoolahoop** (national)—https://schoolahoop.org
  **GreatSchools** (national)—www.greatschools.org
  **My School Choice** (national)—https://myschoolchoice.com
  **Micro Schools Network** (national)—https://microschools.com

- **State-Based Parent Advocacy Groups:** There are some incredible grassroots parenting and education advocacy groups springing up across the United States, especially as school choice policies expand and parents learn they have greater access to new learning options. Look for these organizations in your state—or create one if it doesn't yet exist. Examples include: West Virginia Families United for Education (www.wvfue.org), PA Families for Education Choice (https://paedchoice.org), and Minnesota Parents Alliance (https://minnesotaparents.org).

*Specific Resources*
- **Acton Academy:** A fast-growing network of more than three hundred learner-driven microschools: www.actonacademy.org
- **Agile Learning Centers:** A global network of self-directed schools and co-learning communities: www.agilelearningcenters.org
- **Alliance for Self-Directed Education (ASDE):** Focused specifically on self-directed education and unschooling learning models, ASDE provides a global directory of SDE learning communities: www.self-directed.org
- **Alternative Education Resource Organization (AERO):** Founded in 1989, AERO supports parents and practitioners in the alternative education space, including offering a worldwide school directory: www.educationrevolution.org
- **Black Minds Matter:** A national directory of Black-owned schools and spaces: www.blackmindsmatter.net
- **Charlotte Mason in Community:** A searchable directory of Charlotte Mason–inspired homeschool programs and microschools: http://charlottemasonincommunity.com
- **Latinos Homeschooling:** A resource-rich hub of information and support for Latino homeschooling families: https://latinoshomeschooling.org
- **Liberated Learners:** A network of self-directed learning centers for tweens and teens throughout the United States: https://liberatedlearners.net
- **National Association of University Model® Schools:** A national network of dozens of faith-based hybrid homeschool programs: https://naumsinc.org
- **Prenda:** Founded in 2018, Prenda is a national network of learner-centered microschools: www.prenda.com
- **Primer:** A network of microschools currently operating in Arizona and Florida: https://primer.com

- **Wildflower Schools:** Montessori microschools run by teacher-entrepreneurs: www.wildflowerschools.org

**For Entrepreneurs: Networks, Incubators, and Accelerators**

It's a great time to be an education entrepreneur. There are myriad networks, startup incubator and accelerator programs, consultants, courses, and platforms to help you get your idea off the ground. You'll notice some overlap with the resources for parents above, as some of these organizations offer tools for both founders and families. You may find these supports valuable, or you may be content to go it alone. Either way, go for it!

- **Acton Academy:** A fast-growing network of more than three hundred learner-driven microschools: www.actonacademy.org
- **Agile Learning Centers:** A global network of self-directed schools and co-learning communities: www.agilelearningcenters.org
- **Alternative Education Resource Organization (AERO):** Founded in 1989, AERO offers periodic school-starter workshops: www.educationrevolution.org
- **Black Minds Matter:** A national directory of Black-owned schools and spaces: www.blackmindsmatter.net
- **Drexel Fund Founders Program:** A one-year paid fellowship for founders planning to launch high-quality private schools in several key states: http://drexelfund.org
- **Getting Smart Learning Innovation Fund:** Offering grants to microschools and other innovative education programs: www.gettingsmart.com/learning-innovation-fund
- **Herzog Foundation SchoolBox:** Resources and roadmaps for prospective founders looking to create a Christian microschool, hybrid homeschool, or similar program: http://hfschoolbox.com
- **Institute for Self-Directed Learning:** An organization helping teachers implement self-directed learning practices in their schools, as well as encouraging prospective founders to launch

self-directed learning communities through its New School Models Design Lab program: www.selfdirect.school
- **KaiPod Catalyst:** A microschool accelerator program offering support and information to help founders launch sustainable small businesses: www.kaipodlearning.com
- **Launch Your Kind:** An entrepreneur startup support program affiliated with Kind Academy, a nationally recognized, Florida-based microschool: www.kindacademy.org/launchkind
- **Liberated Learners:** A network of self-directed learning centers for tweens and teens throughout the United States that offers frequent school starter courses and support: https://liberatedlearners.net
- **Microschool Solutions:** Offering different tiers of service to help aspiring microschool founders successfully launch and lead their schools: http://microschool-solutions.com
- **National Association of Black Microschool Leaders:** An organization dedicated to accelerating and amplifying the work of Black microschool educators: https://nabml.org
- **National Hybrid Schools Project:** An initiative out of Kennesaw State University in Georgia, the organization hosts conferences for alternative education practitioners and provides resources and research on its website: www.kennesaw.edu/coles/centers/education-economics-center/national-hybrid-schools-project/
- **National Microschooling Center:** Providing resources and community for founders: https://microschoolingcenter.org
- **Prenda:** Prenda makes it easy for nurturing adults to launch a microschool (in their homes or neighborhood locations) as part of the popular Prenda microschool network: www.prenda.com
- **VELA:** Considered to be the largest network of founders creating alternatives to conventional schooling, VELA offers a resource-rich platform for education entrepreneurs, with opportunities for

community-building, professional development, and knowledge-sharing, as well as information on grants and seed funding: http://vela.org
- **Wildflower Schools:** Activating teacher-entrepreneurs who want to lead Montessori microschools: www.wildflowerschools.org

*Other Resources*
- **Grassroots Entrepreneur Networks:** Connecting with local founders can be one of the best ways to gain support and encouragement on your entrepreneurial journey. Look in your area for groups such as the **Innovative Educators Network** (InEd—www.innovativeeducatorsnetwork.com), **Homeschool, Unschool, Microschool, Alternative** (HUMA Collaborative, https://humacollab.org), or **Wichita Innovative Schools and Educators** (WISE, www.wisetogether.org)
- **State-Specific Accelerators:** In some states, you may find organizations offering resources and grants to new and wannabe founders. An example is **Embark Mississippi**, which helps to support education entrepreneurs in the Magnolia State through community engagement, training workshops, and access to microgrants: http://embark.ms. In Utah, the **Education Innovators Association** supports current and prospective school founders with professional development resources, networking opportunities, and entrepreneurial advocacy: https://edinnovators.org

# Appendix 2

### S.T.A.R.T.U.P.S. Roadmap Worksheet
**Strategic Vision:** What is your vision for your new business?

**Type of Business:** Will you be a nonprofit or a for-profit business, and what type of business entity will you choose (e.g., LLC, partnership, corporation, etc.)?

**Action Plan and Budget:** What is your action plan and budget?

Describe your school/space and your services, as well as why you think families in your local area would be interested in your service and how you are different from other local schools/spaces.

Budget and financial projections:

(A) Revenue: What are your revenue sources? How often will revenue be coming in?
- Revenue source #1 (e.g., tuition):
- Revenue source #2 (e.g., donations/fundraisers):
- Revenue source #3 (e.g., grants):
- Revenue source #4 (e.g., government programs):
- Revenue source #5 (other):

(B) Expenses*: Projected vs. Actual
- Business formation fees/permits:
- Classroom supplies:
- Computers/technology:
- Curriculum costs:
- Furniture/desks:
- Insurance:
- Legal/accounting fees:
- Marketing/advertising:
- Miscellaneous set-up costs:
- Renovation/maintenance costs:
- Rent/utilities:

- Staff salaries/benefits:
- Taxes:
- Website development/hosting:

**Rules and Regulations:** What are the local, state, and federal rules and regulations that could affect your operations?

**Trusted Advisors:** Who are some trusted advisors you can call upon for business advice?

**Understanding Your Customers:** What do families in your area want for their children's education? How do you know? How can you connect with them to share more about your new program? By what date will enrollment contracts and tuition deposits be due?

**People, Places, and Policies:** Who do you need to hire, and how will you find them? Where are you going to be based? What policies and procedures have you created for staff, students, and families?

**Sustainability and Scale:** What is your plan for ongoing financial sustainability? When will you start taking a salary? Do you want to expand someday?

*Don't forget: For your first few startup months (or longer), your expenses may exceed your revenue. It's important to know the amount of money that you will need to cover any shortfall between your revenue and your expenses. For example, your startup costs may include the first month's rent, last month's rent, and a security deposit on your leased property, as well as insurance, business formation fees, website hosting, and so on. These expenses may accumulate before you have any tuition coming in, so be sure to account for these costs—as well as any contingencies, such as lower enrollment—as you launch your new business.

# NOTES

**Introduction**

Epigraph note: Reid Hoffman and Ben Casnocha, *The Startup of You* (New York: Currency, 2022), 3.

1. Rick Hess, "What the Heck Are Microschools?" *Education Week*, May 31, 2023, www.edweek.org/policy-politics/opinion-what-the-heck-are-microschools/2023/05.

2. Peter Jamison et al., "Home Schooling's Rise from Fringe to Fastest-Growing Form of Education," *Washington Post*, October 31, 2023, www.washingtonpost.com/education/interactive/2023/homeschooling-growth-data-by-district/.

3. "Innovative Educators by the Numbers," Innovative Educators Network, accessed August 31, 2024, www.innovativeeducatorsnetwork.com.

4. Ashley Soifer, email message to author, April 16, 2024.

5. Laura Meckler, "How Homeschooling Left the Kitchen Table and Became a Big Business," *Washington Post*, August 17, 2023, www.washingtonpost.com/education/interactive/2023/homeschooling-microschools-pods-esa-vouchers/.

6. Don Soifer and Ashley Soifer, "American Microschools: A Sector Analysis," *National Microschooling Center*, April 2023, https://microschoolingcenter.org/american-microschools.

7. Milton Friedman, *Capitalism and Freedom: Fortieth Anniversary Edition* (Chicago: University of Chicago Press, 1982), preface.

8. "Average Private School Tuition Cost," Private School Review, accessed September 30, 2024, www.privateschoolreview.com/tuition-stats/private-school-cost-by-state; Kaylee Anesta, "Spending per Pupil in Public Schools Averaged $15,633, up 8.9% in FY 2022," US Census Bureau, April 23, 2024, www.census.gov/library/stories/2024/04/public-school-spending.html.

9. Soifer, "American Microschools."

**Chapter 1: Changes**

Epigraph note: Mark Zuckerberg, quoted in Samantha Rhodes, "Obama, Zuckerberg Promote Entrepreneurship at Stanford," CNET, June 24, 2016, www.cnet.com/tech/tech-industry/obama-zuck-entrepreneurship-stanford-brexit-facebook/.

1. Thomas Dee, "Where the Kids Went: Nonpublic Schooling and Demographic Change During the Pandemic Exodus from Public Schools," Urban Institute, February 9, 2023,

www.urban.org/research/publication/where-kids-went-nonpublic-schooling-and-demographic-change-during-pandemic.

2. Mike McShane, "Opinions on Homeschooling Have Changed During the Pandemic," *Forbes*, March 9, 2021, www.forbes.com/sites/mikemcshane/2021/03/09/opinions-on-homeschooling-have-changed-during-the-pandemic/.

3. Terry Moe, *The Politics of Institutional Reform: Katrina, Education, and the Second Face of Power* (Cambridge, UK: Cambridge University Press, 2019), introduction.

4. Douglas N. Harris and Matthew F. Larsen, "Taken by Storm: The Effects of Hurricane Katrina on Medium-Term Student Outcomes in New Orleans," Education Research Alliance for New Orleans, July 15, 2018, https://educationresearchalliancenola.org/files/publications/Harris-Larsen-Reform-Effects-2021-05-17.pdf.

5. Kerry McDonald, "The World's Homeschooling Moment," *Forbes*, March 11, 2020, www.forbes.com/sites/kerrymcdonald/2020/03/11/the-worlds-homeschooling-moment/.

6. Dee, "Where the Kids Went."

7. Peter Jamison et al., "Home Schooling's Rise from Fringe to Fastest-Growing Form of Education," *Washington Post*, October 31, 2023, www.washingtonpost.com/education/interactive/2023/homeschooling-growth-data-by-district/; Lauraine Langreo, "Charter School Enrollment Holds Steady After Big Early Pandemic Growth," *Education Week*, November 30, 2022, www.edweek.org/policy-politics/charter-school-enrollment-holds-steady-after-big-early-pandemic-growth/2022/11.

8. Peter Jamison et al., "Home Schooling's Rise."

9. Angela R. Watson, Homeschool Hub, The Johns Hopkins Institute for Education Policy, 2023, https://education.jhu.edu/edpolicy/policy-research-initiatives/homeschool-hub/.

10. Cooper Conway, "2025 EdChoice Funded Eligibility Rankings," EdChoice, January 23, 2025, www.edchoice.org/engage/2025-edchoice-funded-eligibility-rankings/.

11. Todd Rose, quoted in "Study Reveals Crisis of Confidence in American Education," eLearningInside News, January 18, 2023, https://news.elearninginside.com/populace-study-reveals-crisis-of-confidence-in-american-education/.

**Chapter 2: Alternatives**

Epigraph note: Sam Walton, *Sam Walton: Made in America* (New York: Bantam Books, 1993), 317.

1. Allen Graubard, *Alternative Education: The Free School Movement in the United States* (Stanford, CA: ERIC Clearinghouse on Educational Media and Technology, 1972), https://eric.ed.gov/?id=ED066059.

2. Ron Miller, *Free Schools, Free People: Education and Democracy After the 1960s* (Albany, NY: State University of New York Press, 2002), 130.

3. John Holt and Patrick Farenga, *Teach Your Own: The John Holt Book of Homeschooling*, rev. ed. (New York: Da Capo Press, 2003), 279.

4. Milton Gaither, "Why Homeschooling Happened," *Educational Horizons* 86, no. 4 (2008): 226–237, https://files.eric.ed.gov/fulltext/EJ799390.pdf.

5. Katherine Schaeffer, "9 Facts About Bullying in the U.S.," *Pew Research Center*, November 17, 2023, https://www.pewresearch.org/short-reads/2023/11/17/9-facts-about-bullying-in-the-us/.

6. Eric Wearne, *Defining Hybrid Homeschools in America: Little Platoons* (Lanham, MD: Lexington Books, 2020), chapter 2, Kindle.

7. Wearne, *Defining Hybrid Homeschools*, chapter 1.

8. Kerry McDonald, "Got Teacher Burnout? Launch A Microschool," *Forbes*, November 24, 2021, www.forbes.com/sites/kerrymcdonald/2021/11/24/got-teacher-burnout-launch-a-microschool/.

9. Elizabeth D. Steiner and Ashley Woo, "Job-Related Stress Threatens the Teacher Supply: Key Findings from the 2021 State of the U.S. Teacher Survey," RAND, June 15, 2021, www.rand.org/pubs/research_reports/RRA1108-1.html.

10. Sy Doan et al., "Teacher Well-Being and Intentions to Leave: Findings from the 2023 State of the American Teacher Survey," RAND, June 21, 2023, www.rand.org/pubs/research_reports/RRA1108-8.html.

## Chapter 3: Founders

Epigraph note: Vinod Khosla, "We Need Large Innovations," Medium, June 1, 2018, https://medium.com/@vkhosla/we-need-large-innovations-58e3eaaf8138.

1. "America's Entrepreneurial Boom Continued Apace in 2021," *The Economist*, January 13, 2022, www.economist.com/graphic-detail/2022/01/13/americas-entrepreneurial-boom-continued-apace-in-2021.

2. Melissa Angell, "New Small-Business Applications Surged by 5.5 Million in 2023, Marking Yet Another Record," *Inc.*, January 12, 2024, www.inc.com/melissa-angell/new-small-business-applications-surged-55m-in-2023-marking-yet-another-record.html.

3. Abha Bhattarai, "American Entrepreneurship Is on the Rise," *Washington Post*, September 14, 2023, www.washingtonpost.com/business/2023/09/14/small-business-entrepreneurship-gem-report/.

4. Kenan Fikri and Daniel Newman, "How the Pandemic Rebooted Entrepreneurship in the U.S.," *Harvard Business Review*, January 17, 2024, https://hbr.org/2024/01/how-the-pandemic-rebooted-entrepreneurship-in-the-u-s.

5. Robert Fairlie, "National Report on Early-Stage Entrepreneurship in the United States: 2021," Ewing Marion Kauffman Foundation, March 2022, https://indicators.kauffman.org/wp-content/uploads/sites/2/2022/03/2021-Early-State-Entrepreneurship-National-Report.pdf.

6. Bhattarai, "American Entrepreneurship Is on the Rise."

7. Denisha Merriweather, "Black Minds Matter," RealClearEducation, July 17, 2020, www.realcleareducation.com/articles/2020/07/17/black_minds_matter_110443.html.

8. Andrew Bacher-Hicks, Stephen B. Billings, and David J. Deming, "Proving the School-to-Prison Pipeline," *Education Next*, December 20, 2023, www.educationnext.org/proving-school-to-prison-pipeline-stricter-middle-schools-raise-risk-of-adult-arrests/.

9. Jessica Perez, "New Law Prohibits Suspension of Students Pre-kindergarten to Second Grade," KETV7-Omaha, June 20, 2023, www.ketv.com/article/omaha-new-law-prohibits-suspension-students-pre-kindergarten-second-grade/44273028.

10. Ellena Sempeles and Jiashan Cui, *Parent and Family Involvement in Education: 2023* (Washington, DC: National Center for Education Statistics, September 2024), https://nces.ed.gov/pubs2024/2024113.pdf.

11. Laura Meckler et al., "Home Schooling Today Is Less Religious and More Diverse, Poll Finds," *Washington Post*, September 26, 2023, www.washingtonpost.com/education/2023/09/26/home-schooling-vs-public-school-poll/.

12. "Attendance and Absenteeism: 2022–23," Omaha Public Schools, www.ops.org/cms/lib/NE50000695/Centricity/Domain/204/Attendance%20Report%202022-23%20BOE%20Report.pdf.

13. Lauren Wagner, "OPS Board Talks Achievements and Deficiencies in Recent State Test Scores," *Omaha World-Herald*, November 27, 2023, https://omaha.com/news/local/education/ops-board-talks-achievements-and-deficiencies-in-recent-state-test-scores/article_422d3be8-8d3a-11ee-9a5c-a74b28de9f68.html.

14. "Survival of Private Sector Establishments by Opening Year," US Bureau of Labor Statistics, www.bls.gov/bdm/us_age_naics_00_table7.txt.

15. Friederike Welter et al., "Everyday Entrepreneurship—A Call for Entrepreneurship Research to Embrace Entrepreneurial Diversity," *Entrepreneurship Theory and Practice* 41, no. 3 (2017): 311–321, https://doi.org/10.1111/etap.12258.

16. Timothy Butler, "Hiring an Entrepreneurial Leader," in *HBR's 10 Must Reads on Entrepreneurship and Startups* (Boston: Harvard Business Review Press, 2018), 9.

17. Mark Thornton, "Turning the Word Upside Down: How Cantillon Redefined the Entrepreneur," *Quarterly Journal of Austrian Economics* 23, no. 3–4 (2020): 265–280, https://doi.org/10.35297/qjae.010071.

18. Joseph A. Schumpeter, *Capitalism, Socialism and Democracy*, 3rd ed. (New York: Harper Perennial Modern Thought, 2008), 84.

19. Joseph A. Schumpeter, "The Creative Response in Economic History," *The Journal of Economic History* 7, no. 2 (1947): 149–159, https://doi.org/10.1017/S0022050700054279.

20. Clayton M. Christensen, Michael E. Raynor, and Rory McDonald, "What Is Disruptive Innovation?" *Harvard Business Review*, February 16, 2024, https://hbr.org/2015/12/what-is-disruptive-innovation.

21. Steve Denning, "Fresh Insights from Clayton Christensen on Disruptive Innovation," *Forbes*, December 3, 2015, www.forbes.com/sites/stevedenning/2015/12/02/fresh-insights-from-clayton-christensen-on-disruptive-innovation/?sh=78c16cdf4702.

22. Barbara Gomez-Aguinaga, George Foste, and Jerry I. Porras, "2023 State of Latino Entrepreneurship," Stanford Graduate School of Business, March 2024, www.gsb.stanford.edu/faculty-research/publications/state-latino-entrepreneurship-2023.

23. Rebecca Klein et al., "The New Homeschoolers: More Diverse, Very Committed," *Hechinger Report*, February 9, 2022, https://hechingerreport.org/the-new-homeschoolers-more-diverse-just-as-committed/.

24. Anne Marie Chaker, "Amid Coronavirus, Parents 'Pod Up' to Form At-Home Schools," *Wall Street Journal*, July 21, 2020, www.wsj.com/articles/amid-coronavirus-parents-pod-up-to-form-at-home-schools-11595323805.

25. Melinda Wenner Moyer, "Coronavirus Pods, Microschools and Tutors: Can Parents Really Solve the Education Crisis on Their Own?" *New York Times*, July 22, 2020, www.nytimes.com/2020/07/22/parenting/school-pods-coronavirus.html.

26. Megan Brenan, "K–12 Parents' Satisfaction with Child's Education Slips," Gallup, August 25, 2020, https://news.gallup.com/poll/317852/parents-satisfaction-child-education-slips.aspx.

27. Adam Thierer, *Evasive Entrepreneurs and the Future of Governance: How Innovation Improves Economies and Governments* (Washington, DC: Cato Institute, 2020).

28. Alli Aldis, "Poll Suggests 10% of School Parents Are Microschooling Their Kids," EdChoice, May 15, 2024, www.edchoice.org/engage/poll-suggests-10-of-school-parents-are-microschooling-their-kids/.

**Chapter 4: Families**

Epigraph note: "Anita Roddick: The Radical Woman," The Body Shop, www.thebodyshop.com/en-au/about-us/activism/anita-roddick/a/a00077.

1. "Elon Musk Talks About a New Type of School He Created for His Kids 2015," Elon Musk best videos, November 30, 2015, YouTube, 31:23, www.youtube.com/watch?v=y6909DjNLCM.

2. Populace Inc., "Populace Insights: Purpose of Education Index," accessed October 13, 2024, https://static1.squarespace.com/static/59153bc0e6f2e109b2a85cbc/t/63e96b44a0e46d79a10ecf26/1676241761790/Purpose+of+Education+Index.pdf.

3. Lydia Saad, "Americans' State of the Nation Ratings Remain at Record Low," Gallup, February 5, 2025, https://news.gallup.com/poll/656114/americans-state-nation-ratings-remain-record-low.aspx.

4. Lord Acton, letter to Archbishop Mandell Creighton, April 5, 1887, https://history.hanover.edu/courses/excerpts/165acton.html.

5. Zach Hrynowski, "K–12 Schools Struggle to Engage Gen Z Students," Gallup, August 21, 2024, https://news.gallup.com/poll/648896/schools-struggle-engage-gen-students.aspx.

6. Tim Hodges, "School Engagement Is More than Just Talk," Gallup, October 25, 2018, www.gallup.com/education/244022/school-engagement-talk.aspx.

7. Rebecca T. Leeb et al., "Mental Health–Related Emergency Department Visits Among Children Aged < 18 Years During the COVID-19 Pandemic—United States, January 1–October 17, 2020," US Centers for Disease Control and Prevention, *Morbidity and Mortality Weekly Report* 69, no. 45 (2020): 1675–1680, https://doi.org/10.15585/mmwr.mm6945a3.

8. Ellen Yard et al., "Emergency Department Visits for Suspected Suicide Attempts Among Persons Aged 12–25 Years Before and During the COVID-19 Pandemic—United States, January 2019–May 2021," US Centers for Disease Control and Prevention, *Morbidity and Mortality Weekly Report* 70, no. 24 (2021): 888–894, https://doi.org/10.15585/mmwr.mm7024e1.

9. Elizabeth M. Gaylor et al., "Suicidal Thoughts and Behaviors Among High School Students—Youth Risk Behavior Survey, United States, 2021," US Centers for Disease Control and Prevention, *Morbidity and Mortality Weekly Report. Supplement/MMWR Supplements* 72, no. 1 (2023): 45–54, https://doi.org/10.15585/mmwr.su7201a6.

10. "Data and Statistics on Children's Mental Health," US Centers for Disease Control and Prevention, March 8, 2023, accessed July 13, 2024, www.cdc.gov/childrensmentalhealth/data.html; Asha Z. Ivey-Stephenson et al., "Suicidal Ideation and Behaviors Among High School Students—Youth Risk Behavior Survey, United States, 2019," US Centers for Disease Control and Prevention, *Morbidity and Mortality Weekly Report. Supplement/MMWR Supplements* 69, no. 1 (2020): 47–55, https://doi.org/10.15585/mmwr.su6901a6.

11. Clayton M. Christensen et al., *Competing Against Luck: The Story of Innovation and Customer Choice* (New York: HarperCollins, 2016), 7.

12. Thomas Arnett, "Families on the New Frontier: Mapping and Meeting the Growing Demand for Unconventional Schooling," Christensen Institute, January 9, 2024, www.christenseninstitute.org/publications/microschools-families/.

13. "By the Numbers," Kansas City Public Schools, 2023, accessed July 13, 2024, www.kcpublicschools.org/about/kcps-numbers.

**Chapter 5: Startups**

Epigraph note: John Mackey, Steven McIntosh, and Carter Phipps, *Conscious Leadership: Elevating Humanity Through Business* (New York: Portfolio, 2020), xix.

1. Daphna Bassok, Scott Latham, and Anna Rorem, "Is Kindergarten the New First Grade?" *AERA Open*, 2, no. 1 (2016): 1–31, https://doi.org/10.1177/2332858415616358.

2. Walter Isaacson, *Elon Musk* (New York: Simon & Schuster, 2023), 92–93, Kindle.

3. Jeffrey E. Garten, *The Mind of the CEO* (New York: Basic Books, 2001), 143, Kindle.

4. Amy Fass, "What the World Gets Wrong About Nonprofits," *Stanford Social Innovation Review*, June 7, 2022, https://ssir.org/books/excerpts/entry/what_the_world_gets_wrong_about_nonprofits#.

5. "Khan Academy, Inc.," ProPublica Nonprofit Explorer, 2022, https://projects.propublica.org/nonprofits/organizations/261544963.

6. Stella Kotik, "Dean's Speaker Series: Sal Khan on How 'Delusional Optimism' Led to Free, World-Class Education for Anyone, Anywhere," Berkeley Haas, September 28, 2003, https://newsroom.haas.berkeley.edu/deans-speaker-series-sal-khan-on-how-delusional-optimism-led-to-free-world-class-education-for-anyone-anywhere/.

7. Tom Eisenmann, *Why Startups Fail: A New Roadmap for Entrepreneurial Success* (New York: Currency, 2021), 22, Kindle.

8. "Education Entrepreneur Freedom Index," Yes. Every Kid. Foundation., February 29, 2024, https://yeseverykidfoundation.org/education-entrepreneur-freedom-index-report/.

9. "The School Starter Checklist: Understanding the Regulatory Landscape for Private Schools in America," EdChoice, 2024, www.edchoice.org/wp-content/uploads/2024/06/School-Starter-Checklist.pdf.

10. Alli Aldis, "Poll Suggests 10% of School Parents Are Microschooling Their Kids," EdChoice, May 15, 2024, www.edchoice.org/engage/poll-suggests-10-of-school-parents-are-microschooling-their-kids/.

11. Eric Ries, *The Lean Startup: How Today's Entrepreneurs Use Continuous Innovation to Create Radically Successful Businesses* (New York: Currency, 2011), 124, Kindle.

12. "Hedda Hopper's Hollywood," *The Lima News*, July 15, 1957, accessed July 13, 2024, https://media.snopes.com/2022/04/The_Lima_News_Mon__Jul_15__1957_.pdf.

13. Sherin Shibu, "Side Hustles Are Soaring as Entrepreneurs Start Businesses Working Part- or Full-Time Elsewhere, According to a New Report," *Entrepreneur*, April 10, 2024, www.entrepreneur.com/business-news/side-hustles-are-driving-new-businesses-entrepreneurship/472507.

## Chapter 6: Searches

Epigraph note: "Annie Malone and Madam C. J. Walker: Pioneers of the African American Beauty Industry," National Museum of African American History and Culture, accessed October 28, 2024, https://nmaahc.si.edu/explore/stories/annie-malone-and-madam-cj-walker-pioneers-african-american-beauty-industry.

1. Carl Kaestle, *Pillars of the Republic: Common Schools and American Society, 1780–1860* (New York: Hill and Wang, 1983), 4.

2. William D. Swan, ed., "Immigration," *The Massachusetts Teacher (1848-1855)* 4, no. 10 (1851): 289–291, http://nationalhumanitiescenter.org/pds/triumphnationalism/hickoryhs/massteacher.pdf.

3. Samuel Bowles and Herbert Gintis, "The Origins of Mass Public Education," in *History of Education: Major Themes, Volume II: Education in Its Social Context*, ed. Roy Lowe (London: RoutledgeFlamer, 2000), 78.

4. Shannon Najmabadi, "Missouri Supreme Court Upholds Law That Allows Jailing Parents of Truant Children," *Wall Street Journal*, August 15, 2023, www.wsj.com/articles/missouri-supreme-court-upholds-law-that-allows-jailing-parents-of-truant-children-cd9caa07.

5. David B. Tyack, *The One Best System: A History of American Urban Education* (Cambridge, MA: Harvard University Press, 1974), 28.

6. Paul E. Peterson, Samuel Barrows, and Thomas Gift, "After Common Core, States Set Rigorous Standards," *Education Next* 16, no. 3 (2016): 9–15, www.educationnext.org/after-common-core-states-set-rigorous-standards.

7. Kevin Mahnken, "Classical Academies: What If Education's Next Big Thing Is 2,500 Years Old?" *The 74*, March 22, 2023, www.the74million.org/article/amid-the-pandemic-a-classical-education-boom-what-if-the-next-big-school-trend-is-2500-years-old/.

8. Don Soifer and Ashley Soifer, "American Microschools: A Sector Analysis," *National Microschooling Center*, April 2024, https://microschoolingcenter.org/sectoranalysis2024.

## Chapter 7: Solutions

Epigraph note: Brian Chesky, quoted in Kerry Close, "4 Things Airbnb's Brian Chesky Thinks All Young Entrepreneurs Need to Know," *Inc.*, October 9, 2015, www.inc.com/kerry-close/4-lessons-from-airbnb-co-founder-on-building-your-own-company.html.

1. "Youth Risk Behavior Survey Data Summary & Trends Report 2011-2021," US Centers for Disease Control and Prevention, accessed October 13, 2024, www.cdc.gov/healthyyouth/data/yrbs/pdf/YRBS_Data-Summary-Trends_Report2023_508.pdf.

2. Ama Mazama and Garvey Musumunu, *African Americans and Homeschooling: Motivations, Opportunities and Challenges* (New York: Routledge, 2015), 43, Kindle.

3. Casey Eggleston and Jason Fields, "Census Bureau's Household Pulse Survey Shows Significant Increase in Homeschooling Rates in Fall 2020," US Census Bureau, March 22, 2021, www.census.gov/library/stories/2021/03/homeschooling-on-the-rise-during-covid-19-pandemic.html#:~:text=Homeschooling%20rates%20are%20increasing%20across,12.

4. Cynthia Reuben and Nazik Elgaddal, "Attention-Deficit/Hyperactivity Disorder in Children Ages 5-17 Years: United States, 2020–2022," US National Center for Health Statistics, NCHS Data Brief no. 499, March 20, 2024, https://doi.org/10.15620/cdc/148043.

5. Dongying Li et al., "Exposure to Nature for Children with Autism Spectrum Disorder: Benefits, Caveats, and Barriers," *Health & Place* 55 (2019): 71–79, https://doi.org/10.1016/j.healthplace.2018.11.005.

6. Sarah Carr, "Too Many Schools Are Misdiagnosing Dyslexia," *Scientific American*, December 1, 2023, www.scientificamerican.com/article/too-many-schools-are-misdiagnosing-dyslexia1.

7. Alejandra O'Connell Domenech, "The US Is Experiencing a Boom in Microschools. What Are They?" *The Hill*, April 6, 2024, https://thehill.com/changing-america/enrichment/education/4574859-the-us-is-experiencing-a-boom-in-microschools-what-are-they.

8. Jackie Mader, "Kids' Access to Recess Varies Greatly," *Hechinger Report*, May 12, 2022, https://hechingerreport.org/kids-access-to-recess-varies-greatly/.

## Chapter 8: Metrics

Epigraph note: Richard Branson, "My Metric for Success? Happiness," LinkedIn, April 20, 2016, www.linkedin.com/pulse/my-metric-success-happiness-richard-branson/?trk=mp-reader-card.

1. "Bob Parsons' 16 Rules for Success in Business and Life in General," BobParsons.com, https://bobparsons.com/16-rules/.

2. Thomas Sowell, *Knowledge and Decisions* (New York: Basic Books, 1980), 79, Kindle.

3. Sebastian Suggate, Elizabeth Schaughency, and Elaine Reese, "Children Learning to Read Later Catch up to Children Reading Earlier," *Early Childhood Research Quarterly* 28, no. 1 (2013): 33–48, https://doi.org/10.1016/j.ecresq.2012.04.004.

4. Abigail L. Larrison, Alan J. Daly, and Carol VanVoore, "Twenty Years and Counting: A Look at Waldorf in the Public Sector Using Online Sources," *Current Issues in Education* 15, no. 3 (2012), https://cie.asu.edu/ojs/index.php/cieatasu/article/view/807/386.

5. "Measuring What Matters: How Founders of Unconventional Models Define and Measure Learner Outcomes," VELA, July 2024, www.learneroutcomes.vela.org.

6. Livia Gershon, "A Short History of Standardized Tests," *JSTOR Daily*, May 12, 2015, https://daily.jstor.org/short-history-standardized-tests/.

7. J. Scott Payne and Jeff Allen, "ACT Composite Scores Among Homeschooled Students Trended Up from 2001 to 2019," ACT.org, June 2020, www.act.org/content/dam/act/unsecured/documents/R1831-act-homeschool-stats-2020-08.pdf.

8. Josh Moody, "Some Colleges Slow to Drop Testing for Homeschooled Students," *Inside Higher Ed*, December 12, 2021, www.insidehighered.com/admissions/article/2021/12/13/some-colleges-slow-drop-testing-homeschooled-students.

9. Sarah Wood, "Some Colleges Are Requiring Test Scores Again: What It Means for Applicants," *U.S. News & World Report*, May 13, 2024, www.usnews.com/education/best-colleges/applying/articles/some-colleges-are-requiring-test-scores-again-what-it-means-for-applicants.

10. Martina Raudenska et al., "Johann Gregor Mendel: The Victory of Statistics over Human Imagination," *European Journal of Human Genetics* 31 (2023): 744–748, www.nature.com/articles/s41431-023-01303-1.

11. "About Gregor Johann Mendel," Office of the President, Villanova University, n.d., www1.villanova.edu/villanova/president/university_events/mendelmedal/aboutmendel.html.

12. "2023 Schooling in America: What Do the Public and Parents Say About K–12 Education?" EdChoice, 2023, www.edchoice.org/wp-content/uploads/2023/07/SIA-2023-REPORT-FINAL.pdf.

13. Jill Barshay, "Proof Points: High Schoolers Account for Nearly 1 Out of Every 5 Community College Students," *Hechinger Report*, July 24, 2023, https://hechingerreport.org/proof-points-high-schoolers-account-for-nearly-1-out-of-every-5-community-college-students/.

14. Daniel Hamlin, "Do Homeschooled Students Lack Opportunities to Acquire Cultural Capital? Evidence from a Nationally Representative Survey of American Households," *Peabody Journal of Education* 94, no. 3 (2019): 312–327, https://doi.org/10.1080/0161956X.2019.1617582.

15. Cynthia K. Drenovsky and Isaiah Cohen, "The Impact of Homeschooling on the Adjustment of College Students," *International Social Science Review* 87, no. 1–2 (2012): 19–34, www.jstor.org/stable/41887517.

16. Jill Radsken, "Homeschooled En Route to Harvard," *The Harvard Gazette*, February 21, 2018, https://news.harvard.edu/gazette/story/2018/02/three-harvard-students-on-lessons-of-homeschooling/.

17. Don Soifer and Ashley Soifer, "American Microschools: A Sector Analysis," National Microschooling Center, April 2024, https://microschoolingcenter.org/sectoranalysis2024.

18. Sarah G. Wood et al., "Test Anxiety and a High-Stakes Standardized Reading Comprehension Test: A Behavioral Genetics Perspective," *Merrill-Palmer Quarterly* 62, no. 3 (2016): 233–251, https://doi.org/10.13110/merrpalmquar1982.62.3.0233.

## Chapter 9: Challenges

Epigraph note: Steve Jobs, interviewed by Daniel Morrow, Smithsonian Institution Oral and Video Histories, April 20, 1995, https://americanhistory.si.edu/comphist/sj1.html.

1. "Entrepreneurial Dreams: Key Findings from Right to Start's Bipartisan Voter Poll on Entrepreneurship," RighttoStart.org, accessed October 14, 2024, www.righttostart.org/poll.

2. "Education Entrepreneur Freedom Index," Yes. Every Kid. Foundation., February 29, 2024, https://yeseverykidfoundation.org/education-entrepreneur-freedom-index-report/.

3. Chris Edwards, "Occupational Licensing," Empowering the New American Worker, The Cato Institute, December 15, 2022, www.cato.org/publications/facilitating-personal-improvement-occupational-licensing.

4. Linda Jacobson, "Exclusive Data: Thousands of Schools at Risk of Closing Due to Enrollment Loss," The 74, January 9, 2024, www.the74million.org/article/exclusive-data-thousands-of-schools-at-risk-of-closing-due-to-enrollment-loss/.

5. Andrea Torres, "Here Is a List of Broward Schools Under 'Consideration' for Closure, Changes," Local10.com, April 29, 2024, www.local10.com/news/local/2024/04/30/developing-here-is-a-list-of-broward-schools-under-consideration-for-closing/.

6. Gabriella Gage, "Can Catholic Schools Be Saved?" *Boston Magazine*, May 5, 2024, www.bostonmagazine.com/education/2024/05/05/catholic-schools/.

7. Jon Marcus, "Colleges Are Now Closing at a Pace of One a Week. What Happens to the Students?" *Hechinger Report*, April 26, 2024, https://hechingerreport.org/colleges-are-now-closing-at-a-pace-of-one-a-week-what-happens-to-the-students/.

8. Andrew Atterbury, "'Microschools Could Be the Next Big School Choice Push. Florida Is on the Cutting Edge," *Politico*, July 24, 2024, www.politico.com/news/2024/07/24/microschools-florida-school-choice-00169887.

9. Allen Graubard, *Alternative Education: The Free School Movement in the United States* (Stanford, CA: ERIC Clearinghouse on Educational Media and Technology, 1972), https://eric.ed.gov/?id=ED066059.

10. Alix Martichoux, "These Cities and Towns Are Most Dangerous in the US, Study Finds," *The Hill*, December 22, 2023, https://thehill.com/homenews/nexstar_media_wire/4366668-these-cities-and-towns-are-most-dangerous-in-the-us-study-finds/.

## Chapter 10: Expansions

Epigraph note: Donna Levin, quoted in Kara Baskin, "How to Scale a Startup," MIT Management Sloan School, October 3, 2016, https://mitsloan.mit.edu/ideas-made-to-matter/how-to-scale-a-startup.

1. Sawdah Bhaimiya, "Netflix's Co-Founder Says Blockbuster Execs Tried Not to Laugh When They Pitched a $50 Million Partnership—It's Now Worth $149 Billion," *Business Insider*, April 19, 2023, www.businessinsider.com/netflix-blockbuster-pitch-meeting-rejected-50-million-partnership-deal-2023-4.

2. Catherine Allen, "Public School Enrollment in the U.S. Slipping as Alternatives Gain Political Support," *NBC News*, April 21, 2024, www.nbcnews.com/data-graphics/public-school-enrollment-us-states-map-chart-rcna119262.

3. Peter Thiel and Blake Masters, *Zero to One: Notes on Startups, or How to Build the Future* (New York: Currency, 2014), 51, Kindle.

4. Brandy Anderson and Karen Amesse, "California Independent Study Charter Schools: Summary of Home-Based Pedagogies, Enrollment Trends, and Student Demographics,"

*American Journal of Distance Education* 36, no. 4 (2022): 265–287, https://doi.org/10.1080/08923647.2022.2068316.

5. James Vaznis, "Public School Enrollment Plummets Across Massachusetts amid Coronavirus Pandemic," *Boston Globe*, November 24, 2020, www.bostonglobe.com/2020/11/24/metro/public-school-enrollment-plummets-across-massachusetts-amid-coronavirus-pandemic/.

6. Ben Gilbert and David Rosenthal, hosts, "NVIDIA CEO Jensen Huang," *Acquired* (podcast), October 15, 2023, www.acquired.fm/episodes/jensen-huang.

7. Max Marmer et al., "Why Startups Fail: Premature Scaling." Startup Genome, August 1, 2011, https://startupgenome.com/reports/startup-genome-why-startups-fail-premature-scaling.

**Chapter 11: Intrapreneurs**

Epigraph note: "Larry Ellison USC Commencement Speech," USC, May 3, 2016, YouTube, 23:29, www.youtube.com/watch?v=5DJaWWwITRM.

1. Kerry McDonald, *Unschooled: Raising Curious, Well-Educated Children Outside the Conventional Classroom* (Chicago: Chicago Review Press, 2019), 128.

2. Kathleen McNerney, "Somerville School Committee Votes Against 'Innovation School' Plan," *WBUR*, March 18, 2019, www.wbur.org/news/2019/03/18/powderhouse-studios-innovation-school.

3. Mr. Futrell et al., "Minutes of the Somerville School Committee Meeting on March 18, 2019," City of Somerville, Massachusetts, March 18, 2019, https://somerville.k12.ma.us/sites/default/files/Minutes%20for%20SC%20Meeting%20031819-%20Final.pdf.

4. Felix Richter, "Charted: There Are More Mobile Phones than People in the World," World Economic Forum, April 12, 2023, www.weforum.org/agenda/2023/04/charted-there-are-more-phones-than-people-in-the-world.

5. Elliot Kaufman, "The Teachers Union's Tiny New Enemy," *Wall Street Journal*, October 14, 2020, www.wsj.com/articles/the-teachers-unions-tiny-new-enemy-11602709305.

6. Sofoklis Goulas, "Breaking Down Enrollment Declines in Public Schools," Brookings, March 14, 2024, www.brookings.edu/articles/breaking-down-enrollment-declines-in-public-schools/.

**Chapter 12: Trends**

Epigraph note: Peter Thiel and Blake Masters, *Zero to One: Notes on Startups, or How to Build the Future* (New York: Currency, 2014), 137.

1. Peter Jamison et al., "Home Schooling's Rise from Fringe to Fastest-Growing Form of Education," *Washington Post*, October 31, 2023, www.washingtonpost.com/education/interactive/2023/homeschooling-growth-data-by-district/.

2. Angela Watson, "Homeschool Growth: 2023–2024," Johns Hopkins University Institute for Education Policy, September 2024, https://education.jhu.edu/edpolicy/policy-research-initiatives/homeschool-hub/homeschool-growth-2023-2024/.

3. Andrew Atterbury, "School Choice Programs Have Been Wildly Successful Under DeSantis. Now Public Schools Might Close," *Politico*, May 26, 2024, www.politico.com/news/2024/05/26/desantis-florida-school-closures-00159926#.

4. Nicholas Bloom et al., "Survey: Remote Work Isn't Going Away—and Executives Know It," *Harvard Business Review*, August 28, 2023, https://hbr.org/2023/08/survey-remote-work-isnt-going-away-and-executives-know-it.

5. Ben Wigert, Jim Harter, and Sangeeta Agrawal, "The Future of the Office Has Arrived: It's Hybrid," Gallup, October 9, 2023, www.gallup.com/workplace/511994/future-office-arrived-hybrid.aspx.

6. Kara Miller, "Private Schools in Boston Suburbs Are Seeing a Student Boom. Why?" *Boston Globe*, September 9, 2024, www.bostonglobe.com/2024/09/09/business/private-schools-brookline-cambridge-newton-public/.

7. Michael Strong, *Be the Solution: How Entrepreneurs and Conscious Capitalists Can Solve All the World's Problems* (Hoboken, NJ: John Wiley & Sons, 2009), 15, Kindle.

8. Lydia Saad, "Historically Low Faith in U.S. Institutions Continues," Gallup, July 6, 2023, https://news.gallup.com/poll/508169/historically-low-faith-institutions-continues.aspx.

9. Sarah Krouse and David Marcelis, "What's on TV? For Many Americans, It's Now YouTube," *Wall Street Journal*, May 14, 2024, www.wsj.com/business/media/youtube-viewership-cable-25bf3589.

10. Alex Sherman, "YouTube Dominates Streaming, Forcing Media Companies to Decide Whether It's Friend or Foe," *CNBC*, June 26, 2024, www.cnbc.com/2024/06/26/youtube-streaming-dominance-media-strategy.html.

11. Gerrit De Vynck, "Big Tech Wants AI Regulation. The Rest of Silicon Valley Is Skeptical," *Washington Post*, November 9, 2023, www.washingtonpost.com/technology/2023/11/09/ai-regulation-silicon-valley-skeptics/.

12. Tennessee State Board of Education, "Rules of the State Board of Education, Chapter 0520-07-02, Non-Public School Approval Process," August 2023, https://publications.tnsosfiles.com/rules/0520/0520-07/0520-07-02.20230815.pdf.

13. Tonyaa Weathersbee, "Tennessee Students' Results Improve on Reading, Math Tests, Extending Post-pandemic Recovery," Chalkbeat, June 25, 2024, www.chalkbeat.org/tennessee/2024/06/25/tennessee-students-tcap-reading-and-math-scores-improve-slightly-in-2024/.

14. Angela Watson and Jeremy Newman, "Homeschool Regulatory Changes: Do Adjacent Policy Changes Matter?" Working Paper, September 12, 2024, https://papers.ssrn.com/sol3/papers.cfm?abstract_id=4954517.

15. David Figlio, Cassandra Hart, and Krzysztof Karbownik, "Competitive Effects of Charter Schools," National Bureau of Economic Research, Working Paper No. 32120, February 2024, www.nber.org/papers/w32120.

16. "Measuring What Matters: How Founders of Unconventional Models Define and Measure Learner Outcomes," VELA, July 2024, www.learneroutcomes.vela.org.

# INDEX

absenteeism, 66, 282
academic progress evaluation, 9, 21–22, 165, 179–180, 181, 189–194
accelerator programs, 119–121, 137, 253
accountants, 125
accreditation, 22, 40, 43, 169–171, 212–213
*Acquired* (podcast), 242
ACT, 186
action plans, 118–122
Activate, 166–169, 170–171, 173
Acton, Lord, 86
Acton Academy, 47, 85–88, 203, 208, 217, 225, 245, 276
Acton Academy Fort Lauderdale, 276–277
Adamo Education, Inc., 50–53, 59
Adams, Kanesha, 218–220
Ad Astra, 83
ADHD. *See* attention-deficit/hyperactivity disorder (ADHD)
administration, 166
Advanced Placement (AP) classes, 188
advisors, 125–126
advocacy, 226, 251
AERO. *See* Alternative Education Resource Organization (AERO)
afterschool programs, 8, 132, 172, 247–248
agency-based education, 275–277

age segregation, 24, 42, 87, 144–145
AI. *See* artificial intelligence (AI)
Airbnb, 70, 76
Al Hadi Learning Organization, 122–123
Allen, Denisha, 61–62
Alleyne, Iman, 71, 117–118, 119, 121
alternative education models, 9, 35–37, 202–203, 229, 247–249, 282. *See also* unconventional educational models
Alternative Education Resource Organization (AERO), 267, 282
alternative schools, 36
alumni outcomes, 182
American Dream, 75
America Online (AOL), 115
anxiety, test-related, 194–195
Apple, 247
apprenticeship programs, 144, 262
architects, 125, 169
Arizona State University (ASU), 29
Arizona State University (ASU) Prep Digital, 28–29
Arnett, Thomas, 94–97, 128
ARROWS Christian Academy, 147–152
artificial intelligence (AI), 25, 276–277, 279, 283
ASD. *See* autism spectrum disorder (ASD)

## Index

assessment
  academic progress, 9, 21–22, 165, 179–180, 181, 185–187, 189–194
  benchmark testing, 51
  Charlotte Mason approach, 194–197
  KPIs, 174, 180–182
  quality, 174–180
  social-emotional progress, 181–182
  standardized testing, 22, 43, 64, 146–147, 175, 178, 185–187, 194–195, 262–263, 279–281
attention-deficit/hyperactivity disorder (ADHD), 54, 97, 99, 149, 156, 164–166, 171
autism spectrum disorder (ASD), 72, 73, 136, 147, 149, 165, 214
Azeez Academy, 123

Babson College, 60
background checks, 131
Bair, Sherrilynn, 5, 257–260, 264
Baquedano, Darla, 156–159, 171
Barnard, Amy, 99–100
Barnard, Matt, 99–101
Bassok, Daphna, 109
Becker, Tamara, 50–53, 59
*Be the Solution* (Strong), 275
Bethune, Mary Jane McLeod, 62
Bethune-Cookman University, 62
Bezos, Jeff, 67
Big Bad Wolf House, 78
BIPOC students, 5, 9, 156, 159–164, 171, 214, 219
Birdine, Regina, 6, 65–66, 80
Black founders, 61–67
Black Inquiry Project, 1
Black Lives Matter movement, 61
BlackMindsMatter.net, 62, 80
Black Minds Matter Summit, 62
Blanco, Adriana, 41
Blanco, Arianne, 41
Blockbuster, 230

Bloom Academy, 206
Boston University, 63
bots, 276
Boudreaux, Donald, 183–184
Bradley, Bernita, 79
Branson, Richard, 173
BreakOut School, 164–166
Brookings Institution, 260, 2099
Broward County Public Schools (FL), 209–210
Brown, Greg, 5, 166–169, 170–171, 173
budgets, 118–122
building codes, 212–213
bullying, 41, 65, 157–158
Bureau of Indian Affairs, 258
Bush, George W., 146
businesses
  failures, 67–68, 202–210, 242
  licensing, 205–206
  types of, 115–118
*The Business of Nonprofit-ing* (Fass), 117
busy work, 42
Butler, Timothy, 68

Canary Academy Online, 189
Cantillon, Richard, 69
Canyon Creek Christian Academy, 2–3, 195–197
capstone ceremonies, 262–263
Case, Stephen, 115
Cato Institute, 185, 204
Center for Educational Freedom, 185
certificates of occupancy, 212–213
challenges, startup
  failure, 202–210
  funding, 218–222
  regulatory roadblocks, 210–217
charity schools, 144
Charlotte Mason educational philosophy, 3, 7, 114, 165, 194–197, 220
charter schools, 18, 26, 45, 51, 55, 239, 258, 259, 274, 279, 282

# Index

ChatGPT, 276
Chesky, Brian, 70, 155
childcare licensing requirements, 122–125
Children's Scholarship Fund, 141
CHOICE: An Acton Academy, 217
Christensen, Clayton, 70, 94–95
Christian private schools, 39, 99–103
churches, use of, 21, 39–40, 64, 88, 101, 121, 125, 129, 149, 211
Clark, Jenny, 143
classical education, 148
Clayton Christensen Institute, 94–95
coaching services, 8, 132
co-learning communities, 4. *See also* learning pods
Coles College of Business, 43
collective illusions, 84–85
*Collective Illusions* (Rose), 84
college admissions, 190–191
college-entrance exams, 186
Colossal Academy, 233–236
Colossal Miami, 234–236
Commencement ceremonies, 261
common school movement, 145, 185
community-based education, 4
community spaces, use of, 39, 64, 129
Compass Outreach and Education Center, 20–23, 26, 130
Compass Prep Academy, 40–45, 49, 211
competency-based learning, 261–263
*Competing Against Luck* (Christensen), 94–95
compulsory attendance laws, 144–145, 186, 217
Concordis Education Partners, 148
confidence in institutions, 277–278
consultants, 148
*Contemporary Miseducation* (Goodman), 36
content creators, 278
CORE Butte Charter School, 45

costs. *See* tuition costs
countercultural revolution, 35–37
countertrends, 279–282
*Courage to Grow* (Sandefer), 86
COVID-19 pandemic
 author's experience, 27–31
 Black homeschooling rates and, 161
 disruption of, 18–20, 157, 241, 253, 268
 emergency childcare centers, 167
 entrepreneurship and, 59–60
 mental health impacts, 90–91
 openness to alternative schooling and, 6, 8, 25–26, 49–50, 54, 79, 102, 212, 214, 272
 pandemic pods, 14, 75–79, 167, 211–213, 232–233
 remote learning, 14, 17, 20, 42, 54, 76, 97, 98–99, 232, 272
 school closures, 14, 16–17, 19, 27, 64, 76, 90, 97, 220, 272
 teacher burnout, 52
 test-optional admissions practices during, 186
creative destruction, 69–70
creativity, 25, 269
critical thinking skills, 202–203
cultural capital, 190
cultural diversity, 2, 72, 74–75, 161–164
Cultural Roots, 161–164
curiosity, 25, 113, 191
curriculum evaluation, 140
customers, understanding, 126–129, 172

dame schools, 144
Danford, Kenneth, 45–47, 48, 49, 205
decentralization, 277–278
Dee, Thomas, 26
*Defining Hybrid Homeschools in America* (Wearne), 44
De Leon, Yamila, 205–206, 210
*Deschooling Society* (Illich), 36–37
DiNino, Hank, 92

# Index

DiNino, Heather, 92–93, 96
Disney, Walt, 132
disruption events
   alternative education models as, 229–231
   COVID-19 pandemic, 6, 8, 14, 16–17, 18–20, 25–26, 27–31, 42, 90–91, 157, 235, 241, 253, 268
   emerging technologies as, 277–278
   Hurricane Katrina, 18–19
   September 11 attacks, 13–14
disruptive innovation, 70
diversity
   cultural, 2, 72, 74–75, 161–164
   entrepreneurship, 60
   founder, 61–67
   within homeschooling, 270
   racial, 2, 5, 61–67, 163–164
   *See also* BIPOC students; LGBTQ+ students; neurodiverse students
dual enrollment programs, 29, 43, 188, 262
due diligence, 138–143
Duke University, 69, 161
Duolingo, 185
dyslexia, 5, 51, 149, 156, 166–169, 171

EdChoice, 26, 79, 125, 128, 153, 187
Ed-Prize, 220
educational philosophies
   Charlotte Mason, 3, 7, 114, 165, 194–197, 220
   classical, 148
   freedom-focused, 36–37
   Montessori, 7, 47, 77, 85, 220–221
   nature-based, 165
   P.L.A.Y., 72
   project-based learning, 108
   Sudbury-model, 30
   unschooling, 7, 27–28, 29, 36, 77
   Waldorf, 7, 77, 109, 175–180, 185
educational priorities, 139
educational renaissance, 236–238

educational therapies, 8, 136, 150–151
Education Entrepreneur Freedom Index, 124–125, 203
education entrepreneurs
   boom in, 60, 79
   challenges facing, 201–202, 241–243
   evasive entrepreneurs, 76
   grassroot networks, 236–238
   as innovators, 70
   niche entrepreneurship, 172
   parents and teachers as, 3–5, 7–10, 107, 147, 151–152, 155–156, 164
   private-venture teachers, 144
   qualities of, 68–69
   side projects, startups as, 132, 166–167
   types of, 8
   use of term, 9
   *See also* founders; S.T.A.R.T.U.P.S. Roadmap
education savings account (ESA) programs, 54–55, 152
Edwards, Chris, 204
Eisenhower Center for Innovation, 251–257
Eisenmann, Tom, 121
Elder, Becky, 10
Elementary and Secondary Education Act, 186
Elements Academy, 91–94, 96
Elliott, Brandt, 6, 90–94, 96, 102–103
Elliott, Farrin, 90–94
Elliott, Nox, 91–94
Elliott, Sara, 6, 90–93, 96, 102–103
Ellis, Rebecca, 2–4, 25, 194–197
Ellison, Larry, 247
Embark Mississippi, 273
emergency childcare centers, 167
Employer Identification Numbers (EINs), 59, 116
Engaged Detroit, 79
Enlow, Robert, 153
enrichment programs, 8, 132
enslaved persons, 144

# Index

entrepreneurship
  boom in, 8, 60
  COVID-19 pandemic and, 59–60
  defined, 67, 121
  economics of, 69–70
  evasive entrepreneurs, 76
  everyday, 67–68
  immigrants, 60, 70–75
  innovation and, 69–70
  Latino-owned businesses (LOBs), 60, 70–75
  niche, 172
  risks, 67–68, 201, 241–242
  Silicon Valley, 67, 68
  stereotypes, 68
  stress of, 148
  teaching, 234
  wealth creation, 231–232
  white-owned businesses (WOBs), 73
  word origins, 69
  *See also* education entrepreneurs
*Entrepreneurship Theory and Practice* (periodical), 68
equity, 249–250
evaluation
  curriculum, 140
  of schools/spaces, 138–143, 223–224, 244
  of student progress, 9, 21–22, 165, 179–180, 181, 185–187, 189–194
  *See also* assessment
evasive entrepreneurs, 76
Every Student Succeeds Act (2015), 146

Facebook, 62, 75, 80, 126, 130, 137, 143, 152, 171, 178
Fáilte Microschool, 178–182
failure(s)
  business, 67–68, 242
  fear of, 201
  of traditional schooling, 61
Fairfax County Public Schools (VA), 85
faith-based programs, 2–3, 6, 45, 99–100, 122–123, 147–152

families. *See* parents and families
Fass, Amy, 117
feedback, 8, 131
Fikri, Kenan, 60
financial analysis, 118–122
financial professionals, 125
financial risk, 121–122, 201, 219, 225
fire marshal inspections, 212–213, 215
Fish, Candace, 126–129
flexible work arrangements, 271–273
Florida Virtual School, 29
Floyd, George, 61
Foley, Rebecca, 113–114, 121
Forbes.com, 16, 19, 51, 269
forest schooling, 7, 165
for-profit organizations, 115–116, 117
founders
  Black, 61–67
  as bold visionaries, 108
  challenges facing, 201–202, 241–243
  community building, 225–226
  considerations for pursuing alternatives, 56–57
  as education entrepreneurs, 8
  grants for, 52
  as intrapreneurs, 264–266
  motivations to consider, 32–33, 103–104
  qualities of, 68–69
  questions for, 139
  resources and network connections, 80
  scalability considerations, 244–245
  school choice program participation considerations, 153
  specialization considerations, 172, 198–199
  startup considerations, 224–226
  startup planning, 134
  use of term, 9
  *See also* S.T.A.R.T.U.P.S. Roadmap
Fralicciardi, Toni, 236–237
Fralicciardi, Uli, 237
franchising, 231–236
freedom-focused education, 36

313

# Index

Freedom Preparatory, 127–128
free school movement, 35–37, 218
Friedman, Milton, 6
funding challenges, 201, 218–222

Gallup, 75–76, 84, 89, 277
Gandhi, Priti, 234–236
Gardea, Rachel, 53–54
Gates, Bill, 67
Gebbia, Joe, 70
General Education Development (GED), 42
George, Laura, 38–45, 49, 211
George Mason University, 183
Georgia Accrediting Commission, 40
Global Entrepreneurship Monitor (GEM), 60
GoDaddy, 174
Goodman, Paul, 36, 37
Goodwill of Central and Northern Arizona, 156–157
Grace Preparatory Academy, 44
grade levels, 42
Granberry, Jen, 5, 147–152, 155
Granberry, Zane, 147–152
Grant, Mercedes, 119, 120–121, 129–130, 133
grant programs, 52, 168, 219–220, 222
Graubard, Allen, 218
Greenberg, Sunny, 221
Griffin, LeDonna, 62–67, 80
*Growing Without Schooling* (newsletter), 37
growth planning, 133, 142, 151, 207–208
Guzman, Danna, 5, 76–79

Hamlin, Daniel, 190
Hammon, Joel, 47
Hantman, Andrea, 72–75
Hantman, Danny, 73
Hantman, Sofia, 73
*Harvard Business Review* (periodical), 60
Harvard Business School, 68, 70, 94, 120, 121

*Harvard Gazette* (periodical), 191
Harvard Graduate School of Education, 27
Harvard Kennedy School, 146
Harvard University, 63, 84, 191, 255
Head Start, 5, 65, 77
Hepworth, Todd, 5, 108–112, 113, 121, 217
"hero's journey", 86, 209, 276
Hoffman, Reid, 1, 112
Holt, John, 36–37
homeschool charter school programs, 239
homeschool co-ops
    cultural diversity, 161–164
    defined, 38–39
    vs. hybrid homeschools, 3, 44
    parent-directed education, 66–67
Homeschool EmpowerED, Inc., 187, 189
Homeschool Hub, 26, 161
homeschooling
    Black families and, 160–161, 214
    Christian, 37, 43, 45
    compared to traditional schooling, 87–90
    conferences, 49–50, 52
    COVID-19 pandemic and, 241
    deregulation of, 281
    diversity, 270
    emergence of modern movement, 35–38
    growth of, 26, 76, 161, 267–268, 270–271, 281, 283
    Latino families, 74–75
    laws, 49
    as a legal designation, 15–16, 30, 49, 179
    legal recognition of, 38
    nineteenth century, 144
    public, 239
    reasons for, 65
    secular, 37
    stereotypes, 270
homeschooling collaboratives, 4, 164
homeschool learning/resource centers, 46–47, 49, 79, 205–206, 239, 269. *See also* microschools
HOPE Scholarship program, 43

*How Children Fail* (Holt), 36
*How Children Learn* (Holt), 36
Huang, Jensen, 242
HUMAcollab.org, 80
human intelligence, 25
Hurricane Katrina, 18–19
hybrid homeschool programs, 2–4, 7, 211
   defined, 39, 43–44
   faith-based, 45
   vs. homeschool co-ops, 3, 44
   national networks, 44
   popularity of, 44
   secular, 45
   tuition costs, 40
hybrid work schedules, 272
Hyman, Elmarie, 5, 238–240, 242

Idaho Virtual Academy, 258, 259
ideological conflicts, 184–185
Ignite Learning Academy, 137
Illich, Ivan, 36–37
immigrants
   compulsory school attendance laws and, 144–145
   entrepreneurship, 60, 70–75
income, 132–133
Indeed.com, 130
individualization, 24–25, 42, 84, 133, 149, 186, 261–262
individualized education plans (IEPs), 65, 165
industrialization, 144, 146
information sessions, 128–129
innovation, 23–25, 69–70, 144–146, 248, 275–277, 279–280
Innovation Schools, 247
innovative education, 9. *See also* unconventional educational models
Innovative Educators Network (InEd), 236–237
Instagram, 131
Institute for Justice, 213
institutional confidence, 277–278

insurance professionals, 125, 169
intelligence
   artificial, 25, 276–277, 279, 283
   human, 25
   IQ assessments, 186
Internal Revenue Service (IRS), 59, 116
International Association of Learner-Driven Schools, 170
internship programs, 262
intrapreneurs, 9
   defined, 251
   founders as, 264–266
   new district schools, 257–260
   school-based microschools, 251–257
Invictus: An Acton Academy, 87, 96
Iowa Test of Basic Skills, 185
IRS.gov, 116
Isaacson, Walter, 112
Isra-Ul, Nasiyah, 187–191
IXL, 185

Jackson, Imani, 5, 220–222
Jersey City Public Schools (NJ), 13
Jobs, Laurene Powell, 247
Jobs, Steve, 67, 201, 247
Jobs-to-be-Done (JTBD) theory, 94–96, 98, 103–104, 128
Johns Hopkins University Homeschool Hub, 26, 161
Johns Hopkins University School of Education, 161, 270

Kaestle, Carl, 144
KaiPod Catalyst, 81, 119–121
KaiPod Learning, 119, 137–143
Kaplan, 235
Kauffman Foundation, 60
Kempin, Jennifer, 175–180, 185
Kennesaw State University, 43, 49
Key Performance Indicators (KPIs), 174, 180–182, 186, 191–192, 266
Khan, Sal, 117
Khan Academy, 117, 185, 188, 276

Khosla, Vinod, 59
Kind Academy, 71, 117
KPIs. *See* Key Performance Indicators (KPIs)
Kumar, Amar, 119–120, 121

The Lab School of Memphis, 2, 26, 280
land use ordinances, 216–217
language used in defining schools
   attracting parents with, 128
   regulatory considerations, 123–124, 213–214
Latinos, as entrepreneurs, 60, 70–75
Launch Your Kind, 81, 118, 119
Leaders to Legends Academy, 64–67, 80
Leaders to Legends LLC, 64
Leading Little Arrows, 214–216
*The Lean Startup* (Ries), 131
Learn Beyond the Book LLC, 239–240
learner-directed education, 275–277
learning centers. *See* homeschool learning/resource centers
The Learning Lounge, 219
Learning Pod Protection Act, 211, 213, 269
learning pods, 4, 14, 57, 71, 75–79, 211–213, 215
legal assistance, 116–117, 125–126
LegalZoom.com, 117
Levin, Donna, 229
Lexia, 185
LGBTQ+ students, 5, 6, 9, 90–94, 103, 156–159, 171
*LiberatED* (podcast), 17
Liberated Learners, 47, 48, 49, 81
Libertas Institute, 216
Liberty Self-Directed Learning Center, 49
libraries, use of, 39, 64, 129
licensing requirements, 122–125, 203–204
Life Rediscovered, 241–243
Life Skills Academy, 202, 204–210
LinkedIn, 112
Llewellyn, Grace, 46
Lloyd, Heather, 148

location selection, 129–130, 139, 169, 206–207
Lomax, James, 5, 202–210
Louisiana Department of Education, 18
LoveYourSchool.org, 143
low-income families, 2, 5, 61, 153, 204, 219, 233, 257
Lyft, 76, 282

Mackey, John, 107, 116
Mann, Horace, 185–186
marginalized families, 5, 62–63, 257
marketing, 128–129, 131
Masinelli, Sharon, 5, 211–213
Mason, Charlotte, 3
*The Massachusetts Teacher* (periodical), 144–145
Mastery Transcript Consortium (MTC), 262
Max, Sarah, 87–88, 90, 96
Mazama, Ama, 160
McCluskey, Neal, 185
McCosh, Sarah, 127–128
McDonald, Brian, 28
McDonald's, 234
McLeod Society Fellows, 62
Meckler, Laura, 4
media networks, 278
Meldau, Robby, 5, 251–257, 264
Memphis-Shelby County Public Schools (TN), 280
Mendel, Gregor Johann, 187
mental health
   COVID-19 pandemic and, 90–91
   learner-directed education and, 275
   LGBTQ+ students, 157–158
   as a metric, 193
   test-related anxiety, 194–195
metrics, 173–174, 189–194. *See also* assessment; evaluation
MicroschoolFlorida.com, 80
microschools, 2, 3–4, 5, 7
   defined, 15

## Index

enrollment, 79
  growth of, 270–271, 283
  legal considerations, 57
  legislation defining, 216–217
  measuring outcomes, 192–194
  Montessori, 47
  national networks, 47, 119–120
  partnership, 156
  personalization, 22–23
  reasons for choosing, 94–97
  school-based, 251–257
  secular, 47, 233–236
  tuition costs, 2, 7, 15, 23, 168
Microschool Solutions, 81
Microsoft, 67
Migrant and Seasonal Head Start, 77
Minimum Viable Product (MVP), 131–132, 265–266
minority populations, 144. *See also* BIPOC students; LGBTQ+ students
Mintz, Jerry, 267
mission statements, 115, 134, 182
Missouri Supreme Court, 145
Moe, Terry, 18
Moesta, Bob, 94
Montessori, Maria, 47, 221
Montessori schools, 7, 47, 49, 85, 170, 220–222, 282–283
Moonrise, 268–269, 272–273
Morefield, Coi, 1–4, 25, 280–281
Morning Consult, 79
Motorola, 248
MrBeast, 278
Musk, Elon, 67, 83, 112
Musumunu, Garvey, 160
Mynatt, Cheryl, 6, 97–103
Mynatt, Gabe, 97–103
Mynatt, Randy, 6, 97–103

Narvaez, Gaby, 5, 70–75
Narvaez, Joaquin, 71
Narvaez, Luis Carlos, 71–72
National Council of Negro Women, 62

National Education Association, 256
National Hybrid Schools Project, 43
National Institutes of Health, 195
National Microschooling Center, 7, 81, 148, 170, 192, 205, 225, 273
NBC News, 230
Neill, A. S., 36
Netflix, 230, 268
network connections, 80–81, 143, 236–238
neurodiverse students, 5, 6, 9, 51, 72, 73, 74, 148–150, 155, 164–166, 171, 214, 219
New England Association of Schools and Colleges, 170
Newman, Daniel, 60
new schools, 36
*New York Times* (periodical), 75
niche entrepreneurship, 172
No Child Left Behind Act (NCLB) (2001), 146, 186
nonprofit organizations, 115–117
Northern Cass School District (ND), 260–263
North Star, 46–47, 205
Northwestern University, 282
*NPR*, 248
NVIDIA, 242
NWEA MAP test, 185

Obama, Barack, 146
occupational licensing requirements, 122–125, 203–204
Office of Veteran's Business Development, 110
Okolo-Ebube, Amber, 5, 214–216
Omaha Public Schools (NE), 63, 66
one·n·ten Youth Center, 156–158
online learning, 4, 7, 17, 28–29, 137, 189, 258–260
open enrollment policies, 55
OptionsForEducation.com, 80
Orchard STEM School, 108, 110–112, 121, 217

# Index

originality, 25
outcomes, measuring, 9, 21–22, 165, 179–180, 181, 183, 189–194
outdoor education movement, 165

pandemic pods, 14, 75–79, 167, 211–213, 232–233. *See also* learning pods
Pannell, Jack Johnson, 274, 279–280
parent-directed education, 66–67. *See also* homeschool co-ops
parents and families
   collective illusions, 84–85
   considerations for pursuing alternatives, 56
   as customers, 126–129
   as education entrepreneurs, 3–5, 7–10, 107, 147, 151–152, 155–156, 164
   encouraging innovation, 264
   evaluating schools/spaces, 138–143, 223–224, 244
   fears of, 135–136, 137–138
   intuition, 142
   motivations to consider, 31–32, 103–104
   quality assessment, 174–180, 197–198
   researching school choice programs, 153
   resources and network connections, 80, 143
   satisfaction and testimonials, 180, 196–197
   startup planning, 134
   students with unique needs, 171
   subjective values of, 182–185
   test score priorities, 187
parks, use of, 39, 129
Parsons, Bob, 174
partnership microschools, 156
Passion Learning Approach Year-Round (P.L.A.Y.), 72
Path of Life Learning, 119, 129–130
paying yourself, 132–133
PayPal, 112, 231
Perez, Jill, 13–17, 25

permissionlessness, 76, 210
Permission To Succeed Education Center, 23, 26
Perry Normal School, 23–25
personalization, 16, 22–23, 24, 51, 126, 133, 165, 171, 261–263, 275–276, 278, 286
Personalized Learning Institute, 263
Peterson, Paul, 146
Pew Research Center, 41
Philadelphia Public Schools (PA), 176
philanthropic funding, 219–220, 250
PLAY K–12, 72–74
Poinciana Montessori, 222
policies and procedures, 131, 140
*Politico* (media company), 271
*The Politics of Institutional Reform* (Moe), 18
Popcorn Academy, 71
Populace, 84
Portland Public Schools (OR), 166
Powderhouse Studios, 247–251
Prenda, 47, 81, 245, 252–257
Prenda Code Club, 252
Private School Review, 7
private schools, 4, 144
   Christian, 39, 99–103
   enrollment, 26, 271, 273
   occupational licensing requirements, 203–204
   openness to, 17
   school closures, 210
   secular, 48, 168
   tuition costs, 7, 102, 236
private-venture teachers, 144
problem-solving, 70
project-based learning, 108
ProPublica, 117
protective policies, 213–214
Providence Hybrid Academy, 113–115, 121
public homeschooling, 239
Public Schooling Battle Map, 185
public schools. *See* traditional schooling
public spaces, use of, 39, 64, 129

# Index

quality assessment, 174–180
questions to consider, 138–143

racial diversity, 2, 61–67, 163–164
RAND Corporation, 51–52
Rattigan, Shiren, 231–238
Rattray, Amnon, 19–20
Rattray, Felicia, 19–20, 23, 25, 26
reading instruction, 109, 177
real estate agents, 125, 129
referral rates, 180–181
Refine KC, 99–103
reform movements, 144–146
regulatory considerations, 122–125, 141, 205–206, 210–217, 279–282
remote learning, 14, 17, 20, 42, 54, 76, 97, 98–-99, 220, 232, 272
remote working, 272
Resnick, Alec, 247–251, 265
resource centers. *See* homeschool learning/resource centers
resources and network connections, 80–81, 143
retention rates, 180, 196
Rhode Island School of Design, 70
Richardson, Dallin "Doc", 5, 164–166, 171
Ries, Eric, 131
Rizvi, Rida, 122–123
Roddick, Anita, 83
Rodriguez, Maritza, 254–255
Roosevelt, Franklin D., 62
Rose, Todd, 27, 84
Rutgers University, 14

salaries, 132–133
Salazar, Troy, 48–49
Salie, Ada, 240–243
Salsman, Richard, 69
Sandefer, Jeff, 85–86
Sandefer, Laura, 85–86
SAT, 186
Say, Jean-Baptiste, 69
Saysian economics, 69

scalability, 133, 230, 231
  challenges, 240–243
  franchising, 231–236
  grassroot entrepreneur networks, 236–238
  smart scaling, 238–240
schedules, 140
scholarship programs, 21, 23, 43, 61, 109, 141, 168, 204, 233
school, use of term, 123–125
school boards, 184–185
school choice programs
  advocacy, 226
  Arizona, 54–55, 119, 136, 137, 141, 143, 150, 152, 155, 157, 240, 253, 274–275
  Arkansas, 218
  declining public school enrollment and, 230–231
  expansion of, 26–27, 152–153, 253, 273–275, 281
  Florida, 21, 23, 26, 61, 74, 233, 271
  Mississippi, 273
  Nevada, 204
  participation considerations, 153
  Tennessee, 2, 26
  Utah, 109–110, 165, 218
school closures, 14, 16–17, 19, 27, 64, 76, 90, 97, 209–210, 220, 272
school culture, 41, 140–141
school districts
  new schools within, 257–260
  overhauling, 260–263
school founders. *See* education entrepreneurs; founders
"Schooling in America" survey, 187
school shootings, 65
School Starter Checklist, 125
School Startup Journey, 282–283
school-to-prison pipeline, 63–64
Schumpeter, Joseph, 69–70
self-directed education, 6, 27–28, 29, 77, 205
Seling, Beth, 52

# Index

September 11 attacks, 13–14
Seton Hall University, 14
Shah, Kadin, 136–143, 152
Shah, Melissa, 6, 136–143, 152, 155
Shirley, Hailey, 41–42
side projects, startups as, 132, 166–167
Silicon Valley, 67, 68, 120, 253
Slaven, Martina, 276
Slaven, Tobin, 276–277
small businesses, 67–68, 73, 230
Smith, Kelly, 252
Snake River Online, 259–260
Snake River School District (ID), 258
social-emotional progress, 181–182
social reformers, 144–146
The Socratic Experience, 274
Soifer, Ashley, 192–194, 204–205
Soifer, Don, 192, 204–205
Sowell, Thomas, 175
SpaceX, 83
Spark Community Schools, 156–159
special needs students, 9, 51, 55, 74, 75, 136, 147, 150–151, 166–169, 171
staffing, 130–131
standardized testing, 22, 43, 64, 146–147, 175, 178, 185–187, 194–195, 262–263, 279–281
Stanford University, 18, 26, 73, 146
Startup Genome, 242
S.T.A.R.T.U.P.S. Roadmap
   from vision to launch, 9, 108–112, 131–132
   strategic vision (step 1), 113–115
   type of business (step 2), 115–118
   action plan and budget (step 3), 118–122
   rules and regulations (step 4), 122–125
   trusted advisors (step 5), 125–126
   understanding your customers (step 6), 126–129
   people, places, and polices (step 7), 129–131
   sustainability and scale (step 8), 131–133

statements of faith, 45
"State of Latino Entrepreneurship" report, 73
State Policy Network, 201–202, 220
Steiner, Cory, 5, 260–263, 264, 265
Steiner, Rudolph, 109
St. John the Baptist Hybrid School, 211–213
strategic vision, 113–115, 134
Strong, Michael, 274–275
student engagement, 180
student handbooks, 131
Suarez, Laurel, 20–23, 25, 26, 130–131
subjective value theory, 182–185
Sudbury Valley School, 30, 35, 37, 48, 49, 285–286
suicidal ideation, 90–91
summer camps, 8, 132, 166, 172
*Summerhill* (Neill), 36
Summerhill School, 36
Surf Skate Science, 237
suspension rates, 63–64
sustainability, 131–133, 142
Swan, William, 144–145

Tanner, JeVonne, 217
Tanner, Paul, 217
Tavernetti, Sarah, 205–206, 210
tax credits, 21, 152, 204
teachers
   burnout, 51–52
   as education entrepreneurs, 3–5, 7–10, 107, 147, 151–152, 155–156, 164
   licensing requirements, 122–125, 203–204
   recruiting, 130–131
   satisfaction, 181–182
teachers' unions, 256
Teach for America, 251
*Teach Your Own* (Holt), 37
technological innovation, 275–277, 283
*The Teenage Liberation Handbook* (Llewellyn), 46

# Index

Tennessee State Board of Education, 280
testing. *See* assessment; standardized testing
Thiel, Peter, 67, 231, 267
Thierer, Adam, 76
traditional schooling
  absenteeism, 66, 282
  age segregation, 24, 42, 87, 144–145
  bullying, 41, 157–158
  changing standards, 108–109
  coercive qualities, 46
  collective illusions, 84–85
  common school movement, 145, 185
  compared to homeschooling, 87–90
  compulsory attendance laws, 144–145, 186, 217
  declining reputation, 278
  disciplinary policies, 63–64
  disillusionment with, 45–46, 48, 64, 175–176
  educational quality, 281
  encouraging innovation within, 264–266
  enrollment, 209–210, 230, 260
  experiences of, 83–84
  failures of, 61
  grade levels, 42
  intrapreneurs, 247–266
  mandates in, 64
  new district schools, 257–260
  occupational licensing requirements, 203–204
  one-size-fits-all, 143–147
  recess time, 171
  school-based microschools, 251–257
  school boards, 184–185
  school closures, 209–210
  school district overhauls, 260–263
  school-to-prison pipeline, 63–64
  spending on, 102
  standardized testing, 22, 43, 64, 146–147, 178, 185–187, 194–195, 279–281
  teachers' unions, 256
  toxic social culture, 41
  uncoupling education from, 274–275
  *See also* teachers
training, 130–131
Tran, Tim, 6, 85–88, 90, 96, 103
Tranquil Teachings Learning Center, 15–16
transcripts, 43, 262
trauma, school related, 41–42
*A Treatise on Political Economy* (Say), 69
trends
  adoption of flexible work arrangements, 271–273
  countertrends, 279–282
  expansion of school choice policies, 273–275
  growth of homeschooling and microschooling, 270–271
  new technologies and AI, 275–277
  openness to new institutions, 277–278
  unconventional educational models, 267–269
Trinity Arch Preparatory School for Boys, 274
tuition costs
  free schools, 36
  hybrid homeschool programs, 3, 40
  microschools, 2, 7, 15, 23, 168
  private schools, 7, 102, 236
  questions to consider, 141
  *See also* school choice programs
Turner, Chris, 268–270, 272–273, 274
tutoring services, 8, 132, 150–151, 166–167
twice-exceptional students, 136
Tyack, David, 146

Uber, 76, 282
unconventional educational models
  appeal of, 8–9
  author's experience, 27–31, 285–286
  defined, 6–7
  language used in defining, 123–125
  transformative nature of, 189–190
  trends in, 267–268
  use of term, 9

# Index

University-Model® schools, 44
University of California, Davis, 282
University of Colorado Boulder, 63
University of Oklahoma, 190
University of Rochester, 282
University of Virginia, 109
unmet demand, 181, 196, 231
*Unschooled* (McDonald), 6, 17, 30, 247, 248, 267
unschooling, 7, 27–28, 29, 36, 77, 175
US Census Bureau, 59, 76, 161, 219, 230
US Centers for Disease Control and Prevention (CDC), 90–91, 164
US Department of Education, 65
US Naval Academy, 202
US Small Business Administration (SBA), 67
Utah Fits All Scholarship, 109
Utah Small Business Administration, 110

values, subjectivity of, 182–185
VELA Education Fund, 52, 80–81, 168, 185, 219, 225, 238, 282–283
Vietnam War, 35, 37
virtual schooling, 4, 7, 17, 28–29, 55, 240, 258–260
vision statements, 108–115, 134
voucher programs, 152, 218

Wakeman, Angie, 113–114, 121
Waldorf schools, 7, 49, 109, 175–180, 185
Walker, Madam C. J., 135
Wallace, Dalena, 237–238
*Wall Street Journal* (periodical), 75, 256, 278

Walton, Sam, 35
*Washington Post* (periodical), 4, 26, 60, 65, 270
Watson, Angela, 161, 270
wealth creation, 231–232
Wearne, Eric, 43–44, 49–50
wedding planning language, 124
what-if scenarios, 142
Whole Foods Market, 116
Wichita Innovative Schools and Educators (WISE), 128, 238
Wildflower Foundation, 222
Wildflower Montessori network, 47, 81, 220–222, 225, 245, 282–283
WiseTogether.org, 80
World Health Organization, 19
Wright, Alex, 159–164
Wright, Alycia, 5, 159–164, 171

XQ Super School Project, 247

Yass Prize, 220
Y Combinator, 120, 253
yes. every kid. foundation, 124, 126
yeslegal.org, 126
YouGov, 84
Young, Julie, 29
YouTube, 278

Zaring, Amanda, 100–101
Zaring, Ryan, 100
Zearn, 185
zoning laws, 206–207, 215, 216–217
Zuckerberg, Mark, 13, 67

Credit: Hope Mabry Photography

**Kerry McDonald** works at the intersection of education and enterprise, spotlighting the entrepreneurs who are building creative schooling options across the United States. She is a Senior Fellow at the Foundation for Economic Education, where she leads the Education Entrepreneurship Lab and hosts the *LiberatED* podcast. She is also the Velinda Jonson Family Education Fellow at State Policy Network, an adjunct scholar at the Cato Institute, and a regular contributor at Forbes.com and The 74. The bestselling author of *Unschooled: Raising Curious, Well-Educated Children Outside the Conventional Classroom*, Kerry has a BA in economics from Bowdoin College and a master's degree in education policy from Harvard University. A mom of four, she lives in Cambridge, Massachusetts.